EMO

FANDOM & CULTURE

*Paul Booth and Katherine Larsen, series editors*

# EMO

## HOW FANS DEFINED
## A SUBCULTURE

JUDITH MAY FATHALLAH

University of Iowa Press, Iowa City

University of Iowa Press, Iowa City 52242
Copyright © 2020 by the University of Iowa Press
www.uipress.uiowa.edu
Printed in the United States of America

Design by Ashley Muehlbauer

Printed on acid-free paper

*Library of Congress Cataloging-in-Publication Data*
Names: Fathallah, Judith–author.
Title: Emo: How Fans Defined a Subculture / Judith May Fathallah.
Description: Iowa City: University of Iowa Press, [2020] | Series: Fandom and Culture | Includes bibliographical references and index.
Identifiers: LCCN 2020007861 (print) | LCCN 2020007862 (ebook) | ISBN 9781609387242 (paperback) | ISBN 9781609387259 (ebook)
Subjects: LCSH: Emo (Music)—Social aspects. | Rock music fans. | Gender identity. | Emo (Music)—History and criticism. | Subculture—History.
Classification: LCC ML3918.R63 F38 2020 (print) | LCC ML3918.R63 (ebook) | DDC 781.66—dc23
LC record available at https://lccn.loc.gov/2020007861
LC ebook record available at https://lccn.loc.gov/2020007862

# CONTENTS

# ACKNOWLEDGMENTS

I thank everyone at Iowa University Press for their enthusiasm and support, especially Paul Booth and Kathy Larsen. Special thanks go to Heather Savigny and Rosemary Hill for their valuable comments on the manuscript.

# INTRODUCTION

## THE PREMISE

*Emo is bullshit. It's something for girls who are fifteen. . . . There is no movement, there is no way of thinking, there are no musicians. You guys confuse punk, hardcore, you confuse screamo, you combine all the currents, just to give meaning to your stupid and idiotic movement.*

—**DJ Kristoff**, during the runup to a spate of
violence against emo kids in Mexico City[1]

Insult, identifier, genre, youth scene: the label "emo" has a difficult history. The full term "emotional hardcore" first emerged in 1980s zines and trade press to describe a handful of post-punk bands in US cities, such as Rites of Spring and Embrace. These bands developed as a reaction against and in modification of the all-macho, all-rage, intermittently racist excesses of local hardcore punk scenes.[2] In the 1990s, the term became associated with softer, more pop punk sounds (Sunny Day Real Estate, Dashboard Confessional), then in the early 2000s broke suddenly into the relative mainstream as bands like My Chemical Romance and Fall Out Boy leveraged the emergent social media landscape to engage a new fanbase composed of digital immigrants and natives. At the same time, music journalists and bands sought either to disassociate themselves from the term "emo" or deny that the label meant anything. As senior music journalist Andy Greenwald notes, it may always have been "slightly derisive," suggesting something a little too earnest or unironic for proper critical respect.[3] As the opening epigraph demonstrates, this derision is intensely gendered. It is part of a long, dense, and solid discourse seeking to align "real," "authentic" music with hegemonic masculinity, policing and warding off the threat of feminine hysteria and excess.[4]

In the early 2000s, it was still common for young people to dismiss bands and styles for being "gay," a charge so ubiquitous against emo bands that Fall Out Boy eventually produced a song titled "Gay Is Not a Synonym for Shitty." Williams, Peters, Carillo-Vincent, Ryalls, and de Boise all discussed the relationship of emo to subordinate and Othered forms of masculinity.[5] Boys in Mexico and Iraq have been assaulted for dressing in styles and listening to music associated with the scene, with varying degrees of state and police co-operation.[6] Yet Greenwald maintains that the term is indefinable: "every generation that loves emo bands simultaneously rejects the term while claiming ownership of it," he writes, "meaning if they won't admit that they love emo, they will certainly say how much they hate everything that's been called emo since then. But still, no-one knows what it means."[7] His book gives the impression that while we can chart musical consistencies running all the way from Rites of Spring to the bands called emo today, we are then in realms of generality so broad that we might as well just call it "alt-rock" and could substitute hundreds of other bands without changing the parameters of the discourse. Discourse—in this case, all the statements from trade press, marketers, musicians, critics, and fans—is that dynamic, active property of language that defines and defends the boundaries of ideas, such as music genres or ideas of quality music.

In this book, I argue that the meaning of emo as a genre has been shaped by its fandom, a process with significant implications for fan studies and fandom–industry relations. Fabian Holt wrote in 2007 that "struggles about names and definitions are often an integral part of the histories of individual musics and their cultural dynamics"; and that "genre boundaries are contingent upon the social spaces in which they emerge and upon cultural practices, not just musical practices."[8] Now, although it is never particularly useful to assume determinate timelines or posit that as technology progresses, certain changes are "caused," it does seem that we can chart a trajectory in the invention of modern emo that moves gradually from sites and practices that are more like a broadcast, top-down media model toward sites and practices that are more like "bottom-up" user-generated content (UGC). This is part of why I claim that fandom shaped it. To be clear, I don't wish to suggest some kind of absolute temporal narrative, as though meaning were collected along a timeline from less to more or from top-down to user-generated. Discourse is always in flux—signifiers are never closed totally—but it is nonetheless reasonable to posit that sites like MySpace helped establish the terms and boundaries that initiated this discursive struggle in the early 2000s, even though most MySpace users would not have described themselves or their bands as emo at the time.

As readers may have realized, one key point of my argument is that the genre's meaning is constructed in large part retrospectively—just as a meme points backward to all its past iterations to consolidate and subvert them, what emo "was" has primarily been constituted by fandom's practice of commentary and archiving after the fact. Online discourse is now an important aspect of most genre constructions, and emo provides a particularly salient example to the development of fan cultures. By charting the shaping of emo, we can observe how fandom's statements and categorizations—not to mention humor—work their way back around into the statements of subcultural celebrities and the music press. The definitions become retrospectively "author-ized." Through this process, the term "emo" has become what discourse theorists Laclau and Mouffe might describe as "fixed."[9] Its meaning or referent has been struggled over, pulled back and forth, and gradually come to the point that fans know precisely what is meant by a one-word meme or joke. This degree of referential shorthand is only possible in a well-defined discourse. It seems that, contra Greenwald, online emo fandom knows precisely "what it is." Most strikingly, and in illustration of this "fixing" process, fandom's creative definitional work has come full circle, being adopted back into the music press and even the statements of musicians who once dismissed it.

On one hand, this book answers Oliver Marchart's call for the reconnection of micro and macro aspects of sociopolitical practice in the field of subcultural studies.[10] Furthermore, it contributes to the feminist project instigated by Angela McRobbie, demonstrating the creative uses of male-dominated media by girls and women.[11] Genre and gender are intricately connected, and as well as providing a key case study for updated ways to consider fandom–

industry interactions, the construction of emo has significant implications for millennial discourses of gender. Adapting the methodological tools I developed elsewhere,[12] I am concerned to show how fans' creative work resonates in broader cultural constructs. In this book, I argue that at least in some cases, we need to abandon the idea that the media produce texts and ideologies that fans reshape and adapt—this is ultimately still a reception studies argument. That was Holt's discursive perspective when he claimed that "mass mediation plays an enormous role in genre formation," and then went on to discuss how fans interpret and negotiate those definitions.[13] Now, over a decade later, I have found that rather than taking up and altering a discourse from popular media, there was no coherent referent called emo before fandom shaped it—and now there is. Holt also thought that "online discourse" could be "viewed as an extension of offline discourse, and is often complementary to the professional mass media."[14] I think this was an unsupported and dubious claim even in 2007, and it is clearly not tenable now. This study has significant implications for the changing relationship between fandoms and industry, not just with regard to genre and categorization but also with definitional and boundary construction in general.

There are points in Greenwald's book where he seems to define emo as simply the shared experience of sensitive young people in the digital era: "With the internet, teenagers have the ultimate emo tool—a private medium that their parents don't understand, one where they can easily trade, access, and share music, ideas, news, feelings, and support."[15] This is too broad and neglects the fact that for most fans, emo refers to a group of bands and albums over a historical period. However, Greenwald is correct to stress the centrality of the internet to contemporary emo. Whatever emo was—and I believe that applying the same term to post-punk gigs in Washington basements and contemporary YouTube clips is only useful in constructing a historical retrospective—the phenomenon that is now called emo is primarily digital. Tumblr, for example, will provide a clearer if disjointed definition. Searching the "emo" tag in late 2018 produces the same or similar sets of images. It links constantly to the fandom-invented phrase the "Emo Trinity," which refers to My Chemical Romance, Fall Out Boy, and Panic! at the Disco. Nothing before 2001 exists. There are a range of selfies by (largely white, middle-class) teenagers in band T-shirts and black skinny jeans, faces half-turned artfully from the camera. But overwhelmingly, what emerges is the material of fandom: art, GIFs, links to videos, photographs of merchandise—and hashtags.

The annotations are endless and stylistically distinct. As a rule—and contra Greenwald's association of emo with earnestness—this material is humorous, self-mocking, and fluent in meme, simultaneously acknowledging and reflexively distancing the writer from the content.

Although Greenwald does not sufficiently address the active role online fandom plays in constructing emo, he attributes the importance of the internet to the web's capacity to compress time and connect teenagers who are alienated from their immediate physical communities. This accords with my experience—I discovered emo on MySpace when I was about fifteen. I had not long been released from traumatizing inpatient "treatment" for anorexia (that most problematically gendered of diseases) and was still suffering quite badly from that disorder. I felt entirely alienated from my family and peer group. But having grown up listening to the same and related bands today's teenagers are now discovering, it seems to me that the new fan discourse is more knowing, more (self-)parodic, more reflexive, and far less respectful than early 2000s fandom, in line with the rise of social media and the development of what Paul Booth has called the "philosophy of playfulness" on the internet.[16]

In the following chapters, I aim to identify and analyze the creative process of consolidation by which emo has come to mean what it means in 2020. In the rest of this introduction, I outline some of the paradigms of thought around new media fandom that have informed my approach. As the reader has gathered, I write from the broad perspective of discourse analysis: that is, the understanding of language as something active and creative. We are concerned with what statements do, rather than attempting to "see through" them and discover some essential unchanging meaning behind or inside them. In the next chapter, I give a brief overview of what other critics have made of the term "emo" in its post-2000 application, especially regarding struggles for the meaning of gender/genres. The following chapters present the research, which is organized by website in a loosely chronological order, according to the contemporary importance of each site. Courtesy of the Internet Archive Wayback Machine, chapter 3 begins with MySpace and the linked Fueled by Ramen blogs, which flourished in the early 2000s, before comparing them with the simultaneous development of LiveJournal fandom. Chapter 4 moves on from text-based blogs to compare the similarly co-created space of YouTube, which of course relies on video, to the multimedia microblogging site Tumblr, that vortex of disruption and consolidation that acts almost as a metonym for the polyvocal cacophony on online fandom.[17] Chapter 5 contrasts these processes with the different forms of definitional work we observe on Reddit and 4chan, online communities whose histories and practices are likewise informed by humor but tend to be structured—and gendered—very differently than the fan sites more traditionally studied. Chapter 6 returns to industrial media, exploring the reuptake and consolidation of emo by industry professionals, with a focus on fandom influence, and explores some of ways the term is changing right now and with reference to the future. I conclude with a review and discussion of the implications of my findings, especially the implications for fandom's creative and definitional processes.

## THE PARADIGMS

In the remainder of this introduction, I introduce some recent research on fandom and online culture that helped shape my thinking on this subject, developed especially from Paul Booth on digital fan studies and from Whitney Phillips and Ryan Milner on new media more generally. After all, as Stein has argued, "Fan culture and millennial mainstream digital cultures are, to a degree, discursive fictions."[18] Although we should certainly be wary of "equating" or "assuming causal relationships of influence" between the constructs, any hard distinction between "media mainstream" and "fan culture" has effectively collapsed in the era of digital fandom.[19] To put it another way, a lot of what younger millennials do and make online involves the sort of practices, sociality, and creativity that were once considered hallmarks of subcultural fandom. In addition to the increasing visibility—and economic utility—of fandom, Booth attributes this trend to a certain "philosophy of playfulness":

> What is a "philosophy of playfulness"? . . . The contemporary media scene is complex, and rapidly becoming dependent on a culture of ludism. Today's media field is fun, playful, and exuberant. More so than at any other time, the media we use in our everyday lives have been personalized, individualized, and made pleasurable to use. We play with our media; it is malleable in our hands. The field of media studies needs to take into account this philosophy of playfulness in order to represent the media texts created by fans not just as individual

fan fiction, fan videos, fan songs, or fan research, but rather as pieces of what fans use as a larger multivocal media "game."[20]

Though characteristic of fandom, Booth believes that the philosophy of playfulness structures much online engagement with media content in a way that no longer makes sense to confine to particular affinity groups and spaces. Tumblr's popularity is considered a key factor here. Quite simply, the technological affordances and social practices of Tumblr make all media participation look like what we used to call fandom, with its practices of curation, comment, remix, preservation, and adaptation. Given Tumblr's social norms of irreverence and emotional investment, Stein argues that "step by step, we are moving to a millennial media landscape no longer dominated by fears of the excesses of the unruly fan, one that instead embraces personal investment, performativity, emotion, and excess, within the content of shared digital creativity."[21] Millennial fandom is still primarily feminine-coded but has lost some of the gendered stigma. The reasons for this shift are multiple and complicated, and this is not the place to discuss them. Stein's observation is important to my work for two reasons: first, Tumblr is a primary site at which contemporary emo is constructed, and second, the playful, humorous, affective, often parodic discursive norms in question are so profoundly at odds with the kind of cultural gatekeeping observed in the epigraph to this introduction. In much "serious" trade press, emo was either dismissed or reclaimed as part of the masculinist tradition of punk and hardcore through a process of gatekeeping attempting to separate "real" emo from feminized sell-outs and mainstream pretenders enjoyed by (shock horror) women and girls.

The focus on playfulness, as part of an argument for fannish practice as an increasingly mainstream style of engagement with industry, is key to Booth's 2015 book, *Playing Fans*. Booth argues that given the "continual, shifting negotiation and dialogue" between fans and industry, we ought to bear in mind that although many specific fan practices can be resistant, transformative, and critical of media practices, the underlying affective connection between identity and activity marks fans as in an always liminal state between resistant and complicit in institutional contexts.[22]

The point is salient because early fan studies and early studies of musical subcultures were heavily invested in seeing people's discursive/semiotic practice as resistant to industry,[23] mainstream society, and (to an extent in Fiske's case) capitalism. The Birmingham School critics that pioneered subcultural studies believed that subcultures were eventually subsumed by industry, then resold to the consumer in a process of appropriation and diffusion. But they didn't believe this necessarily negated their resistant potential. As I will map out more thoroughly in the next chapter, much has been written on the ambiguous relationship of emo to heteronormative gender models, particularly its uses by boys. But the social and technological codes of new media fandom render discrete statements increasingly difficult to trace or attribute to individual users, as opposed to how style of dress is displayed as being "authored" by its wearer. The fannish/subcultural/cultural discourse that now confronts us is so anarchic, so mimetic, so ironically knowing and self-reflexive that attempting to categorize elements as simply resistant or complicit is futile, particularly concerning a discourse as flexible, contentious, and messy of that of gender.

Booth observes that in keeping with his philosophy of playfulness, the practices of parody and pastiche have taken a central place in fandom. Pastiche (the appropriation and recombination of textual elements) is not necessarily critical or satirical but could include digital art, mood boards, Pinterest collections, and so on—Booth suggests it as a "bare-bones reflection" of the emotional investment that characterizes fandom.[24] I am a little wary of the term "reflect" in speaking of media—as established, I tend to read text more in terms of action and effect, but that is largely a result of the fact that Booth's work tends to be more psychoanalytically oriented and mine oriented more toward discourse as a social/material effect, rather than any fundamental disagreement in characterizing the phenomenon. Parody tends to have a more cynical, critical, or satirical element, yet the criticism is never total. Linda Hutcheon has argued that there is a paradox at the heart of parody,[25] which is related to the paradox I identified in the workings of fan fiction.[26] Hutcheon contends that "in imitating, even with a critical difference, [parody] always reinforces."[27] Even as it deconstructs the original media text, parody emphasizes it as source and basis for the current statement. This is why it is important to recall that, for all fandom's creative work, it is only once the term "emo" gets taken up again by the music press and bands that we can say the discourse has consolidated. The authority of traditional gatekeepers has been compromised by new forms of digital fandom, but it hasn't vanished.

I also want to build on some ideas regarding what, in the age of digital fandom, comprises the idea of a "text" and where its boundaries might lie.

Matt Hills wrote in 2007 that "the bounded 'text' may no longer exist for audiences navigating their way through dispersed yet organized networks of textuality."[28] Booth, Williams, and Stein have discussed how the definition of a "text" is increasingly hard to delineate.[29] These writers mostly discuss transmedia franchises that combine film or televisual properties with digital storytelling, wikis, tie-in books, computer games, and more. If we take "contemporary emo" as our text and agree that texts are made out of discourse, there is no way we could imagine that music channels, radio, or even the trade press delimit its boundaries. As Hills wrote in his foreword to the second edition of *Digital Fandom*, "The amazing array of texts, images, and alternatives created by and within digital fandom means that we cannot quite be sure where media texts begin and end anymore. . . . Although 'official' parameters can be re-established around the latest *Game of Thrones* or *Doctor Who* episode, much of the brand value and cultural meaning surrounding these (and other) shows surely emanates from all the digital fan activity clustering around them."[30]

In (somewhat boldly) subtitling this book "how fans defined a subculture," I indicate my argument that the example of emo actually takes this further, that the working definitions of what emo is have actually been produced by fandom, or at least significantly shaped by it. The genre is thus "fandom-shaped" in another sense as well: the contours of its discourse adhere to the kinds of irony, humor, and reflexivity we find in fan culture online. There is a broader argument here about the potentials for fan culture to actively intervene in and alter public discourse. The example here is of gender, a much contested, highly wrought, and ever-shifting construct. Is it possible that in the way "emo" has been reuptaken by artists and popular press, we can demonstrate the definitional powers of fandom chronologically? I explore this throughout the book. How does one measure the burden of definition? Though it would be silly to posit that texts—or whole ideologies—are x percent defined by fandom and x percent by industry, I do think that this research demonstrates a genuine shift in influence at the negotiating table over time. This work of definition has come about largely through the complementary processes Booth calls "narractivity" and "intra-textuality."[31]

"Intra-textuality" is coined to contrast "intertextuality," which is the linkage of disparate texts through exophoric reference, quotation, and gesture.[32] Intra-textuality, by contrast, "finds unity within disparate elements within a text."[33] Booth illustrates this with reference to a blog post and its comments, but I am going to take a liberty with his concept and suggest that in emo fandom, intra-textuality works as the process by which very diverse elements in the broader text that makes up emo are connected by fans as part of the definitional process. In 2007, My Chemical Romance frontman Gerard Way complained that the term "emo" was used by journalists and record execs to group bands with "no similarities" together.[34] This assessment was made strictly from the perspective of (audio) music criticism. But clearly, fandom's investment/invention comprises much more than audible content. Through intra-textual processes of curation, archive, collage, commentary, fan fic, and remix, the disparate elements of emo are made to have similarities, a process I demonstrate in the coming chapters.

Acts of intra-textuality are part of a broader process Booth conceptualizes as "narractivity." This coinage, joining the words "narrative" and "activity," is an obvious fit with the conception of discourse as an active process of meaning-making. In discussing the work of discourse theorist Michel Foucault, Robert J. C. Young conceptualized a "statement" as an "incision into a discursive field."[35] By this, he means we should see each statement an action that has an effect on a preestablished set of meanings, consolidating or altering them, rather than reflecting or imitating a prior existing reality. Booth defines narractivity as "a fandom's communal construction of a narrative," which reconciles the traditionally opposed forms of "narrative" and "database."[36] Much of fandom's archival work takes the form of databases, either literally as wikis like Fanlore or in the looser sense of a collection of knowledge and ideas. As I will illustrate, the narrative databases fandoms construct contest "the traditional split between what is told (the story) and the telling of that tale (the discourse)."[37] In her book *Rogue Archives*, Abigail De Kosnik argues that informal practices of archiving by fans and volunteers are enacting the construction of new cultural institutions of memory, displacing traditional, official, and state-sanctioned archiving practices in constructing social meaning. She writes: "Fan archiving is driven by a political longing: a longing to protect and sustain female and queer communities and cultures. . . . In chapter 2, I explained that fan fiction archives fulfil the functions of all three major types of rogue digital archives: they are, at once, universal archives, community archives, and alternative archives."[38]

Universal archives are driven by an impetus to cohesiveness and gathering as many relevant entries as possible; community archives seek to preserve and promote texts of importance of oppressed and overlooked communities, and alternative archives use nontraditional and nonnormative standards of aesthetic judgement in the valuation of a "good" or valuable text. But De Kosnik recognizes that "digital cultural memory is composed of two threads, woven around each other like the double helix structure of biopolymer strands in a DNA module."[39] One thread consists of "actual archives," which are the searchable and organized repositories of texts, and the other of "conceptual archives," the shared metaphorical storehouse of ideas out of which meaning is created.[40] The sites this project considers are not always archives in the actual sense, because they do not necessarily seek to preserve texts, nor are they always easy to navigate. Tumblr is particularly notorious for instability and poor search functions. But they all contribute to the broader metaphorical archive of meanings through which fandom has shaped contemporary emo. The construction of "primers" on LiveJournal—a fandom trend for piecing together commonly told histories of emo bands and band members with photo and video evidence—is a good example of the narrative database, as these primers are key resources for fan fic. Primers arguing for a particular interpretation of events, relationships, controversies, and so on are also called manifestos. Manifestos and primers are narrative databases and community alternative archives.

De Kosnik points out that the individual end user now has a far more active role in curating and constructing the flow of material to which she is exposed. Because all materials are made equally available, "so users of an Internet archive may 'activate' whichever of the materials they wish, constructing their own personal canons based on the materials that they use."[41] This is the process in action when people select images, GIFs, and quotations from primers to create fic and an illustration of the phenomenon noted earlier, of a movement from sites and practices that are more like a broadcast model, toward sites and practices that are more like bottom-up UGC. To illustrate, we might place De Kosnik's and Booth's work next to Daniel Cavicchi's 1993 monograph, *Tramps Like Us: Music and Meaning among Springsteen Fans*. There are not many monographs in fan studies working on music subcultures, something Cavicchi attributed to musicology's relatively late turn to user agency in the construction of meaning. Although Cavicchi perceives his work in the active audience tradition, his interviewees and survey respondents were very much responding to a received/broadcast set of images and sound, which they interpreted with regard to music theory, their lived experiences, and trade press accounts of Bruce Springsteen's life. I am not suggesting that Cavicchi's fans are cultural dupes by another name, but the limit of their textual production was hard-copy fanzines with a necessarily small circulation. Compared with the generative and archival practices of contemporary online fandom, there has clearly been a shift in the kind and degree of activity we can now understand as productive of cultural meaning.

The shifting powers of construction between industrial texts and fanwork can also be illustrated by examining how online culture has facilitated fandoms for texts with some barrier to direct experience. Booth explores the fandom invention of "SuperWhoLock," a hypothetical mashup or crossover of the cult shows *Supernatural*, *Doctor Who*, and *Sherlock*. Through the construction of fan fic, GIFs, art, videos, and GIF fics (short stories told through the juxtaposition of GIFs with captions), these fans literally "create the text they are fans of" by "linking the texts . . . with the practices learned from other fan communities."[42] As Booth notes, the three source texts have certain things in common: "each features a white male protagonist (or two) who is troubled and emotional; each features story arcs as well as monster of the week episodes [and] each has a strong fan audience."[43] But the invention of SuperWhoLock is fan work. Relatedly, fans of the NBC sitcom *Community* have created an entire backstory for *Community*'s text-within-a-text, a *Doctor Who* parody by the name of *Inspector Spacetime*. Inspector Spacetime fandom is a subsection of Community fandom, which through a process of collective authorship, has invented an entire history, canon, and a large amount of fan art and fan fic for the hypothetical text. *Inspector Spacetime* provides a variation on the process of fandom coming "full circle" in its relationship with industry. Inspired by the fandom's enthusiasm and creativity, actor Travis Richey has launched the web series *Untitled Web Series about a Space Traveller Who Can Also Travel through Time*. Williams has studied the affordances of online communities for what she calls "post-object fandom": fandom of and around texts that are officially over, such as television series that have ended or bands that have broken up.[44] As My Chemical Romance (MCR) broke up in 2013 and did not reunite until 2019, when this research was concluded, the MCR fandom was studied technically as a form of postobject fandom, though one uniquely ratified by frontman Gerard Way's departing statement that "My Chemical Romance is done. But it can never die. It is alive in me, in the guys, and it is alive inside all of you. I always knew that, and I think you did too. Because it is not a band—it is an idea."[45] An idea indeed, and one that, in Williams's words, "is kept alive through the creation of both official para-texts and fanfiction, videos and other user-generated texts."[46]

Digital fandom compresses time and space: new fans discover MCR through "emo fandom" and find themselves confronted with a back catalog of albums and immediately available interviews/press material/fan work from every period of the band's career. MCR fandom seems as intense as it ever was, contra Williams's suggestion that "in the absence of live gigs to attend or a lack of new material to enjoy, a fan of a rock group may still occasionally listen to CDs or wear a T-shirt but consider themselves to have a lessened investment in this group."[47] The affordances of YouTube and the carefully preserved community archives of scanned magazines, combined with the fact that all MCR members have released new music since 2013 and are active on social media, creates an experience of currentness that was always available to new fans after the breakup. The live experience was lost, of course, which necessarily makes their fandom of a different quality to those of us who grew up with MCR—several younger fans expressed to me their envy that I have "seen MCR live," a sort of impossible holy grail that could only ever exist as an idea(l).

Finally, I want to introduce some recent work on online culture more generally and raise the question of how theories around trolling, memes, and humor associated with new media creativity(/destructiveness) interact and overlap with fan spaces. If we accept that fandom is increasingly merging with online culture at large, and that a philosophy of playfulness underlies new media engagement, it is necessary to consider how these forces alter the construction of text and its reuptake by the industry. As someone who first became a fan of the Emo Trinity bands as a teen in the early 2000s (not that the name had been invented!), my first encounters with younger millennials' digital fandom were equally surprising, provocative, and hilarious. These affective practices appeared less serious, less earnest, more self-aware, more ironic, and far less respectful than I would have thought—had I, at the age of sixteen or so, been confronted with an image of Emo Pepe, decked in black eyeliner, crying a single tear or reciting a frog-appropriate version of the lyrics to "Welcome to the Black Parade," I would have been confused and disconcerted. Here, contrasting the infamous cooptation of Pepe as a white nationalist symbol, we observe a key example of fandom's capacity to alter social discourse in the broader sense. Much activity positioned as fandom appears to exist along the borderline of laughing at oneself and laughing at the genre, quite in opposition to the serious, gendered policing of musical hierarchies one finds around rock subgenres in the trade press.

Most emo fans are girls. Greenwald has commented quite rightly that if boys dominate the bands, "girls rule the (message)boards,"[48] an extension of the "bedroom cultures" McRobbie and Garber first recognized as fundamental to girls' identity construction in adolescence.[49] Burgess and Green remind us that girls' "cultural performance have always been part of the repertoire of these semi-private spaces of cultural participations."[50] They discuss girls who turn the camera on themselves in producing content, but the production and manipulation of text, particularly as part of a shared culture with developing and changing social codes, is no less contributory to and transformative of public discourse. Burgess and Green describe this discursive work as a process of "redaction"—"the production of new material by the process of editing existing content."[51] Redaction is not reduction—indeed, it frequently involves addition, such as annotation, illustration, or comment. Girls' fandom of rock bands has been framed as problematic since the era of so-called Beatlemania:[52] hypersexual, naive, out of control, and somehow threatening to the bands' status as serious musicians. While the last of these charges might apply, it seems to me that on the contrary, the redaction we observe from MySpace to Tumblr is increasingly sophisticated: highly controlled, only ambiguously complimentary, and perpetually amused.

We have established, then, that the question of what emo is in 2019 is complex, fundamentally entailing questions of gender, genre, gatekeeping, and participation in public discourse. Its development also provides a striking insight into the shifting relations of authority between music labels, the trade press, artists, and fandom, providing a vital case study of fandom's definitional abilities in the new media environment. The question of definition—of what kind of statements, and in what context, count as definitive—cuts to the heart of questions about social hierarchies, oppressions, and power struggles. As we will see in chapter 1, music has always been a nexus of cultural anxiety regarding masculinity, femininity, and authority, the problem of genre being intricately tied up with gender in both professional discourse and fandom. In chapter 1, I examine how critics up to now have addressed emo and gender, before I more properly explain the discursive theory and method used in the rest of the book.

# 1

## THE PROBLEM OF GENDER AND GENRE

### EMO IN CONTEXT

When Panic! at the Disco released the single "Girls/Girls/Boys" from their 2013 album *Too Weird to Live, Too Rare to Die*, it was hailed in some progressive media as a "bisexual anthem."[1] The title plays on the cliché of being a rock star surrounded by groupies, but the song acknowledges bisexual possibilities. It seems initially that some of these admirers might be male and that the artist/singer embodied in frontman Brendon Urie might be interested in them. But a close look at the lyrics suggests otherwise. In the song's refrain, it is "girls," specifically, who "love girls and boys": the narrator's dilemma is that the female object of his attention is more interested in another woman than she is in him. While the hypothetical bisexual woman holds all the cards in this scenario ("If you change your mind you know where I am") it is ultimately only girl–girl relationships as framed and contained by the male gaze that are up for affirmation. In other words: look guys, hot lesbians. In this double-edged promise of gendered/sexual rebellion that at the end of the day still upholds and centers male desire, the male gaze, and the masculine subject, writers such as Emily Ryalls and Sam de Boise would argue we could find an encapsulation of gender in emo: a performance of reformist masculinity that ultimately shores up male privilege and centrality.[2] In this chapter, I explore how emo and gender have been constructed in popular and academic music criticism, in opposition to and as a development of rock, punk, and hardcore. This provides necessary context for the chapters that follow. I elaborate a little on the method used in later chapters before beginning the discursive study properly in chapter 2. The few extant studies on emo specifically lead on from academic histories of rock, punk, and hardcore, both critiquing and consolidating their discourses of gender. This is because the bands that came to be called emo mostly developed from this musical tradition. Remember that emo is short for "emotional hardcore" and although the full term is rarely used, its connotations still exert a framing power that lingers by association.[3] In the following discussion, the reader should bear in mind that as always, the genre labels used are semi-retrospective discursive functions rather than essentialist descriptions.

The study of popular music is concerned with the relationship between music, society, and culture. With regard to gender and sexuality, Susan McClary's landmark *Feminine Endings*, published in 1991, was the first monograph from a music scholar that set out to demonstrate how music "*participates actively* in the *social organization* of sexuality" (emphasis added) rather than reflecting or illustrating some preexisting state of human life.[4] She argued that the reason certain musical codes are recognizable over long stretches of history is not because of a timeless "universal language" of music but "because certain social attitudes concerning gender have remained relatively constant throughout the stretch of history," such as the association of femininity with weakness and softness and masculinity with hardness and strength.[5] She further demonstrated how women composers had to adopt discursive strategies coded as masculine to be taken seriously. This accords with the perspectives of Nicholas and Agius that in discussing gender, we should be less concerned with simple oppositions such as "men versus women" and more with the pervasive privileging of ways of thinking, speaking, and behaving socially coded as "masculine" over those coded "feminine."[6] They call this process "masculinism," a concept that is useful to us in this book, because it recognizes that although masculinities can vary according to time and place, masculinism (the privilege and preference of whatever is coded masculine) is much more persistent.

McClary's work did much to introduce a social constructivist perspective to musicology and open musicology to cultural studies' perspectives more generally. Frith and McRobbie's critical essay "Rock and Sexuality" was originally published in 1978, but before McClary, it had not made much impact on musicology because of disciplinary boundaries in place at the time. "Rock and Sexuality," which provides contextual background to my study, argued that "rock has become synonymous with a male-defined sexuality," coining the phrase "cock rock" to describe the aggressive, physical, macho style of traditional rock music.[7] Rejecting the concept of a natural human sexuality that music expresses, they contended that "the most important ideological work done by rock is the *construction* of sexuality" (emphasis in original),[8] which renders women as passive objects of exchange between men: "Rock offers a framework within which male sexuality can find a range of acceptable, heterosexual expressions. These images of masculinity are predicated in sexual divisions in the appropriation of rock. Thus we have the male consumer's identification with the rock performer; his collective experience of rock shows which, in this respect, are reminiscent of football matches and other occasions of male camaraderie—the general atmosphere is sexually exclusive, its euphoria depends on the absence of women."[9]

Frith and McRobbie argue that cock rock constructs a cultural Other to define itself against. Cock rock's Other is feminine and incorporates feminized fan practices (gossip, crushes, feminine sexuality) and performances of "teenybop" pop music. Norma Coates argued that according to this binary, "rock is metonymic with 'authenticity' whilst pop is metonymic with 'artifice.' Sliding even further down the metonymic slope, 'authentic' becomes 'masculine' whilst 'artificial' becomes 'feminine.'"[10] Cock rock is aggressively (white) masculine. The sexuality it constructs is based on the subjugation and objectification of women—the guitar and microphone become phallic symbols of male power. Emo bands perform an explicit rejection of cock rock masculinity, as culturally feminine attributes like sensitivity and softness are valued in lyric content. Rosemary Hill has analyzed a gendered process of gatekeeping in the UK magazine *Kerrang!*, traditionally devoted to metal, rock, and hardcore, which started featuring emo bands in the early 2000s. She writes that the presence of these bands in the magazines and the female readers they attracted "caused a revolt amongst fans of more established metal bands, who represent the magazine and emo as feminised, akin to the mainstream."[11] Hill hoped that "the presence of many vocal young fans open to ideas of fluidity of gender" may have a transformative effect on gender constructions, and although this project in some ways demonstrates fulfillment of that hope, we should also bear in mind that fandom practices perceived as too overtly feminine, not to mention actual women, are quite frequently denigrated in emo lyrics and in fan communities, a tension I explore in the coming chapters.

Punk by definition is a disaffected response to both politics and music's ability to change politics. As Grossberg reminds us, punk was discursively positioned in response to the institutionalization and dilution of rock and roll:

> Punk emerged at, and responded to, a particular moment in the history of rock and roll. It is, after all, not coincidental that in 1976 the first of the baby boomers were turning thirty. Punk attacked rock and roll for having grown old and fat, for having lost that which puts it in touch with its audience and outside of the hegemonic reality. It attacked rock and roll in the guise of megagroups and arena rock, hippies and baby boomers who had clearly become part of what was supposed to be outside of rock and roll.[12]

Rock had become associated with huge stadiums, expensive shows, and hierarchy and distance between performers and audience. Punk introduced a DIY ethos; a rougher, less technical sound; and an egalitarian, communal rhetoric wherein bands and audience shared performance space in small venues. Some bands that went on to become successful in the mid-2000s got their start this way. Figure 1 shows an early Fall Out Boy gig with no effective space between the band and the (somewhat unenthused) audience. They display several discursive markers of punk and hardcore shows: a flat stage, plain dark-colored clothes, and wires, amps, and equipment on messy display, connoting authenticity, lack of pretension, and equality of all present in the space.

Because of punk's radical posture and checkered history with regard to gender and sexism, many studies of the genre employ a feminist lens. Some of this work has come from musicians themselves. Mavis Bayton of feminist punk band The Mistakes conducted an ethnography concerned with the particular obstacles for women in the scene.[13] Her participants discussed

FIGURE 1: Early Fall Out Boy show, January 16, 2002, LaGrange, Illinois. Filmed by Christopher Gutierrez. Screencapped from https://www.youtube.com/watch ?v=BGyXnty4tRM.

the prejudices they encountered in a male-dominated sphere, the lack of female mentoring system in the genre, and the anxieties they felt around technology.[14] Her interviewees report being startled by "their first experience with amplification" and having an "initial fear of feedback."[15] This "fear of being loud" is clearly born out of cultural expectations for women. Similarly, Brockmeier quotes punk legend Ian MacKaye as attributing the lack of women in hardcore to "a certain kind of aggressiveness that leads the boys to pick up instruments."[16] This statement implies that women and girls do not have this aggression. In the individual cases where women have been accepted as musicians, it tends to be on a backing instrument, such as a bass guitar. Brockmeier comments that as well as being perceived as "easier" to play, "bass is [discursively constructed as] the least aggressive instrument. It is supportive and is in many cases heard in the background, where women take their place."[17]

In addition to these cultural and physical barriers, Helen Reddington has argued that the elision of women and girls in histories of punk and hardcore is an "example of male hegemonic control over popular cultural history."[18]

In a work of feminist reclamation, she documents the "large and productive presence of young women in the subculture from its very beginning," from musicians to organization and promotional work.[19] Brockmeier likewise documents girls' involvement in the punk and hardcore scenes, describing hardcore as a form of protest music for and by a variety of "outsiders."[20] However, it could be questioned whether punk and hardcore were ever popular or widespread enough to effect meaningful social change. The hardcore scene in particular was inward-looking: less concerned with changing society than creating an alternative bubble. Emo has been likewise characterized as an alternative space, rather than a rebellious or challenging one.[21] More seriously, for those who would uphold hardcore as a progressive social movement, "events and concerts frequently ended in brawls and attracted white-power skinheads" drawn by the "aggressive style of music."[22] Fall Out Boy's drummer, Andy Hurley, and bassist/lyricist, Pete Wentz, cite racism as a major reason for leaving the hardcore scene: their experiments with an antiracist hardcore band, Racetraitor, were short-lived and not particularly successful.[23] These stories position the bands that came to be called emo as the better alternative, constructing FOB (Fall Out Boy) as part of a movement that takes up and corrects the social legacy of hardcore. Compare the following comments from My Chemical Romance frontman, Gerard Way, being interviewed with rhythm guitarist Frank Iero in 2011:

> **Interviewer:** All of you guys are married right now
>
> **FI and GW:** Mm hmm (affirmative)
>
> **Interviewer:** So there's no use for meeting girls on the road and stuff like that
>
> **GW:** There never was that's actually the funny part
>
> **FI:** Yeah
>
> **Interviewer:** But I like that uh (.) you say that you have given rock bands bad name [*sic*] because of that (.) because you have never done any stuff like that
>
> **FI:** (laughs)
>
> **GW:** Oh yeah (.) absolutely I (.) I (.) let's just say (.) without mentioning names (.) I've sensed frustration or tension around certain kinds of bands (.) because we don't play that kind of game (.) like we've just

never been that kind of band and I think (.) we're a bummer to those kind of bands 'cos we represent kind of the direct opposite which is you know like respecting women and (.) not objectifying them and (.) and (.) not (.) not basically starting a rock band to get laid . . . (.) that's frustrating for some people that we take the high road and some people don't like that.[24]

There are two points of note here. First, artists and interviewer are concerned to construct My Chemical Romance (MCR) as "rock," rather than "emo," as the latter term had not yet been taken up again and author-ized by industry figures. Second, contra the interviewer's promptings, Way is constructing MCR as part of a new, better kind of rock, distancing his band from the cock rock tradition.

Brockmeier writes that while unlike cock rock, hardcore's ideals included gender equality, the scene frequently failed to live up to its progressive self-image. Raha noted that it was "a community which proudly rejects societal and cultural norms, yet, that same community falls prey to those same traditions and confining notions of behaviour in regards to gender and sexual identity."[25] The problem of women in emo has genealogical roots here. Brockmeier quotes an introduction from the only live show by the influential if short-lived Alone in a Crowd in 1988:

This next song goes out to specific type of person that comes into this scene, it's a type of girl that thinks that they can find some kind of respect and status by knowing people who are influential in the scene. Who will stoop to any level just to be fucking respected. You cannot be respected if you are not a human being. This song is not about the people who are real, it's about the people who are fake. And this song is about the people who think it's not who you are, it's who you know.[26]

The "fake" who "stoop[s] to any [implied, sexual] level" in pursuit of subcultural capital is the genealogical predecessor of the scene queen, the token unfaithful female figure who appears in so many emo lyrics. Hardcore was likewise difficult for women to negotiate as performers. While the scene gave rise to breakaway bands featuring or made up solely of women (notably Black Flag, a strong influence on My Chemical Romance), Brockmeier argues that "the raw sound of hardcore had no room for a female voice."[27] Here we see a key example of how masculinity (associated with the assumed deepness and power of the male voice) is socially constructed as more serious and authentic than higher-pitched female tones. There is no a priori reason the male scream should be read as more serious or "raw" than a female voice; the "authenticity" of the masculine is a purely discursive construct.

The first wave of bands that were called emo came directly from this US hardcore scene. Whether they really "sounded like" the 2000s Emo Trinity bands is a moot point—the genealogical connection, and thus the inherited politics, has been discursively built and maintained by fans and the trade press alike. This is an ongoing process of narractivity. Bands like Rites of Spring, Jawbreaker, Embrace, and Fugazi maintained much of the hard-core sound but introduced lyrical content focusing on sadness, heartbreak, and depression as opposed to just anger. Content became more focused on interpersonal relations than on politics in the narrower sense. Furguson considers that "emo spread worldwide" during the 1990s, when bands like Sunny Day Real Estate and Dashboard Confessional began to get radio air-play, even though "emo" was still not an established discourse/identifier outside a small, restricted scene.[28] Meanwhile, the rise of home internet usage was rapidly transforming the music industry, music fandom, and their relationships with broader social discourse. Hodkinson believes that "the onset of the Internet served to consolidate and strengthen . . . subcultural boundaries" (through creation of an echo chamber effect),[29] other scholars have argued that the condensation and overlap of many kinds of culture facilitate discursive osmosis and social change online and off. Given Stein's observations on the overlap and diffusion between fan culture and millennial culture more generally, I think the latter view is now more warranted.

Overell observes that in the early 2000s, the success of the bands now called the Emo Trinity "overlapped with the popularity of online social networking sites 'MySpace' and 'LiveJournal' . . . These sites hosted a plethora of emo-related online communities, with MySpace being known anecdotally as 'emospace.'"[30] Meanwhile, smaller imprints and independent labels were working to distinguish their brands against the rapid homogenization of the music industry, using the affordances of new technologies and connectivity with young audiences. In the wake of the 9/11 terrorist attacks and the unpopular wars that followed, disaffection, cynicism, and anxiety increased among young people. The scene was set, and emo was poised for reinvention.

On November 23, 2015, *Rolling Stone* ran the headline "How Emo Night Vindicated the Scene," reporting on a themed club night that has "become an emotional traveling circus of sorts, visiting everywhere from Seattle to Omaha and gathering a diverse crowd of emo fans and scene legends to perform and attend."[31] The event constructs itself rather ironically—at the end of the year, Spanos reports, "they'll celebrate #1YearofTears and the first anniversary of Emo Night LA"—clearly influenced by pervasive use of irony and ambiguity in online fandom. Dashboard Confessional's Chris Carrabba, who performed on the anniversary, is quoted as commenting: "What made our scene so unique was the bonding of the bands just like the bonding of the fans. . . . All the bands that started out together, from My Chemical Romance to Thursday to Saves the Day to the Get Up Kids, still talk all the time, tour all time. We have that special bond together after building a whole scene up with all the heavy-lifting of the fans."[32]

Emo is thus constructed retroactively and self-consciously in the trade press, via genealogical descent from Saves the Day to MCR. Asked to reflect on MCR's former rejection of the term, bassist Mikey Way (younger brother of Gerard) is quoted:

> "We used to detest the word," [Mikey] Way remembers with a laugh. "We were pretty against it for a while because we thought it was a dishonest term record labels were using at the time to get them to buy things they were selling. If the band had the right hair or the right look, they would call them emo. If they were on a specific label, they would call them emo. That's why we had kind of a negative take on it for a while. It's aging nicely."[33]

"Aging" is one way to put it, but in the context of discourse analysis, we might say emo has "consolidated" as a genre definition.[34] The three bands it has consolidated around are MCR, Fall Out Boy, and Panic! at the Disco. Fans were calling MCR emo since the LiveJournal days, while the band was still rejecting the term as an empty signifier used by marketers. Speaking to *Rolling Stone* in 2007, Gerard Way called the concept of emo "a pile of shit" and claimed it "has never been accurate to describe us": "I think there's bands that unfortunately we get lumped in with that are considered emo and by default that starts to make us emo. All I can say is anyone actually listening to the records, put the records next to each other and listen to them and there's actually no similarities. I think emo's a pile of shit."[35]

In 2015, he tweeted a picture of himself with Pete Wentz and the caption "I actually knocked and [*sic*] Pete's door and asked him if he wanted to take a 'legends of emo' selfie."[36] Naturally, the tweet has become fandom-famous, recirculated and annotated with expressions of extreme delight (and mockery). By contrast, in his 2005 biography, music journalist Tom Bryant was at pains to construct MCR as a cock rock band in opposition to the feminine. He quotes "reputable" rock periodicals like *Q* and *NME*, and seeks to demarcate their music's difference from "'whiny [read: feminine] emo."[37]

The Emo Trinity bands are all male, though Panic! did briefly hire a woman as a touring bassist, and Fall Out Boy has collaborated with and featured female performers. As I discuss in chapter 4, the most notable of these is Courtney Love, a key punk rock example of a successful woman whose primary media construction is through her late husband, Kurt Cobain. We might compare the in-scene standing of Lindsey Way (née Ballatto), the bassist of Mindless Self Indulgence, who is married to Gerard Way. Despite the fact that she is a successful musician and visual artist in her own right, her construction by fans is primarily as a wife and mother, though Tumblr users have started to exhibit some pushback against this. Some bands on the Decaydance/Fueled by Ramen label feature women: Paramore and The Hush Sound are sometimes considered emo bands, and both have female singers. The long-standing binary in Western thought that aligns women with nature and men with culture has meant that historically, women have been more readily accepted as singers than as composers and instrumentalists. There is a prevalent misconception that singing, even at a professional level, is somehow "natural," whereas musical instruments require learned technical mastery. Victoria Asher was the keytarist in the semi-joke band Cobra Starship (2006–15). Cobra Starship's songs and videos frequently featured flamboyant gender play, including a song about male prostitution sung first-person by frontman Gabriel Saporta.

With regard to gender, Asher's role was notable for its lack of note—she was a full participant in interviews and on stage, and the fact of her being a woman was scarcely mentioned. She dressed in a way that both signified femininity (skirts, long hair) and allotted her into the band as a group (matching color schemes, for instance). If Cobra Starship had actually been an emo band, her presence would have forestalled the objection that only men can be artists/

instrumentals in emo. Despite sharing a label and frequent collaborations with emo bands, Cobra Starship was presented more as a commentary on emo than an emo band itself. Saporta had once been the frontman of Midtown, one of the New Jersey punk bands that inspired the Emo Trinity, before supposedly receiving a vision from a mystical cobra. This often repeated story is visualized in the 2007 video to the single "Send My Love to the Dancefloor, I'll See You in Hell," with the cobra's instructions subtitled. Having transported Saporta to a futuristic starship, the cobra appears and reveals that Saporta's true destiny is "to teach hipsters to not take themselves so seriously, and emo kids to stop being pussies."[38] Here again is Nicholas and Agius's masculinism in action. The construction of female musicianship and its absence is quite complex—women, it seems, cannot really lay claim to the status of artist in emo—yet emo is criticized and self-criticized for feminine properties, metaphorically attached to male bodies.

To see how fandom has shaped emo, we first need to examine the statements of the trade press and academics regarding emo as a concept. This is not a top-down, authority-to-subversion model by which we can observe the definition changed, for as we have established, several senior music critics don't believe that emo is workable as a genre label. Our purpose is to examine what Foucauldian discourse analysts might call the "genealogy" —that is, the inherited predecessors to current discursive constructs—of the statements this research goes on to examine. In his book *Nothing Feels Good: Teenagers, Emo and Punk Rock*, Andy Greenwald initially denied that the term "emo" has any coherent meaning, arguing that it is simply the label applied to whatever music is favored by sensitive, alternative-leaning youth at a particular point in history.[39] A mere page later he seems to contradict himself, citing independent record label Jade Tree co-owner Darren Walters for a working definition: "Originally [emo] was a genre of hardcore punk that was less focused on politics and heavy music and more on personal politics and melody. It looked to address issues of a personal nature that were being overlooked in the extremely political punk landscape of the Reagan era."[40]

Elsewhere in his book, Greenwald describes emo as a "subgenre of punk" that deals with emotion and vulnerability, and suggests Rites of Spring's 1985 debut album as its inception.[41] Likewise, in his history of emo's development, Aslaksen claims that "Rites of Spring represents a change in the emotional character of hardcore," slowing down "the pounding hardcore influence to bring a much more personalized expression of personal anguish and pain."[42]

Phillipov calls emo "a melodic subgenre of punk rock music, characterised by 'emotional' or personal themes."[43] As we observed, early emo records were released on hardcore labels, and emo bands promoted themselves by association. Statements from emo band members consolidate this: Fall Out Boy's frontman Patrick Stump recalls that at the band's inception, their friends in hardcore bands would offer them slots at shows, to a lukewarm response from audiences who "really just came to mosh."[44] "Moshing" is an aggressive style of dance native to hardcore shows and consists primarily of headbanging and pogoing. Most of FOB's output is too soft in rhythm and melody to support such movement. Regardless of the empirical validity of these statements, they consolidate a history and genealogy for emo, usually tracing a direct line from Rites of Spring to Thursday to MCR, simultaneously to FOB then through to Panic!. De Boise identifies some moshing-repellent sonic qualities that distinguish emo from hardcore and punk: "[early emo bands] experimented with different chord progressions (there was a widespread use of minor seventh chords) and a greater variety of rhythms, frequently involving half-time 'breakdowns.' In contrast to punk's aversion to musical pretentiousness musicians were often more unashamedly technically adept and did not rely almost exclusively on basic I, IV, V 'power-chord' patterns."[45]

The revaluation of technical musicianship clearly marks out a class division from punk: most if not all emo band members are middle class with a middle-class musical and literary education.[46] Moreover, de Boise and Williams claim that there is a distinctive "emo voice," a "slightly prepubescent nasal quality with a diaphragmatic push that resembles the arrogant vocalizations of British punk."[47] As Mack has noted, the alternating use of "high pitched head tones" with chest and throat voice, in conjunction with the "fetishized" use of falsetto, constructs the vocalist's masculinity as fluid, unstable, and continuously improvised.[48] Finally, emo lyrics display a preference for complexity: polysyllaby, irony, long song titles ("The Only Difference Between Suicide and Martyrdom Is the Press Coverage"; "I Slept with Someone in Fall Out Boy and All I Got Was This Stupid Song Written about Me"; "You Know What They Do to Guys Like Us in Prison"), and literary topoi like punning and metaphor. Most emo bands are signed initially to independents and move to major labels later in their careers, to predictable dissatisfaction and accusations of selling out from some of their fanbase.

Picking up the strands from research on punk, several critics have discussed emo's relationship to gender and class politics. Williams relates it to the much-vaunted "crisis of masculinity" of the late twentieth and early twenty-first century: "In many ways, current emo rock embodies what journalists and sociologists have referred to as a so-called crisis of masculinity . . . emo captures the changes in cultural attitudes about masculinity [through] the musical signifiers of emotional weakness—that is, such 'undesirable' qualities like vulnerability, femininity, weakness—while attempting to retain the musical signifiers of aggression that are the bedrock of the punk/hardcore musical style."[49]

Williams argues that the juxtaposition of aggressive and soft instrumentation, timbre, and lyrics reflect contemporary demands for men to show increased emotion. She reads emo as an "attempt to reconcile the long-established codes of masculinity—musical representations of aggression, pomp, stoicism, misogyny, and determination—with more multifaceted human expressions of heartache, weakness, longing and loss."[50] As a discourse analyst, I am wary of suggesting that music "reflects" culture in any simple way or of claiming intention behind it, seeing music instead as one of the texts through which culture is constructed. I would rather argue that emo partakes in and contributes to the construction of new, fractured masculinities, composed of contradictory statements, as we will observe.

Greenwald believes that despite certain continuities with punk, emo is more alternative than oppositional. Emo kids typically accept capitalism as part and parcel of their musical experience: "the middle-class suburban kids buying these records are children of a . . . late-nineties mentality: greed might not be good, but wealth certainly is."[51] Emo's "proposed way out" of middle-class suburban ennui, "accessible concerts" and online communities to which parents have no access, "seems a lot more doable, if not considerably more pleasant, than forming an anticapitalist commune."[52] His teenage interviewees display an awareness and understanding of the music industry that accords with Frith's dictum that incorporation does not diffuse all political potential: "Emo may be marketed, but to us it's fresh and it means something," says Anthony.[53] Likewise, Aslaksen sees the scene as a "challenge to conventional norms of hegemonic middle-class masculinity," born out of discontent with the emotional repression this gender performance entails.[54] He quotes the testimonies of self-identified emo boys he interviewed: "Claudio . . . had a similar statement about emo's expression of feeling. He states, 'I think um emo is about kind of admitting that, "hey guys have feelings."'" Claudio's response is important because it shows that emo allows men to explore feelings that gender norms often do not allow them to express."[55]

Aslaksen's findings are convincing, as far as they go—he is primarily concerned with his interviewees' experience of emo fandom, on which they are of course the authority. Yet describing emo as "oppositional" to hegemonic masculinity is too blunt, particularly in studies that prioritize social/discursive effects over interior experience. Ryan Mack suggests that emo constructs a "synergistic masculinity that dissolves the culturally ascribed border between hegemonic and subordinate masculinities."[56] Building on Connell's insights into the hierarchically organized structure of masculinities, Mack argues first that emo poses a challenge to dominant masculinity, citing assaults on emo boys in Mexico and the Middle East in retribution for their gender performativity. He considers emo masculinity to be "founded upon an emotional earnestness that is oftentimes ascribed to men perceived to act in defiance of hegemonic masculine norms through vulnerability, effeminacy, and passivity."[57] However, he finds in emo "a lyric connection to both hegemonic and subordinate masculinities," notably in frequent references to alcohol, which is "arguably . . . the only signifier of a truly masculine method of coping with loss, or more accurately, the socialized method for men."[58] He considers the emo scream to be a particular locus where hegemonic aggression and subordinated vulnerability and loss synergize. Mack summarizes his concept of synergistic masculinity as "a position within the social organization of masculinity that envelops *both* hegemonic and subordinate masculine polarities and manifests egalitarianism in and between both musical and extramusical conditions."[59] I find the first part of this argument more convincing than the second. As we will find, the construction of masculinity in emo does incorporate and alter statements and signifiers from a wide—and contradictory—range of masculinities, but Mack fails to show how the effect is to "manifest egalitarianism" between gender constructs.

Using a Butlerian discourse analysis from which I take precedent, Mack moves to the study of emo videos, quoting Chris Brickell's distinction that "while the term *performance* implies enactment or doing, *performativity* refers to the constitution of regulatory notions and their effects."[60] "Performativity" refers to physical, embodied acts as statements that contribute to discourse constructions in the social realm. Mack argues that the imagery of isolated figures and open, desolate spaces in emo videos construct a masculinity that is isolated and vulnerable. I am unconvinced and feel Mack misses the citation of an older discourse, one valorizing isolation and the lone male hero excluded from the falsely civilized world. More seriously, there is a fundamental elision in his understanding of gendered discourse. He writes, "Intense and loud dynamics in rock music have signified concepts of hegemonic masculinity such as anger, rage, power, and self-annihilation. In contrast, softness has been related to singer/songwriter traditions and alternative forms of masculinity."[61] Would it not be more accurate to say that softness has been characterized as feminine and identified with women? Mack's "synergistic masculinity" could be just as easily read as an all-encompassing, narcissistic subject position that lays claim to both masculinity and femininity, yet elides actual women to retain all subjectivity to the powerfully androgynous artist-poet.

Sam de Boise disagrees with the claims that emo embodies a crisis of masculinity. "This [erroneously] implies," he writes, "that explicit, male emotional expression is historically incompatible with the performance of Western 'masculinity.'"[62] On the contrary, de Boise contends, the "softening" of masculinity displays "a number of historical continuities with [constructing] masculinities as a means of sustaining gendered inequalities," notably the Romantic artist/subject. He thus "locates emo within a broader strategy of male power, or more properly within a reconfigured continuation of gender inequality."[63] This is an apt illustration of Nicholas and Agius's point: the sensitive man, or man of feeling, is just one variation in historical constructs of masculinity that can be perfectly well incorporated into the broader persistence of masculinism. Relatedly, Carrillo-Vincent finds that rather than outright rebellion or attempting to deconstruct the discourse of gender, emo offers alternative spaces for white middle-class boys to perform masculinity differently. He characterizes emo masculinity as a "peripheral critique of normativity," which "comes largely from otherwise normative subjects: straight, white, middle-class males," and less an overturning than "sideways" critique of the hegemonic subject from people who in many ways embody that subjectivity.[64] This accords with Greenwald's description of emo as alternative rather than oppositional. De Boise even goes on to posit that, in accordance with Connell's theory of hegemony's flexibility, "Emo may actually be an ideological reworking of male power which positions 'sensitive' men above 'Neanderthal' men in light of economic, social and political change. . . . In this way, emo is indicative of societal shifts which guarantee the dominant position of some males rather than a crisis of masculinity."[65]

Once again, I do not believe that popular music is indicative of societal shifts, but that it is part of them: part of the matter that makes up definitions in the social sphere. Nonetheless, I agree with de Boise's broader point that gender hegemony—or masculinism—is flexible enough to incorporate emo masculinities, which have demonstrable predecessors in Romanticism. Moreover, the "sensitive" man's relation to women is not automatically progressive. De Boise argues that the emo scene involves a patronizing concept of chivalry and what he calls "beta-male misogyny"—that is, the expectation of sex from girls in recognition of one's superiority to insensitive, brutish jock types. Girls are frequently the source of male suffering in emo, which de Boise connects back to McClary's analysis of nineteenth-century classical music as "rife with portraits of hapless men who are seduced from their transcendental quest by feminine sensuality."[66] This point is especially applicable to the figure of the scene queen, an imagined object position for women in emo. Not quite a fan, but certainly not a musician, she is frequently the object of address in songs—the artist's muse, lover, and torturer who inevitably betrays him and breaks his heart. The Scene Queen has a long genealogy as a female threat to male strength/creativity/virtue, descended from the cruel mistress of Romantic poetry via the femme fatale. De Boise argues that emo tends to separate sex and love, with the male subject/lyricist "privileging the latter."[67] While acknowledging the divergence from a "normative definition of masculinity" that prioritizes sexual conquest, de Boise points out that "bourgeois ideals of virginity as essential to female respectability have a very long history and it is clear that the double standard around female sexuality still resonates."[68] I am not sure, however, that emo lyrics do maintain a double standard with regard to sexual behavior: the narrator rarely indulges in sex with strangers. He is typically far too obsessed with his muse, his worst crime being semi-pitiful stalking, watching the object of his fantasies enjoy her time with other, more popular boys.

As a former emo kid who grew up listening to the Trinity bands, de Boise writes with a certain insider authority. His work, however, is understandably focused on masculinity and male experience, and it does not really consider the agency of girls in the invention, construction, transformation, and consolidation of the genre. Indeed, this criticism could be leveled at almost all academic work on emo—Aslaksen is a rare exception. This book is primarily concerned with discourse as a public phenomenon; it is difficult, if not impossible, to trace online posts to individual users. Nonetheless, we cannot ignore the fact that girls dominate the kind of social media and on-line fandom practices we are looking at, and that emo today is defined in a space that is, if not feminine, androgynous and queerly gendered much of the time. Notably, the girls Aslaksen interviews are keen to deny structural sexism in the scene:

> **Allie:** Yah I think it could because you're what you're hearing, most emo bands are all guys and they're talking about girls so . . .
>
> **James:** [interrupting Allie] I think women have a better way of looking at things from both sides, rather than men who just kinda have that egotistical, "it's your fault bitch."
>
> **Allie:** Well in some cases it could be like in Taking Back Sunday how the girl is sleeping with both members of the band, [short pause] that's just shitty. [short pause] They write a song about her because she's a bitch.[69]

Ironically, these statements literally play out the privileging of male voic-es, with James speaking over Allie. Allie's input reinforces the construction of the scene queen as bitch/whore and the male as feeling human subject. This emphasizes my point that while the experiences of scene participants are valuable data, we should also attend to the operations of discourse con-structions in the social realm regardless of speaker intention.

Peters's 2010 study of gay emo boys continues the focus on masculinities. His "essay aims to highlight the myriad reactions/responses that emo style signifies to a world that is often far too hegemonic in what it considers mas-culine and/or beautiful."[70] His main contention is that the emo aesthetic and Romantic outlook offer alternatives to the "images of butch masculinity" that dominate the mainstream queer scene. He notes that mainstream gay culture can be just as patriarchal and antifemininity as hetero culture, exclud-ing and Othering feminine boys who must necessarily craft alternative queer identities. In his embrace of androgyny and femininity, the queer emo boy is thus "liberated from the feelings of being insignificant that many masculine-centric social conventions produce."[71] This may be the case, but emo's relation-ship to homosexuality is complex and at times fairly problematic. Of particular note here is the phenomenon known as "stage-gay," that is, the public pres-entation of queer talk and gesture by male performers who identify as straight, up to and including kissing onstage. Such performative statements must be set against and connected to the broader context of the gay marriage debate and its ultimate legalization the United Kingdom and United States—on one hand, stage-gay and the emo articulations of masculinity in general can be read as a progressive rebellion against the homophobia of the hardcore scene, an appeal to queer female desire that subverts the male gaze, and as pushback against hegemonic masculinities that marginalize queer men.[72] On the other hand, it can equally be read as an appropriative capitalist strategy available only to those in the privileged position to use it. Stage-gay is composed of particular performative utterances and gestures between band members, which deliberately "hook" into broader cultural discourses of homosexuality as a way of condensing meanings into a brief or small space.[73]

In this book, I want to make a distinction between stage-gay, which is constituted of specific, highly coded gestures, and queer statements more generally. I use "queer" in the broad sense popularized by theorist Alexander Doty, to cover a whole variety of nonhetero sexualities.[74] Statements I call "queer" often evade or deconstruct the straight/gay binary and normative discourse around relationships. Stage-gay is one kind of queer statement, but queer statements are a broader category than stage-gay. Stage-gay is a key example of Butler's performativity—as discourse analysts, we must read it as positing, constructing, and shaping sexualities in the social realm, regardless of the actual sexuality or feelings of its performers. Furthermore, our readings must vary with context—stage-gay on MySpace in 2002 is a different proposition than queer performance through the present poste-verything assemblages of Tumblr.

Most of the studies I have discussed so far are ethnographies, drawing on interviews and participant observation. This discourse analysis seeks to fill the gap left by lack of attention to textual materials. I have centered the analysis on the internet for ease of data collection and because the internet has been crucial to emo's development. Greenwald is correct to point out the productive intersection between the spread of home broadband and the consolidation of the genre by and for those of us who were adolescents at that time.[75] He writes: "Teenage life has always been about self-creation, and its inflated emotions and high stakes have always existed in a grossly accelerated bubble of hypertime. The internet is the most teenage of media because it too exists in this hypertime of limitless limited moments and constant reinvention. If emo is the soundtrack to hypertime, then the web is its greatest vehicle, the secret tunnel out of the locked bedroom and dead-eyed judgmental scenes of youth."[76]

To this end, Mortara and Ironico have conducted the first "netnography" of the scene, aiming "to analyse the role of creative re-appropriation of goods, symbols, and other manifestations of the dominant material culture in the Emo subculture identity construction process."[77] Using "a purposive sample of social networks, blogs, discussion forums and online platforms for images [*sic*] sharing," the authors' content analysis found that emo kids use and transform commercial cultural materials to accomplish "the aestheticization of inner pain, the sense of alienation and isolation from socio-cultural mainstream, the search for authenticity, and the need for emotional connection."[78] While I am wary of reading participants' subjectivity from texts, their article provides an important precedent in terms of online discourse analysis. The authors write that

> The first stage was to identify the main blogs and discussion forums used by Emos through the special search features offered by Google. Yahoo Answers and Al Femminile had the highest number of threads on Emo lifestyle while the search blog functions immediately brought out Photobucket. . . . The researchers found on Photobucket 420,259 Emo images and decided to analyse the 2000 most recent and the 2000 more viewed (for a total of 4,000 images, summing up photos and drawings). . . . As social networks, the authors examined Netlog and Facebook.[79]

Speaking as a participant, I find this misguided and likely to result in an unrepresentative sample. Emo kids are unlikely to use Google to find sites popular with their peers—they use insider knowledge and word of mouth, and they congregate at the sites music labels use to promote their bands. This is probably why this essay's findings—that emo represents "the aestheticization of inner pain, the sense of alienation and isolation from socio-cultural mainstream, the search for authenticity, and the need for emotional connection"—strike me as one-dimensional.[80] There is no account of humor, reflexivity, or the influence of wider online discourse. As noted, the construction of modern emo began on MySpace and LiveJournal, spreading to YouTube, Tumblr, and so on. Mortara and Ironico are correct, however, to note that in an online context we should pay attention to "de-contextualisation and re-semantisation" of imaged objects and texts, or, to put it in critical discourse analysis terms, the citation and variation of earlier statements in the solidification and transformation of discourse.

Finally, in studying emo, some scholars have engaged with the moral panic that the right-wing UK, US, and Australian media briefly attempted to frame around the scene. I fully address the struggle between the tabloid press and fans, which some magazines dubbed "the war on emo," in chapter 6. Rosemary Overell and Michelle Phillipov discussed the media's treatment of the so-called emo suicides of 2007, where schoolgirls Jody Gater and Stephanie Gestier killed themselves in Melbourne. They were subsequently identified/constructed as emo kids by the popular press, and their use of the internet was pathologized and contrasted with a normative model of girlhood wherein teenagers use new technologies in fun and social ways.[81] In the media narrative, emo kids used the web for secretive, disturbing purposes, which led to isolation and mental illness. Overell's online ethnography of LiveJournal and MySpace and interviews of scene kids found that on the contrary, "the internet enabled group sociality, rather than individual alienation, for emos."[82] Although I agree with Overell that the media pathologization of emo girls is extremely problematic, and likewise with her broader point that in the emo scene, "the internet operates as a form of micro-media, which produces subcultural coherence and sociality," what is missing from her article is some focus on how emo girls use and author texts through the resources of the scene and in response to their media pathologization.[83] This is covered in chapter 6. Moreover, in my experience and the findings of this study, emo girls differentiate themselves from normative girlhood, consciously and deliberately, and certainly would wish to distinguish themselves from "young women [who] bounce happily to pop music [and] giggle as they try on colourful dresses and flirt with young men."[84] Girls who behave in this way would be considered unintelligent, brainwashed, and shallow by many emo girls. Overell's interviewees bear this out—she found that (contra Greenwald on inclusivity) emo kids accumulate and exercise subcultural capital, policing the boundaries of their scene from those deemed inauthentic. Emo kids defined themselves against "posers," as her interviewees put it:

**Manda Bum:** Yeah, there's now emo-poser-barbies who just wear skinny jeans and have the emo mullet.

**Erin:** I hate those mainstream emos!!! . . . Emo has moved into supre— the ultimate "look at me I'm a pretty girl" shop.[85]

The denigration of "pretty girls" and their association with the mainstream is an example of how emo girls separate themselves from "normative girl-hood," and any study of emo kids' art and writing will bear that out. Thornton established that "the mainstream," as a concept, is discursively conflated with femininity in subcultures that seek to distinguish themselves as superior alternatives, a modern development of "the traditional divide between virile high art and feminized low entertainment."[86] We have already established that emo has a problematic relationship with femininities. Studying the patterns of acceptance and rejection from LiveJournal communities, Overell observes that male applicants were "universally accepted" based on "their music likes and opinions," whereas "communities' moderators often positioned female applicants' appearances as the basis for acceptance or rejection" before conflating this with insufficiently discriminating taste in music. "All the 'rejectees' whom I canvassed were women, confirming the feminization of the 'true' emo's 'fake' Other."[87] In other words, boys were accepted as authentically belonging to the group based on their say-so, while girls were held to particular standards of appearance and performance, and femininity was conflated with disparaged constructs like "mainstream" and "inauthentic." These statements thus hook into a solid, well-established binary. Building on Thornton, Hill writes: "To some degree the mainstream stands in for the masses . . . derivative, superficial and *femme*. It is associated with pop music, fashion, herd mentality, passive consumption, and lack of discernment or real taste (Thornton 1995, pp. 99–100). 'Subcultures', on the other hand, are authentic, intelligent, original and independent."[88]

Thus Overell's moderator tells a female community applicant she is unattractive, then slides straight into a dismissal with "you sound like you got your list of emo bands from MTV2."[89] Here is evidence for my argument against Mack—that supposed "synergistic masculinity" is not so much a synthesis of hegemonic and subordinated masculinities but a centering of the variously gendered male subject as fully human at the expense of women and girls.

Angela Thomas-Jones documents the concerns of tabloids and pop psychologists with emo. She is concerned with emo history being overwritten by self-proclaimed experts who are tone deaf to the uses and gratifications emo kids derive from their scene.[90] Hill critiques the *Daily Mail*'s typically tasteless and factually challenged treatment of the scene following the suicide of Hannah Bond, supposedly a happy thirteen-year-old until she succumbed to the "sinister cult of emo." Hill argues that we should "listen to what the young women have to say about their reasons for listening to My Chemical Romance" (and other emo bands).[91] Within the limits of her brief chapter, however, she does not have time to gather more than introductory statements from girls, and she is not concerned with texts. Indeed, this book presents the first project to take a fandom studies perspective in looking at UGC and the textual production of emo—which is strange, given how the scene flourishes online.

On that note, I now take a little space to describe my methodology in more detail. Discourse analysis is the systematic study of language in action. Its key ideas can be traced to Michel Foucault and J. L. Austin, who demonstrated that language in the social sphere is not reflective of meaning but creative of it.[92] There is no objective state of things, or prior reality, behind language: we do not "see through" texts to some truth or reality they succeed or fail in conveying, because discourse *defines* reality. Some examples of this are very obvious—Austin called them "performatives"—where speaking a word or signing a name in particular contexts brings a state of affairs into existence ("Not guilty"; "You're fired"; "I now pronounce you husband and wife"). Foucault demonstrated through a series of book-length studies how language does not merely create social/legal states but actively constructs subjects and objects of knowledge over time, some of which come to be taken as ineffable and unchanging, thus creating a false impression of language's neutrality. He traced the history of several discourses, including sexuality and medicine, to demonstrate that there is no "thing" called, for instance, medicine—what comprises medicine at any given time is what society includes in the books it calls medical books, teaches in the courses the relevant institutions call medical training, is practiced in the offices of the people we call medical professionals, and so on. Clearly, context is crucial—we imbue certain positions with the authority to make pronouncements on what "counts" as medicine and what doesn't—but what matters here is the speaker's position, which is a social construct, not their intention or reason for speaking or their internal state. Discourses are flexible, and change over time; in previous work, I have looked specifically at how the practice of fan fiction changes and/or upholds and solidifies discourse constructions from favored cult texts.[93] Discussing a similar method of online discourse analysis, Marsh usefully describes this sort of process as "a Foucauldian approach to discourse analysis, in which the body of statements which constitute a discourse are examined in terms of how they are created, what can be said and what cannot be said and how practices are both discursively and materially constructed."[94] As I have demonstrated elsewhere, it is important that we pay attention to absences as well as present statements in discourse formations, that is, what is not said, and what sort of statements are rejected and silenced by the broader community.

Norman Fairclough developed these philosophies into his critical discourse analysis, which pays particular attention to power in social and political life.[95] Adding the descriptor "critical" reminds us that discourse is always political in the small-$p$ sense. How could it not be? It addresses the linguistic and textual struggle through which concepts are defined, positions established, changes introduced or rejected. Laclau and Mouffe argue that in studying discourse, what we are actually observing is a struggle for definition, a metaphorical pushing and pulling of signifiers by different interests or participants, who consciously or otherwise attempt to "fix" or pin down the meaning of signifier.[96] Selwyn writes that a critical discourse analysis draws attention to the question of how particular representations of the content, relations, and subjects come to dominate popular understandings and in particular come to be "naturalised" as a generally unchallenged form of "common sense." This is when the ideological character of a discourse is obscured—when "received wisdom" works to obscure the vested interests, dominant agendas, and power imbalances of any situation, especially social relations and power hierarchies.[97]

For an illustration relevant to this study, we might observe that until recently, the signifiers "man" and "woman" were mostly fixed in British English. Now as transgender activists' usage comes into conflict with popular received wisdom and with some streams of feminism, we observe a struggle over where the signifier "woman" (especially) should be pinned down—to refer to whom? To which bodies? Because "woman" is defined by its binary opposition to "man," the signifier "man" is likewise thrust into struggle. If Foucault, Laclau, and Mouffe are correct, the definition of a woman is whichever definition is presently dominant and comes to be generally accepted in the sociopolitical life of the culture in question—though no signifier will ever be fixed permanently and totally, and the degree of fixedness will vary by context.

Foucault was looking primarily at written language, but discourses are constructed from statements made in a whole range of media. We should not confuse the term "statement" in discourse analysis with "sentence" or "utterance"—sentences and utterances are a kind of statement, but not all statements are sentences or utterances. Because I will analyze web networks, I require a tool set that is sensitive to an online context. Chiew suggests that in discourse analysis online, we differentiate between the categories he calls item, lexia, cluster, and web.[98] "Item" refers to what I have previously called a statement, after Foucault: a single unit of meaning, such as an image, caption, typed sentence, or utterance. Seeing as this project is more multimedia focused and my last book focused on the written (digital) word, I think "item" is sometimes more appropriate than "statement" (although the reader should bear in mind that theoretically, the terms are synonymous). "Lexia" refers to a single webpage one can scroll without following a link, such as a blog entry and comments; "cluster" refers to a set of linked websites, and "web" to the World Wide Web itself. Meaning is created in the interaction between these levels.[99] In band fandom, many (if not most) of the still and moving images concern faces and bodies. Judith Butler, whose work develops both Foucault's and Austin's, coined the term "performativity" to describe the physical, bodily statements like gestures, mannerisms, dress, and so forth that operate to construct gender in everyday life. Performativity is different than performance, because it is constant and ubiquitous, and all of us partake in it whether we mean to or not. Performativity works primarily by citation—all of our gestures, movement, choice (or the imposition) of clothing and accessories work by reference to the social history of gender performativity.[100] We cannot get outside discourse—we live in it. Whether I wear a suit, jeans, or a skirt to a job interview, the items solidify and/or work against preconstructed discourse of what it currently means to be a woman and an academic.

In this book, I use multimodal discourse analysis, defined quite simply as the analysis of "discourse . . . which make[s] use of multiple semiotic resources," including "meaning arising from the integrated use of semiotic resources" and their juxtaposition.[101] As Baldry puts it, multimodal text analysis does not accept the notion that the meaning of the text can be divided into a number of separate semiotic "channels " or "codes": the meaning of a multimodal text is instead the composite product/process of the ways different resources are co-deployed.[102]

The caption of an image, for example, might subvert its most obvious connotations, confirm them, or do something else entirely. Roland Barthes recognized two possible functions of text juxtaposed to an image. First, texts can "anchor" interpretation, which is to say, direct the viewer's attention to a certain part or perspective, narrowing it down and guiding the reader to a particular interpretation from the range of possible meanings. Alternatively, the text might work in "relay," that is, the text and image work together to create a unified meaning, like a comic strip.[103] I see no reason to limit this insight to texts that caption pictures—annotations to a playlist or commentary on a video can serve similar functions. There is necessarily some subjectivity in judging the relationship between text and image; in fact, there is a degree of subjectivity in all discourse analysis, a fact Foucault tended to obscure in his desire to present it as a semi-scientific method. The researcher exercises judgment in selecting the sites of interest and picks out the statements and sections for close analysis. I hope that my experience as a longtime fan of emo and participant in online fandom in general, in addition to my training in discourse analysis and the systematic sampling tools I have applied, will ensure that the choices I've made here are as sufficiently representative and notable as any large-scale analysis could hope to be.

Unsurprisingly, multimodal discourse analysis is frequently applied to hypertext. The task is to discern how the affordances of hypertext and the internet operate together and/or against each other as items of discourse, including how a user interacts with the text. Building on Aarseth's description of hypertext as "ergodic" literature, or literature that requires literal exploration, Chiew suggests we understand the digital reader as an "ergodist" or "a choice-making individual" facing a set of paths laid down by the hypertext creator.[104] Though Chiew does emphasize that the ergodist may go off the intended path made most easily usable by the creator, I think there is something missing from his analysis, and that is the impact of the technological platforms themselves. The portability and replicability of online content means that texts change with context. We will see this most obviously in chapter 3 and after, as we progress onto more multimedia-based sites. Band interviews uploaded by journalists or news organizations to YouTube invite the most obvious level of user interaction: simple clicking and then viewing as one would a broadcast. But the affordances of web 2.0, in combination with the social norms and practical examples from older fandoms, have allowed them to be remixed, edited, and adapted. Often, simply moving an image can change its meaning—copying and pasting a candid photo into one of the "manifestos" codes whatever image or GIF is captured as supporting the compiler's argument. As Chiew reminds us, we should never "divorce hypertext from contextual use because as a means of communication, hypertext only acquires its richness and definition from its use in the social realm. The functions of hypertext are not wholly determined either by technology or society, but by technology used in society."[105]

Jones, Chik, and Hafner's 2015 edited volume, *Discourse and Digital Practices: Doing Discourse Analysis in the Digital Age*, attempts to lay out some guidelines for discourse analysts working with digital media. They suggest that while different studies will prioritize different aspects, all digital discourse analysis should take account of four elements that operate together and against each other. They define these as

- **Texts:** How different technologies of entextualization allow us to combine semiotic elements to form socially recognizable texts that can be used to perform different kinds of socially recognized actions.

- **Contexts:** The social and material situations in which texts are constructed, consumed, exchanged, and appropriated.

- **Actions and interactions:** What people do with texts, especially what they do with and to each other.

- **Power and ideology:** How people use texts to dominate and control others and create certain versions of reality.[106]

By "technologies of entextualization," they refer to the specific features of web 2.0 that people use in constructing and maintaining meaning—we have already encountered De Kosnik's examination of online archives as repositories that categorize, organize, and hierarchize texts; Barton's study of tagging on Flickr would be another example.[107] We have also begun to observe how the social and material contexts of fandom and gender interact with the shaping of emo and the examination of "what people do with texts" is fundamental to the study of both fandoms and subcultural scenes. However, I find the authors' description of "power and ideology" as elements of analysis a little blunt. It slides too easily from "power" to "ideology" as conceptual tools when in fact they are distinct terms. Moreover, discourse analysts aren't generally concerned with "intention," considering the effects and operations of text in the social world more important than what the producer meant. On the other hand, I do think that the chronological/site-based progression of the chapters demonstrates a messy, gradual, uneven, but demonstrable shift in power away from professional, corporate media and toward UGC, fandom, and participatory media. Finally, Jones, Chik, and Hafner remind us that "the nature of new media texts doesn't only change practices of reading and writing . . . but also has the effect of disturbing comfortable notions of textual boundaries."[108] A broadcast interview on MTV has clear temporal and spatial limits, in an absolute sense (say, a four-minute "chat" slot between a video and an ad break) and in terms of which items are to be taken as authoritative (utterances from the artist themselves, as opposed to the interviewer/ audience). An interview coheres internally around a question-and-answer format and makes sense in terms of the broader program format. Once the interview moves online, these borders can be shifted. Jones, Chik, and Hafner argue, "The responsiveness of digital texts, however, not only involves the interaction between writers and readers, but also involves interaction between human users and machine algorithms which automatically alter texts based on the ways users use them or on certain characteristics of users such as location or pre-defined user settings."[109] If embedded in a blog post, the text may cohere around the video, recontextualized by user comments and descriptions. If taken apart and reassembled for a "crack vid,"[110] the coherence mechanisms of the original are deliberately broken and subverted, replaced with new context for humor's sake.

In the cut-and-paste culture of web 2.0., intertextuality and interdiscursivity are more prominent than ever. Vasquez writes that while "every spoken utterance, written text, or instance of computer-mediated communication (CMC) always bears traces of texts that came before it," we should still distinguish between intertextuality strictly speaking, which is direct reference to particular previous texts, and interdiscursivity, which is the invocation of broader genres, styles, and traditions.[111] Fanwork is intertextual, being made out of transformed and readapted snippets from broadcast media, but the influence of netspeak and meme culture in general is an example of "interdiscursivity" or the "hybridisation of one genre or text-type with another."[112] Benson found that his study of multimodal interaction on YouTube was illuminated by "draw[ing] upon tools for the analysis of spoken interaction," notably turn-taking and conversational pairs,[113] to a greater extent than when Herring and colleagues found the wider blogosphere only "sporadically conversational."[114] This may suggest that the context of opening a discussion with a video/audio post influences the following text to use a style that mimics spoken language more closely than that which responds to written text. An important part of discourse analysis is identifying how practices common to particular spaces have altered the situation, with endless and ever-changing rec lists and links to collections to create an unmappable catalog of intersecting desires, often incorporating bandom material with texts from other fandoms, united by style, creator, trope, plot device, or any other link imaginable. Memes are a key example of intertextuality, and in keeping with Booth's philosophy of playfulness, they now feature heavily in bandom spaces. Some are produced within the subculture and others imported interdiscursively from the wider web. Shiffman defines an internet meme as a group of digital items sharing common characteristics of content, form, and/or stance; (b) that were created with awareness of each other; and (c) were circulated, imitated, and/or transformed via the internet by many users.[115]

Memes are a key example of how affect, humor, and play take a public role in public discourse and social change, as "socially constructed public discourses in which different memetic variants represent diverse voices." Used by everyone from teenagers in their bedrooms to news corporations to politicians, memes "spread on a micro basis, [but] their impact is on the macro level: memes shape the mindsets, forms of behaviour, and actions of social groups." Most of the memes we observe in the construction of emo (see figures 2 and 3) are what Shiffman calls "founder-based," that is, "sparked by a specific (often viral) text" and endlessly adapted, although we also observe the "egalitarian meme: comprising many versions that seem to have evolved simultaneously."[116] It is not unusual to encounter Emo Trinity wallpapers that consist of the faces of the three bands' respective frontmen badly Photoshopped onto Christian artwork representing the Father, Son, and Holy Ghost, complete with unnatural angles, mixed perspectives, and unnecessary white space to highlight the "messiness" of the process. Whole YouTube channels are devoted to "emo crack": videos cutting up clips of the bands to interrupt them with memes, pausing on unfortunate freeze frames and zooms on comedic facial expressions, adding drawn annotations and reaction GIFs. Davisson writes that "in the mashup process that takes place when fans create music videos, new meanings emerge from old cultural artefacts."[117] Frequently, the comedy of emo mashups is generated by the juxtaposition of footage intended to frame the bands as serious rock musicians in the tradition of white male artistry and the unruly bathos of the internet ugly aesthetic. The critique is thus necessarily gendered: it is queer critique, from Doty's broad perspective on queerness as whatever is opposed or tangential to hegemonic gender constructs.

Figure 2: Emo pepe (Pete Wentz).

"Crack" and "shitposting" are terms specific to fandom and online culture. I prefer them to the better-known "trolling," for as Phillips and Milner
write, in both popular and academic press, online behaviors with even the
slightest whiff of mischief, oddity, or antagonism are often lumped under
the category of trolling. Although specific definitions of the term can vary,
its use tends to imply deliberate, playful subterfuge and the infliction of
emotional distress on unwitting or unwilling audiences.[118]

At times, the behavior emo fandom displays would fall under the broad
definition of trolling, albeit in a relatively harmless mode. For example, being
"G-noted" is the fandom equivalent of being RickRolled— that is, being linked
out of context to the opening piano notes of "Welcome to the Black Parade,"
which is claimed to induce angst and pain in an unsuspecting listener. Likewise,
leaving YouTube comments such as "Last time I was this early, MCR was still a
band," or "Last time I was this early, Panic still had band members" (Panic! at
the Disco has gone through a dramatic series of lineup changes, which upset
some members of fandom) are traditionally met with responses like "Why
do you hurt me?"; "Let me live"; or more self-reflexively "I love suffering."

When I was, a young meme, my frogther, took me into
the city, to see a memeing band, he said, "pepe,
when you grow up, would you be the savior of the
memeless, the tadpoles, and the dankests,"

#meem #meme #me
#so imma add a mil hashtags but u dont need to read them so like yaeh have
a good dday
#pepe #dank #rare #rare pepe #mcr #chemical #romance #my
#frog #frogs #mcrmeme #mcr meme #mcr memes #emo #goth
#rad #cool #tumblr #fun #funny #jok #joke #hilarious #reblog
#trending #funnn

**432 notes**  Jul 22nd, 2015                                  ···

Figure 3: Emo pepe (My Chemical Romance).

Yet Phillips probably would not call this trolling, precisely. If we are going to argue for fandom's effect on social discourse, we must be more specific. In other work, Phillips's definition mostly limits trolling to purposeful conflict with the aim of defeating one's opponent, preferably with humiliation. She argues: "Trolls' privileging of cool rationality over emotionalism, coupled with their emphasis on 'winning,' that is, successfully exerting dominance over a given opponent, represents a logical extension of androcentrism, what cultural theorist Pierre Bourdieu describes as the 'continuous, silent, invisible injunctions' that naturalize a phallocentric (male-focused) worldview. Though androcentrism may manifest itself as violent sexism or misogyny, it is in fact most potent when its effects are taken to be natural and necessary, something that could not be otherwise."[119] This does not describe the sort of practices I observe in emo fandom, which is not an androcentric or masculinist practice at all. Nor could it be characterized as a "feminine" one. If anything, it is antigender, equally mocking the heteronormative-masculine standards emo supposedly rejects and pretensions to undermine it. Moreover, Phillips believes that trolling necessarily privileges logic and rationality over emotion, as the point of troll engagement is to win. Phillips and Milner contrast trolling to online ambiguity, which cannot be categorized as serious, ironic, earnest, aggressive, or benign, but incorporates all. Ambiguous new media content can convey earnest emotion and irony at the same time, as well as negation and approval, mockery and admiration. It deconstructs the false binary equating emotionless reason with "serious" speech, with political public purpose, and affect with the nonserious, private, and trivial. As Zizi Papparchissi has shown,[120] affect and emotion are as much contributors to public discourse as reason is: "Just as anger and frustration can facilitate meaningful public debate, so too can engagement that appears to be 'just' playful. Theorists across disciplines have long affirmed the political potential of play, immediately complicating the notion that play is, or should be, framed as 'just' anything."[121] The exclusion of play, humor, and affect from "serious" public discourse often serves a conservative function, reserving the capacity to speak to those already authorized and positioned to uphold the status quo—say, middle-aged male rock critics who write for *Rolling Stone*, as opposed to teenage girls who play on Tumblr.

Finally, although this study is focused on the internet, there has never been a better time to answer Marchant's call for a subcultural studies that connects micro and macro politics, a method of connecting scenes and subcultures to broader social contexts. Bennett argued in 1999 that we now see more "osmosis" between subcultures and wider society than the Birmingham School addressed, and likewise, just as there is no longer any real distinction between fandom and the ordinary business of teen culture, online/offline distinctions are becoming increasingly obsolete.[122] The internet is no longer just a place we visit but part of our everyday fabric of work and play. A cynical perspective would claim that the mass cultural industries have incorporated everything, subcultures are dead, and emo is merely one consumerist lifestyle choice among all the others, one set of style selections from a depoliticized global hypermarket owned by six or eight corporations. To do so would not only be fictitious, it would unjustifiably depoliticize a scene that was publicly deconstructive of both gender and sexual binaries in the hostile climate of the early 2000s. "Being emo" is provocative enough to incite physical violence, from brutality in Mexico against boys dressed in emo style to young women in Saudi Arabia being arrested for wearing the fashions under their abayas.[123] Its musicians have been hit with bottles at rock and hardcore festivals, a clear sign, to quote Gerard Way's enthusiastic account of one such assault, that music is getting "dangerous" again.[124] At its outset, cultural studies was sometimes guilty of overpoliticizing subcultures, of assigning them meanings and purposes their members would neither recognize nor understand. But we must also take care to avoid the opposite mistake—depoliticizing and flattening the important differences between subculture(s) and the mediatized mainstream. In the contemporary online climate, the shaping of emo has done something to gender. The project of this book is to discover what has happened here and how.

# 2

## GATHERING NOTES

### INTRATEXTUALITY FROM MYSPACE
### AND BAND SITES TO LIVEJOURNAL

The three bands that became known as the Emo Trinity launched their websites between 2002 and 2005. Using the Internet Archive Wayback Machine, I was able to analyze a systematic sample of at least one frame from each site per week between their dates of launch until they went offline or converted to their later incarnations (e.g., typing the early site name of "falloutboyrock .com" now redirects to falloutboy.com, a site built on the Tumblr template, which I address in the next chapter). The bands' sites were initially quite amateurish and clunky: Panic!'s first "About Us" page linked to a downloadable Microsoft Word document. Whether by design or lack of resources, this aesthetic seemed to operate as an invitation to intimacy with young teens just discovering the internet. These were the sorts of sites we made. As of 2004, My Chemical Romance (MCR) and Fall Out Boy had established official

MySpace presences that were consistently linked to their sites, while Panic!'s MySpace page was established simultaneously with their website in 2005. Meanwhile, burgeoning fan communities created "chemicalromance" and "falloutboylove" accounts on LiveJournal in December 2002 and January 2003, respectively, five months before Fall Out Boy even released their first album. MCR and FOB were then signed to tiny independent labels Eyeball Records and Uprising, which had little budget for marketing.

Fan communities were initially composed of local teenagers who knew the bands from small club shows, plus a few of their friends who would drop in with obliging attempts at promotion. By the time LiveJournal overtook MySpace as a primary site of fan engagement, these communities had grown hugely, acquiring hundreds of commenters and multiple posts every day, complete with requisite complaints about how the fandoms had gone to hell since all these noobs joined (I'll come back to this). Fans established a LiveJournal community for Panic! at the start of 2005, to which the then-teenage band members sometimes dropped in to give updates.

MySpace pages and the bands' websites are obviously run in an official capacity. These texts are produced for and addressed to fans (even when the early posts, authored by band members, could hardly be called professional). The LiveJournal accounts are fan inventions. This accords with Baym's observation that "by the time musicians and industry figures realized they could use the internet to reach audiences directly, those audiences had already established their presences and social norms online, putting them in unprecedented positions of power."[1] Although it was common knowledge that band members read the LiveJournals (and referred to particular points of them on their own sites), each LiveJournal community is an explicitly co-created, loosely moderated network of discussions where we see the discursive shaping process I've been referring to start to come to fruition. I have found it necessary to refer back to MySpace and the websites that operated alongside LiveJournal not because I view them as official texts which are then reinterpreted by fandom (the reception studies model) but because elements of them serve as raw material—the material out of which fandom invented the Emo Trinity. This chapter begins the discursive study proper, with the first true online fan communities to develop around what would come to be called the Emo Trinity. The bands' sites were far from the only materials used by fandom. As we will see in this chapter, much older discourses concerning music and gender are woven throughout the

LiveJournals, sometimes in ways that appear less progressive than the professional sites.

The bands' sites make some references to the other bands—especially when Pete Wentz initially signed Panic! at the Disco to his Decaydance Records imprint on Fueled by Ramen—but there is no indication that all three belong to a recognizable genre. They also reference hundreds of other bands, most of which have faded into obscurity. On LiveJournal, MCR, Panic!, and FOB are knit together by intratextuality, constant cross-referencing by fans that persists from the opening of the communities until the entries stop in the early 2010s. Users constantly mention the bands in each other's communities: as 8_light_minutes in the panicatthedisco community notes, "I wonder if everybody here has Fall Out Boy under their [favorite] band list . . . all the ones I have seen do. It's pretty awesome."[2] Blushandrecover laments missing an MCR show in that band's community and adds, "I'm missing out on FOB that night, too."[3] User geraldway links all three, commenting:

> my mum says she doesn't like mcr, but she sings to them all the time.
> she denied liking panic!; but changed her msn name to some of their
> lyrics.
> she plays fall out boy all the time in the car.[4]

The term "emo" was much discussed on LiveJournal, sometimes derisively, sometimes defensively, often in confusion. We will not see much agreement here on what it is. But in the movement from MySpace and the bands' sites to LiveJournal, we can observe how the elements that would make up the discourse of emo are selected and molded in connection with the bands concerned. Though FOB, MCR, and Panic! were constantly connected and compared with each other by their fans, the term "Emo Trinity" had not yet emerged.

Once I gathered the website lexia, I coded them. Coding is a method that brings a more objective, quantitative element to discourse analysis. By sampling one capture of each band's website each week, I could look for developing themes and changing constructs over a period of time and compare the sites fairly. I used the same method for MySpace and LiveJournal web captures—with the exception that on the LiveJournal sites, I also coded pages with an unusually high number of comments compared with the monthly average. I did this because the items on those pages evidently had a greater-than-normal impact on the discourse and thus on the constructs

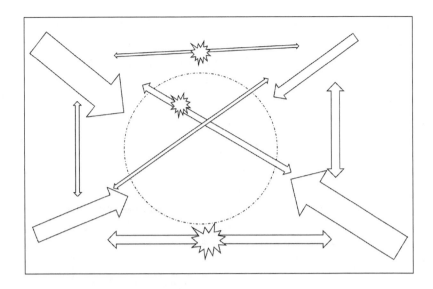

FIGURE 4: The process of discourse construction.

it shaped. In my previous work on fan fiction, I followed Michel Foucault in visualizing discursive constructions like trees, wherein groups of related statements branch out from a root formed out of "governing statements."[5] Here I found that governing statements or items were much harder to identify and the image of a tree was less useful, probably because we are looking at a discourse in the process of coming into being, rather than one that has already been established. Instead, I found that if we consider "emo" as the discursive construct in progress, it makes more sense to visualize the groups of items that form it as tributaries, or smaller rivers running into a central pool. I therefore refer to them as "streams." These streams must frequently flow into and compromise each other, so a diagram of the process might look something like what is shown in figure 4. The centralized discourse is drawn with dotted lines because it isn't fully formed yet. The arrows represent the sets of items feeding into it, clashing, contradicting, and supporting each other to varying degrees. The stars represent points of contradiction.

I located four key sets of items that informed the construction of emo. While present in the bands' sites and MySpace pages, the sets did not originate there: they come through it, not from it. In accordance with Vasquez's insights on interdiscursivity, all four sets have much older and more disparate origins, and the way they are used in the LiveJournal communities is informed by these histories as much or more as by the authorized sites' use. The first was the explicit discussion of gender, for example, the roles and behavior of boys and girls in music scenes and the tastes of boys and girls. I discussed the genealogy of these discussions in the previous chapter. Moreover, as Victoria Cann explores in *Boys Like This, Girls Like That*, media tastes play a large role in the discursive reproduction of gender among teens.[6] Following Bourdieu's famous dictum that "taste classifies, and it classifies the classifier,"[7] Cann found that teenagers' tastes were surprisingly tightly policed in an era of supposed gender fluidity, with young people anxious not to be "shunned" for expressing likes or dislikes inappropriate to their gender. As I have explored, musical tastes and pleasures gendered masculine are discursively constructed as better, more genuine, and more intellectual than those gendered feminine in the West. The LiveJournal communities continue and consolidate this discourse, valorizing instrumentation and technicality, and belittling fan practices judged excessively feminine.

This brings us to the second group of items, which I named "authenticity." This group was concerned with the value of music, the criteria for genuine musicianship, and skill and talent as opposed to musical practices judged to be shallow, talentless, or overly commercial. Authenticity was largely gendered masculine, as one would expect, though the set did need to negotiate the bands' feminine performativity and rejection of masculine hardcore, which led to some important findings. Another complicating factor, as Baym recognized, is that the relational labor that is traditionally gendered feminine, belonging in the sphere of communication and intimacy, has become part of the meaning of "authenticity" in new media culture.[8] There was a certain amount of pushback in defense of girls' tastes and the feminine, which questioned the cultural value of authenticity. The third set concerned fandom itself, the appropriate way to be a fan, and the relationship between the band concerned and their fandoms. Bury, Zubernis, and Larsen and a group of academics featured in Henry Jenkins's blog have all written on the intersections between fan identities and gender.[9] There is a loose consensus that fan activities, which tend to be gendered masculine (such as collecting, reviewing, and encyclopedic knowledge of the fandom-object) tend to be elevated and preferred over those gendered feminine, such as fan fiction and romantic/sexual attraction. This was truer in the early years of LiveJournal's popularity. As time went on, fan fiction, slash, and fan art playing with

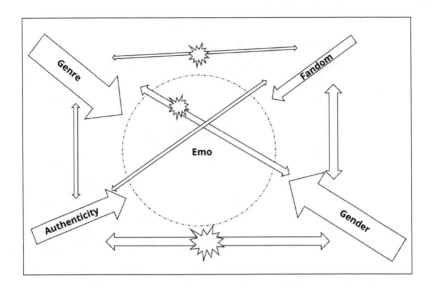

FIGURE 5: The construction of emo in process.

gender gradually became more popular, influenced by the interdiscursive culture of the web. Finally, there was a set of items explicitly concerned with the construction of genre, and a growing discursive struggle over the signifier "emo." So we can refine the diagram by naming the groups of items as seen in figure 5.

In the rest of this chapter, I examine the operations of these sets and how they undermine or reinforce each other. Let us consider one set of items at a time. As we progress, it may strike the reader that the data so far is rather, well, *serious* in tone and content. That impression would be correct. I am not claiming that the LiveJournal communities were devoid of humor—there were funny Photoshop posts and jokes—but overall, fannish practice seemed to be much more "straight" and serious than Tumblr's queer irreverence. The humor when it occurs is more traditional, based on wordplay and overturning expectations, than the more anarchic, pastiche image-based style that came to dominate later. This is partly a matter of how web culture developed and changed as a whole (see Booth), but shifts in preferred platforms have also enabled the shift in tone. Whereas LiveJournal posts allow singular threads with linear branch-offs aimed at specific communities of users, Tumblr supports constant recirculation and annotation, wherein users are free to jump in from a much wider pool of sources. Now I turn to the material itself, considering how each group of items operates in its sociotechnological context.

The LiveJournal communities begin the intratextual process of tying the yet-unnamed Emo Trinity together explicitly. While it's true that the three bands often mentioned each other in favorable terms and appeared on the same tours, this is also true of hundreds of other bands. Many of the same users post across groups, and when asked to decide between the bands in a vote or nomination, fans often comment on the difficulty of choosing. On an MTV vote between Panic! and MCR, truthtruthlie writes in the Panic! community, "like I said in the MCR comm . . . It's like asking a mother to pick between her two children . . . can't do it."[10] Of a 2009 magazine poll for "Most Important Band in the Decade," user 555gehenna666 admits in the MCR community, "I'll be honest, I voted for Fall Out Boy rofl. Shoot me ;)."[11] The abbreviation "rofl" (rolling on the floor laughing), followed by "shoot me" and the text winking face suggest that the commentator has done something slightly inappropriate to the community, but the offense is not grave enough to be taken seriously, presumably on the assumption that most people who love MCR also love FOB. User electroclash posts an "Open Letter to the Warped Tour"[12] to the MCR comm, including a picture and several comments on the FOB set:

To Pete Wentz: Thank you for making such a delicious face.

To my digital camera: Thank you for letting me capture said face.

To Andy of FOB: Throwing your drumstick into the audience was amusing, as was the knot of people (all guys, I think) fighting over it.[13]

No one objects to this focus in the MCR community; on the contrary, the user is thanked twice for that picture specifically. Meanwhile, in a discussion of which band out of several candidates will get the most requested video slot on MTV 2, girl_rotten proposes:

I think they should have the members of Fall Out Boy and MCR pitted against eachother in a gripping wrestling match to determine what band's video will be #1.
I can totally see Gerard in a cape. Mikey and Pete bitch slapping eachother.[14]

FIGURE 6: Fall Out Boy site entrance screen, 2002.

In this item, these two bands out of the many candidates are tied together by their shared failure at masculinity. This brings us to the first set of items feeding the definition of emo, those concerned with gender.

The first homepages of MCR and FOB were distinctive in style. To get to the FOB main page, the user must go through an entry screen (figure 6). Many of the items here are distinctly coded feminine: the color palette, the heart, the swirly font—they all hook into a broad discourse of femininity so well established it is cliché. Yet their collision with the item "rock," which was also part of the URL, complicates this. This is neither an anchor nor relay effect in Barthesian terms: the effect is ironic, but where the irony lands (on "rock"? on the pinkness?) is undetermined. Upon entering, the pale color scheme continues, but turns more neutral: blue, tan, and white are not as immediately symbolic as pink and white (figure 7). The items reference school days, imitating the range of items that might be found on a teenager's bulletin board, reinforced by the sound of a bicycle bell when one clicks on a link. The most distinctively gendered item is the bead bracelet, which inserts hearts between the words in the band's name. This would seem to suggest that, contra discourses of proper/unemotional fandom, fans should feel free to enjoy this band in sentimental/affective ways.

Panic!'s website was themed around the cabaret aesthetic of their first album (figure 8). The items cite a discourse of explicit performativity—the

FIGURE 7: Fall Out Boy official website, 2003, via the Internet Archive Wayback Machine.

flowers, the frames, the colors, the pastiche effect of the album cover. It is difficult to call it masculine or feminine; it fits more as queer—deliberately evasive of gender binaries, self-consciously artificial. By contrast, MCR's site is built on traditional masculine black with orderly white block text and a few small images of the band's logos: a safe choice, one might say. The text, however, is more ambiguous, and in studying the relationships between these items, I came up with the concept of "gendered self-mockery." Gendered self-mockery performs the male self as feminine, generating humor by the gap between expectations of male performers produced by the genealogy of cock rock and actions attributed to the band members. For example, in a site update, Gerard Way of MCR writes: "We'd also like to welcome NJ's own, The Banner, to the Eyeball Records family. Expect lots of fights between me and the singer, Joey Southside, about who gets to use the eyeliner first when we play with them on 9.26.02."[15]

Gendered self-mockery occurred across all the bands' sites. Panic!'s bassist Jon Walker used to sign diary entries "Jon Walker is a boy" as though to

FIGURE 8: Panic! at the Disco official website 2005, via the Internet ArchiveWay-back Machine.

mitigate any doubt. Self-mockery based in sexuality is also prevalent. Pete Wentz used to flatly refer to himself as "gay" in his site blog, long before the term was reclaimed in any meaningful sense:

> Oh yeah is it me or do I have a total crush on "kate was like" from the messageboard. Brighteyes, weakerthans [indie rock bands, presuma-bly favored by the poster in question], super cute and an attitude . . . Swoon. Girls don't come much hotter.
>
> Too bad I'm gay.[16]

The item "I'm gay" functions as a punchline, as spatially emphasized by a large enough gap to effect a pause in reading. In these items, the attribution of queer or feminine properties to boys is a source of humor. Thus feminine characteristics are devalued, even as the artists' readiness to apply them to themselves simultaneously mitigates their stigma. Mocking feminine per-formativity while simultaneously professing enjoyment of that very quality carries over and is amplified in fan discourse on LiveJournal. Here, fans are discussing a television interview with MCR:

did you see the part where frank was sitting beside gerard with his arms wrapped around him? aww, slash love! lol. i really want pictures of that.

was not surprised at leahs [a presenter] stupidness + inability to act. plus she was saying things just to impress the guys.

i laughed at the end when she walked right into the box mikey was holding.[17]

———

*frank was sitting beside gerard with his arms wrapped around him?.* i neeeeeeeeeeeeeeeeeeeeeeeeeeeeeeeeed to see this.[18]

———

it was my favorite part of the whole show! =D i really hope someone rips it.[19]

and gerard can't grow a beard, aw how sad. i actually dont want to see a beard on gerard.[20]

———

why can't he grow a beard? O__o.[21]

———

he said he cant? haha i dont know. maybe he cant grow hair there or something.[22]

———

*snicker* he's such a little woman, i swear.[23]

Properties considered feminine (physical affection with friends, hairless-ness) are considered cute and appealing when men display them—though the "*snicker*" enacts a note of condescension. Moreover, "woman" cannot be read literally due to the male pronoun, and it almost becomes an insult here, a sort of affectionate put-down. Though fans approve and enjoy the exhibition of affection and softness between bandmates, when it comes to actual women in the music industry, the LiveJournal communities are almost universally ready to denigrate. This same comment thread called the female presenter of the show a "bitch" and "whore" multiple times, complaining about her apparently annoying voice. See the first quotation noted, from user _ritalin. This discourse is not inherited from the bands' sites but the broader sexist traditions of music and artistry we explored in chapter 1. Unlike the site mailing lists and MySpace friends lists, these LiveJournal communities are primarily female, as demonstrated by frequent introduction posts. An early thread on the Panic! LiveJournal bemoans: "most of the members here are female, arent they?! WHHHHYY??"[24] with the responses "hahahaha i know. LAMEEEE"[25] and "Thats true huh?? We need more penis in this community!!!!! ::shakes fist::."[26] Exactly why "more penis" would be beneficial is not explained, but we might compare Overell's finding that boys were automatically accepted into the emo community she studied while girls were screened. Girls may dominate the boards numerically, as Greenwald noted, but boys' contributions are apparently more valuable.

So it seems that the streams that came to shape emo aren't as feminine-friendly as one might think. However, the denigration of women did meet some opposition. The MCR community had a tradition of writing in "Gerard Way" as a vote in *Kerrang!*'s annual "Sexiest Female [in rock music]" poll. Some fans took offense to the joke. User svkv writes, "I'm really disappointed in you, guys! I thought that MCR fans are kind people that would never take the liberty to mock at someone [*sic*]. Shame on you, guys."[27] bloodyhands replies acerbically, "cos it's totally not okay for a man to be like a girl. . . "[28] The ellipses inflects the item with irony in the context of web forum lexis. bloodyhands's statement questions why the attribution of femininity is negative, referring to the band's own gendered self-mockery to authorize her statements. Patentpending notes that "Gerard has called himself feminine, girly, a fag and a cupcake. No one is 'mocking' him and no one is being 'mean spirited'. . . No one is calling him anything derogatory or saying anything derogatory."[29] Scorpy808 explicitly invokes the gendered history of rock music:

> I really wasn't gonna even touch this one . . . but you know, I'm in a mood so what the fuck, eh? Here goes . . .
> Kerrang has a long history of being an agro-metal-testosterone-fueled-mag. Yeah sure, they've featured some fine (real) women in the industry, but for the most part, their target market IS those dudes with the backwards baseball hat and no shirt on, listening to Pantera, and wanting to beat the fuck out of a "faggot" like Gerard Way. What a better crowd to make feel squeamish huh? That's the whole fucking point imho

. . . And yeah, as someone who so eloquently already pointed out, a guy who makes out with his guitarist on stage and has been quoted saying, "I looked hot as a chick" would find this all ultimately funny. We all know he's a straight DUDE (at least I hope we ALL know that) . . . sheesh.[30]

Thus the playful vote drive is framed as using MCR to enact real change in the industry, in illustration of Phillips and Milner's point that "engagement that appears to be 'just' playful" can "facilitate meaningful public debate."[31] Bearing in mind the "social and material situations in which texts are constructed,"[32] I should note that when these posts were made in 2008, overt homophobia was relatively accepted. It pops up on the bands' sites now and then, as outsiders drop by to leave relatively uninteresting vitriol ("fuck u ass holes u dick heads ur so gay bitchs i hate u assholes ppl hear ur music cuz ur fucking lyrics jackasses not cuz they like u bitch fuck u fuck u fuck u ur so fucking stupid go have anal sex with ur boy friends u gay ass holes") or accuse male fans of being "fags" for their taste in music.[33] Yet for all this, Scorpy808 is careful to establish that in real life, Way is "a straight DUDE," as if that qualification legitimizes this bit of queer humor: "I hope we ALL know that." This pattern holds true across the sites. In a discussion of Panic!'s habit of performative onstage affection, LiveJournal user ohyoursocool comments:

Why can't people get over it. They're not gay. Why is it such a big deal with talking about them being gay? damn. Almost all the bands I like

"OMFG THEY'RE GAY THEY FUCK EACH OTHER I KNOW THIS" . . . I'm sorry but isn't that childish? But if they were gay I wouldn't care . . .

eh hope no one replys to this.[34]

Two people do reply, and the second is noteworthy: "I seriously doubt very many people here legitimately believe any of the boys—okay, with the possible exception of Brendon *facepalm*—is actually gay. Those that do are teenies and tinhats."[35] The commenter denies that there is anything wrong with being gay—but when she speculates that Panic! frontman Brendon Urie might "actually" be gay, the invoked *facepalm* enacts discomfort and dislike. Heterosexuality is framed as justifying stage-gay: queer performativity is approved because of an imagined straight "reality" behind it. This encapsulates the problematics of stage-gay: transgression is allowed as long as the performance and artificiality are made clear. For all the hugging, kissing, and innuendo between band members, no one in the Emo Trinity has ever come out as being in a real same-sex relationship. Most are married to women.

We have established that male behavior playfully coded feminine or queer is an important discourse stream informing the construction of emo. But the items that make it up are not automatically progressive, first due to the assumption of some "straight" authorizing reality behind queer performativity, and second because of an interesting deflection of what we would now call slut-shaming onto the male body. In the first week of March 2006, Pete Wentz's smartphone was hacked, and his self-taken pictures of his penis were published all over the internet. There was no possibility of a hoax, as Wentz has a very distinctive tattoo on his pelvis. MCR's Mikey Way, one of Wentz's closest friends, posted an uncharacteristically angry response on his MySpace page, which was immediately copied and pasted into LiveJournal by a fan: "Would everyone leave the poor guy alone already? Everyone wonders what drives people in band 'over the edge' or into a 'meltdown' . . . its shit like this. How would you like it if someone posted 'risque' pics of you online. Have some tact people. fuckin weak."[36]

Way didn't use Wentz's name, but fans immediately knew what the post was about, commenting on the spread of the pictures or observing casually that "I wouldn't be ashamed tbh."[37] The commenters' overall conclusion was that "if you don't want your penis on the internet, you shouldn't take pictures of it"[38] and that "to prevent said explicit photography from being 'splashed' around the internetz then maybe you shouldn't keep the pictures on a device that could easily be hacked into? I mean you shouldn't take them to begin with but if you do keep them somewhere safe. I mean . . . he had it coming."[39] *He had it coming.* It strikes me that I'd never seen this sentence in a sexual context. In a striking example of Nicholas and Agius's persistence of masculinism, it seems that feminine performativity can actually attach the language of rape culture to men and boys. This is certainly a change in the construction of gender through popular music, but not a particularly encouraging one. Granted, there is some pushback, as user fetishism comments that "accepting this kind of invasive, irreverent attitude instead of disparaging the perpetrators is otherwise known as enabling,"[40] but emokid__wannabe maintains that:

> You can't act like Pete did nothing wrong. It's not like someone snapped
> a picture while he was changing and posted it everywhere. He took

the pictures HIMSELF and put them on a device that could easily and has been easily hacked into recently. . . . I applaud the hackers for at least giving Wentz a lesson about cam-whoring and the limits one should put on it.

I don't feel bad for him in the least and I think Mikey was out of line to defend someone who had the whole thing coming.[41]

Nowadays, many people would call this victim blaming, and it is notable that the policing of behaviors coded feminine is extended to fans as well as band members. "Cam-whoring" is a dangerous business.

If we envisage the streams of discourse I invoked in figure 5, we can imagine that "policing the performance of gender" operates as a tributary between the categories of gender and fandom, each feeding into the other. Contributors to all three LiveJournal communities are eager to distance themselves from "hysterical fangirls," who mob, scream, and otherwise perform behaviors associated with Beatlemania and young female fans of earlier decades. Several scholars have written on how fan communities create divides between Good Fans and Bad Fans; I have never before seen a fandom make the practice so explicitly gendered.[42] Here, Bad Fans are simply called fangirls, with no hint of reclamation of the term. Their behaviors are constructed as defectively feminine: "They just SQUEAL and cry. If there's one thing I hate more than anything is the sound of pre-pubescent girls shrieking at the top of their lungs."[43] An anonymous poster decries "disgusting teeny bopping ex-backstreet boys fans on this server who claim to have like my chemical romance from the very beginning when that isn't the truth and who care more about their videos and appearance or dressing like them than their fucking music."[44] "Teeny boppers" was the term Frith and McRobbie and Norma Coates used for rock fans' devalued Other. In the Panic! LiveJournal, user fabledfaith writes:

when I think of fangirling, I think of,

"OMG I THINK HE IZ SO CUTE!!!!11! HAVE MI BABIES OK?!!?!?! LOL U SO HAWT

Personally, I don't mind "aw, he's so cute" or crushing or anything. But what really bugs me (and what I consider "fangirling") is the crying/ shaking/squealing like a wounded pig. "HOMIGAWD BRNDN TOTES TOUCHD MEH N IM GUNNA CRI 4 HOURS!" that pisses me off.[45]

Note how similar all the descriptions are. The construction of this hypothetical fangirl is solid and consistent across all the fan sites: she is screechy, obsessed, irrational, hypersexual, doesn't care for or understand the music, and ruins events with her presence. User dstar_ pro longs for the good old days, before so many new fans contaminated all the communities with their feminization: "Most of my favorite bands are punk bands, and I adore those communities. Why? No message boards, no fanfics, no band crushes, no drama. Buncha dudes who turn up to pit and scream into a mic. That's it. I long for the day when bands like My Chem get the same privilege once again—you know they long for it."[46] This item seems to hark back to an imagined pure masculine hardcore, as we discussed in the section on emo's sources. The fact that dstar_pro locates this scene in the past, before feminine fandom began all its meddling, demonstrates again my points that the development of emo was doing something to gender in the music industry, and fandom was a key force in this change. Indeed, dstar_pro imagines that fans have changed MCR into a different kind of band against their collective will, assuming the thoughts of the band members to lend authority to his statements.

There is a little backlash to the denigration of the fangirl figure. User mysti112 responds to a standard list of complaints: "I say, be a fan however you want to be a fan. You're entitled to your opinion, but there's just so many of these pointless rants by people who want to distance themselves from stupid little fangirls. I don't give a fuck which you are as long as you appreciate MCR and they bring you happiness. The important thing is that we know who we really are and what the band means to us, right? So who gives a fuck what anyone else thinks?"[47]

The defenses are rare, don't attract many responses, and aren't really couched in terms of defending feminine/fangirl behavior. They tend more to generalizations about enjoying bands however one pleases and accusations of hypocrisy: "I bet fifty bucks that over 99% of these kids that agree with you[r complaints] are the people that you just ranted about."[48] The construction of fandom by the fans is almost entirely built around this Good Fan/Bad Fan binary, which does not come from the bands' sites or MySpace pages but seems to be a feature of fan culture in general. One-upping with detailed knowledge of the band and claims to insider or exclusive knowledge were common as a means of building subcultural capital and status as a fan.[49] Eventually, self-construction as a Good Fan became so cliché there emerged a copy-paste meme that people would drop into comment streams:

YOU WIN. You're more punk, hardcore, mod, straightedge, emo, indie than me. Your hair is cooler, your pants are tighter, you're skinnier and better looking and you have more tattoos . . . Your glasses are thicker and blacker than mine, the plugs in your ears are bigger. You know more people in bands and your black jelly bracelets are the envy of scenesters everywhere. Your photography is blacker and whiter, your LiveJournal profile is wittier, . . . Your scene points are double, perhaps triple, mine. Because as we all know, that's what really matters. In a scene where the music has taken a backseat to the haircuts, you win and I lose. Congrats.[50]

As ever, parody functions two ways, mocking the idea of the Good Fan/Bad Fan divide and helping reinforce it. "Knowing people in bands" was probably the ultimate claim to capital in these communities. Greenwald argued that a hallmark of emo is a close relationship between fans and band facilitated by new technology. I think this was fairly true in the beginning. Early commenters on the Panic! board were always especially careful to name-drop their interactions with the band, who, after all, were fellow teenagers with LiveJournal accounts at the time. One could follow the band's progress of catching Fall Out Boy's attention via sheer persistence online and eventually getting signed. In 2004, Panic!'s then-seventeen-year old lead guitarist Ryan Ross posted to his LiveJournal:

"take those pics and write the hits"

wow. big things have been happening. pete from f[all ]o[ut ]b[oy] heard the band and liked it. he and i talked today about a lot of things about what we plan to do, as of now he's going to go see us in california. who knows after that. weird that someone in a band i really like is into my music. it feels good.[51]

Similarly, a now-famous post of Ross's on the MCR community reads: "hey im ryan i'm new i live in las vegas my chemical romance makes me dance."[52] The contemporary comments are much as one would expect, welcoming him to the community and complimenting his taste, plus some teenage flirting. Naturally, the post has become legendary and the subject of much humor, with fans posting "~NEVAR FORGET~" in increasingly larger font well into the late 2000s.[53] The progression of this thread over time literally enacts the change to a more distant, humorous, and sophisticated form of fandom via the influence of meme and web culture. As the bands grew more successful and were eventually signed by major labels, the LiveJournal communities grew larger and more impersonal. Accusations of "selling out" began to circulate. An anonymous commenter posts on the FOB MySpace page: "I feel like a woman . . . you guys are such sellouts."[54] This is an odd item: as best I can parse it, the commenter claims to feel feminized by frequenting the site of a band he believes has sold out. The shorthand demonstrates how closely feminization and mainstream commercialization/lack of authenticity are linked in musical discourse.

Certainly, as the bands became more popular and signed by major labels, the claim of close relationships is harder to maintain. Although it's true that all official sites either hosted or linked to band members' LiveJournals, which contained a surprising degree of personal minutiae, from reports of life on tour to the band members' opinions on media to reflections on friendships and relationships, FOB and MCR would typically turn the comments off in their entries. Baym writes that musicians are expected to perform relational communication with listeners via the new media economy, a form of "relational labor" that takes time, energy, and technological and communicative skills not previously required of musicians.[55] She recognizes the rise of as MySpace as a significant point in the development of this economy, and the Trinity bands' MySpaces and LiveJournals might be cited as an early illustration. Yet I'm not sure how relational the practice really is. The impression of intimacy is there, but it's not really a conversation: more like the maintenance of a discourse that constructs bands as being in an intimate relationship with their fans. Thus I don't think it's fair to say with Greenwald that fan–band intimacy is a hallmark of emo, but what might be is the conscious impression and performance thereof. The commodification of emotion is a hallmark of late-stage capitalism in general and the online economy in particular,[56] which probably contributes to the internet's role in the establishment of emo as a genre. Nor is this entirely a marketing gimmick: it is also a quality that grew organically from smaller and more intimate fan communities that really did have strong connections with the performers. Fan–band intimacy is the ideal in emo, as it is increasingly across the music industry, but it isn't really practicable all the time. Nonetheless, the three bands make a practice of appealing to fans for votes and airplay. The common tactic was to frame one's band as the deserving underdog with fewer but better-quality fans than competitors:

THE TRL TAKEOVER—NEW PHONE VOTING TIMES

thanks so much for voting us onto the countdown on TRL today!!! its insane to think about the bands we are up against and how their fans rank in the millions but that we simply have more dedicated and amazing fans!!!! it sent chills down my spine that you guys brought us there. and for everything we've ever put into this band, you paid us back with this. please keep voting on friday, we want to show them we can stay . . .

truefucking love—Peter.[57]

A similar post from the MCR mailing list, which user how_u_disappear copied into the LiveJournal community, actually relates a history of the ancient Battle of Salamis, in which the Greek army defeated the Persians despite having far fewer soldiers, noting the "element of surprise," before going on:

We know that was super long and we love you for reading it. You see, we like learning about underdogs. That is how we grew up. We have had to fight the entire time. Now we feel that it is very important to continue this battle . . . We are so blessed to feel like we have you guys alongside us in this fight. Let's look at ourselves as the Greeks. We do not have the army that some of these other artists we are up against have. We have ourselves and you guys. That is how this whole crazy ride has been, and we would not want it any other way ever. We also want to be part of the future . . . All of that being said, let's go. Please go here to vote for My Chemical Romance for the Viewer's Choice award (you can also vote by playing a game by clicking here) and here for the MTV2 award. Let's use our element of surprise and take all of these other armies out. It is time to show the world why our fans are the best any band could ask for.

Oh and by the way . . . We have a surprise for you soon.

xoxoxox,
Gerard, Mikey, Frankie, Ray & Bob
My Chemical Romance.[58]

Of course, nowadays addressing fans as a group/family with a distinct identity and investment in one's brand is a widely used marketing tactic by celebrities of all types. Rather than responding in earnest, however, some fans mocked the earnestness of the latter invitation. In an illustration of how copying and pasting into a different context changes the item's reception,[59] some users were less than impressed:

> Do you ever wonder if maybe they're taking this a little too seriously. it's fucking mtv.[60]

Could it be that the expression of intense personal emotion—which if Baym is right, should belong to the authenticity construct here—is disparaged because of its feminized discursive heritage? The fan's dry remark positions the overload of emotion as unwarranted, out of place, an improper bid for authenticity: "it's fucking mtv." Others posters used humor and bathos to puncture the serious tone:

> Oooh I wonder what the surprise is?[61]
>
> [. . .]
>
> I bet Gerard's pregnant.[62]

It seems that the performed invitation to intimacy is being turned down here, as commenters enact a more sophisticated, less earnest position, dismissing the bands' attempt at relational labor. The fandom group of items, then, has some surprising implications for the study of gender. First, the Good Fan/Bad Fan divide, which denigrates styles of fandom gendered feminine, is preserved with only a little criticism. Second, the supposedly close relationships posited between bands and their fandoms do have a real provenance, but their practice isn't as straightforward as previous critics have suggested and can be rejected in favor of a more snarky, ironic kind of participation we might expect from more masculine-coded sites such as Reddit and 4chan (see chapter 4).

Unsurprisingly, the next group of items was concerned with the construction of authenticity. As established, this stream of the discourse comes pregendered, aligning authentic musicianship with masculinity with rock music and instrumental playing, and inauthenticity with femininity, pop, commercialization, and singing. The communities certainly continued this tradition, but they also complicated it. Contrasting MCR to 1990s pop groups, LiveJournal user martyrsxhidxme comments:

> was i the only one who noticed that BSB [Backstreet Boys] and NSYNC did not play instruments?

and yet they were called a band?
more like five part singing group.
and thats my two cents.
xoxo-alley.[63]

———

mhm!!! i hate how GROUPS are called bands. or singers with no talent,
who don't even write their own shit, are called artists.[64]

———

pshh.
artists my ass.
that irks me too.[65]

These and similar items are doing a fair bit of ideological work, with a long
genealogical history (see chapter 1). We might draw out the implied binary
to posit masculinity, artistry, creation, originality, culture, the mind, and
value on one side and femininity, performance, imitation, derivation, nature,
the body, and devaluation on the other. Interestingly, on the bands' sites,
authenticity is less strictly constructed in accordance with this discursive
tradition. For one thing, they do not denigrate other artists by name—
although expected in some genres such as rap, that would be too far at odds
with the image of "softer" masculinities at work here. On the bands' websites,
"authenticity" is constructed first and foremost as composing/playing for
its own sake rather than for money. As of 2004, FOB's MySpace page listed
their genre as "pop-punk," but listed their label as "indie." Commenter Jamie
responds "'Type of Label : Indie' Who do you think you're kidding?"[66] User
The Jo Jo Bean replies, "They are kidding their 16 year old fans jamie!"[67]
Here is an example of fandom upholding the masculine/authenticity/indie/
rock tradition more rigidly than the bands did. According to the MySpace
page, there is no contradiction between the loaded item "pop" as a genre
descriptor and belonging to an indie label. Jamie's comment challenges the
authenticity of the claim to indie status, which The Jo Jo Bean denigrates
as something that only (presumably gullible) teenage fans would believe.
On the other hand, FOB's own site was actually quite invested in warding
off the specter of pop music: the band members' profiles state only indie,
hardcore, and metal bands under their favorites, leaving no room for association with pop.

Thus the category of authenticity overlaps with the other sets of items, implicating gender, genre, and fandom. However, if envisaged as a Venn diagram, the segment of authenticity that doesn't overlap the other categories would be concerned with capitalism, money, and selling out. This segment would be most heavily informed by statements from the bands, the others by the fandom, though the fandom's interdiscursive work connects them all. Lovesongwriter posts an MCR interview to the community:

My Chemical Romance Slam Fame-Hungry Musicians on New Album

"Rock 'n' roll is not red carpets and MySpace friends—rock 'n' roll is dangerous and rock 'n' roll should piss people off. Right now, there's not a lot of that happening. What it is is a lot of people trying to be famous. That seems to be the goal."

In Way's opinion, that desire to be famous is messing up the sanctity of rock 'n roll. "It's bled into rock. It came from other places, but it's bled into rock 'n' roll and kind of tainted it a bit," Way says. "This record is really a response to that as well."[68]

The phrase "rock 'n' roll" functions here as a shorthand for an idealized conception of music subcultures than a genre description (MCR's output is pretty far from the mostly acoustic, mid-twentieth-century style of music usually called rock 'n' roll). Responses to the post are enthusiastic, with user innovade quoting the first sentence and adding "this," a common phrase used to indicate reinforcement.[69] Yet none of the bands' sites were shy about trying to sell things—be it tickets, merchandise, or records—which aligns with Greenwald's argument that emo doesn't carry over the anticapitalist energies of its hardcore roots, nor is it approving of greed. FOB posted an apology in July 2004 for canceling a series of shows due to "massive amounts of confusion" that "was beyond the control of the band," stating that they "don't feel its right to charge kids 35 dollars for tickets when the shows are this disorganized."[70] It seems that authenticity in emo can negotiate wanting to profit from one's music, but not overreach or give the impression of taking advantage.

A second aspect to the "authenticity" construct concerns the bands' appearances in media. As they became more successful, their participation in press and broadcast media had to be negotiated. In June 2006, Panic! posted to their own site:

As many of you have heard, we will be doing a "walk on" on TRL January 17th. it was never an intention or a goal for us to be on trl, or carson daly, or any tv show for that matter. but after some serious thinking, we decided to do these things because it is an intention of this band to have our music heard by as many people as will listen. maybe this means that those of you without fuse might be able to catch our video on mtv2 instead of not at all.[71]

TRL stands for *Total Request Live*, an MTV magazine-format show associated more with pop and gossip than with indie or punk. Thus the decision to go on the show is hedged with a justification (as many people hearing the music as possible) to negotiate the specter of feminization. Similarly, in December 2004, user _tune_you_out copy-and-pasted the following from MCR's site to the LiveJournal:

MCR HITS TRL

Yeah—you read that right. The powers-that-be at MTV have seen the light and have asked MCR to play live on TRL on January 17th. We're all just as surprised as you are, but it'll be pretty amazing to see the TRL crowd experience the MCR assault.
To make sure that there aren't the usual TRL Barbie and Ken dolls in the audience, they're looking for 15 of the biggest MCR fanatics to be in the studio live with the band. So, send in a note explaining why you want to be in the audience that day . . .
- Jeff at MCRHQ [72]

To not violate the construct of authenticity, MCR's "assault" is framed as something that will happen to TRL, changing it, rather than the MCR adapting themselves or their music to be on TV. Likewise their fans are called on to literally change the audience demographic, the hyperfeminized and artificial category of "Barbie and Ken dolls" being unworthy of MCR's performance. The direct message to fans comes not from the band themselves—negating its ability to hook into authenticity that way—but someone working a vaguely corporate-sounding "HQ." Fan responses were taken aback:

o-O B-b-but. But. Muuh. Muh?[73]

―――

at least they're happy ??[74]

―――――

hahaha.[75]

―――――

I got that email. It's just . . . wrong.[76]

In time, though, most adopt the same strategy as the bands' spokesman to preserve the structure of authenticity: "aww, yeah. i'll admit, at first when they were on trl i was a bit bummed cos everyone else was convincing me, but later, i realized just how great they are for doing that/ they deserve it more than anyone! . . . MCR didn't go mainstream . . . mainstream went MCR. ;)."[77]

MCR's participation in popular TV is acceptable if they are framed as changing the mainstream text, not changing for it. One category that cannot be recouped, however, is teen magazines. Apparently this is a feminization too far. On Panic!'s site, Ryan Ross is careful to assure fans that the bands have no control over images and pull quotes in the public domain, and thus cannot be held responsible for their appearance in such: "We found out that we are in a great little mag called 'J14' i'm sure you all are just as excited as we are about that one. unfortunately those kind of things are out of our hands, we don't have to give permission to them to put us in there . . at least we aren't stickers. or maybe that would be awesome?"[78]

The sarcasm is established by context and doesn't need to be signaled lexographically. Thanks to the construct identified by Coates, which opposes rock/masculinity/authenticity with pop/femininity/inauthenticity, all fans know that teen magazines are risible. MCR fan untilyoubelieve comments, "i die a little inside whenever i hear they're in yet another teeny bop magazine."[79] User marionnettes tells a story: "So I went to Barnes and Noble today to look for Rocksound, and while we were there my friend Joanna decides she wants to find out who her pop star!boyfriend should be (who places teenie magazines next to Spin and Kerrang and such? I mean, come on!) So she turns to the first page and screams and I look up at her and she's shoving the magazine in my face and saying 'Gerard's in here! What the fuck?'"[80]

This item highlights a thread that runs through the discourse of authenticity, that is, the fear of contagion. Placing the "teenie magazines *next to* Spin and Kerrang" infringes on the masculine, sophisticated, critical tradition of the rock periodical. It is as though there is a fear that the

Trinity bands might not really be quite authentic enough ("Indie? Who are you kidding?"), so the borders of the authenticity construct are carefully policed. Hill attributes this to the cultural feminization of emo bands and the strong association of femininity with the inauthentic: "the trouble is that femininity proves a threat to authenticity so that anything associated with women needs to be restrained from rock to preserve its authenticity."[81] The most popular single comment on early MySpace was "you rock!" This small item does a lot of work. Positioned at the intersection of gender, genre, and authenticity, it hails the bands as part of an "authentic" heritage of music whilst simultaneously expressing fannish delight. It was often accompanied by items that shored up the commenter's masculinity, perhaps as a guard against appearing like a Bad Fan, for example, "omg, i saw u guys last night and u rocked. i had so much fucking fun and got the shit kicked out of me in the pit! Robster."[82] Though the poster is positioned as the object, not the subject of the violence, willingness to endure a bruising in the pit is very much a matter of masculine cultural capital at hardcore shows.

This leads us into the final set of items—those constructing genre explicitly. First, we should note that the actual term "emo" was intensively struggled over in all three communities. Discourse theorists Laclau and Mouffe saw words/signifiers as objects that were struggled over, pulled back and forth between interested parties to become more or less "fixed" in their meaning (never completely; and of course, they can always become unfixed again, as with the man/woman example I made earlier). These communities demonstrate the struggle, but no fix is achieved (yet). There were odd occasions where posters identified themselves as emo fans from the outset—usernames on MySpace included XTheEmoestPirateX and Emo Kidz Have More Fun. Some identified with the label but were aware it may have derogatory overtones and discuss being insulted for their tastes. Galadflower observes, "emo hate? There's LOTS of it. Even metal kids get a lot of respect today, while quite a shocking amount people think of emo kids as trash and scum."[83] User nest_freemark links this "emo hate" specifically to queer performativity, noting, "I don't think it's about the genre emo at all, it's more about people these days being so damn rude and also the fact that a lot of bands that are considered emo play with homoerotism and unfortunately homophobia isn't dead."[84] This was relatively unusual, however: not many commenters identified themselves or the bands with the term "emo" at this point. The other genre labels attached to the bands were:

- rock (very frequently)
- punk pop (frequently)
- punk (quite frequently)
- alternative (occasionally)
- dark indie (very occasionally)
- dance rock (once, regarding Panic!)

We observed how commenters dismissed FOB's claim to an indie label as a bid for authenticity. Flyswatting writes of Panic! fans' claim to "alternative": "alternative my ass; pop-punk and that's about it."[85] The post modifier "about it" assigns "pop-punk" to a lower level than alternative on the respectability-of-genres scale, no doubt because the "pop" item is feminizing. Similarly, here xstainmybladex is feeling uncomfortable about MCR's upcoming MTV appearance: "Afterall [sic], MTV IS a mainstream station, and the majority of things played on there isn't even music, and when it is, its rap or hip hop or pop punkish stuff . . . is that what we want for MCR?"[86] This suggests that rap, hip hop, and "pop punkish stuff" are lower forms of music, to which MCR should not be affiliated. Notice that xstainmybladex has listed genres that require little or no instrumental merit, connecting to the concept of instrumentation as authenticity.

Genre is constructed not just as a means of labeling music but as a key component in identity, which accords with Cann's observations on the importance of taste in self-construction. User leadtheflock posts to the MCR community: "Hey. Ok this might sound rather silly, but are like all the people that go to MCR gigs punks? Because me and my friend are going to see them in Portsmouth in November, and we aren't punks at all, we are very much like the characters from the OC lol. I don't have anything against punks I was just wondering if there was anyone like me lol."[87] Responses ranged from a polite "I guess you get all kinds of people at an MCR gig" to an arch "you might be a problem."[88] Lordfuckie, who writes with a male profile picture, was one of the first posters on the community and upholds a traditional masculinist discourse holding MCR to standards of rock authenticity. In the context of this, the item functions as a put-down, suggesting via interdiscursive connotation that the young female poster is an inappropriate attendee (too young, too female, too unsophisticated) for an MCR show. User brndnw22 hedges: "I personally don't care what people are wearing at the show, as long as they act the right way and are into the music. one 'fuck me gee' and you're down, but if it's just the clothing that's different, who cares? then again, the rest of the people at the show could have a different opinion of you. just play it safe and wear a black tshirt anyway. heh."[89]

The original poster thanks her and states that it's "great to see that most people don't give a shit about stereotypes and stuff. It's just this guy at school was all like 'Why are YOU going to see MCR, you're not emo.'"[90] Thus it seems that "emo" and "punk" are interchangeable here, which is unusual. The genre hierarchy would generally put rock and punk are at the top, while emo is still pulled in all directions. Sometimes, it is dismissed as meaningless. User forlornangel writes:

> People always tell me how EMO MyChemRomance is . . . It's really annoying and then they always ask if I'm EMO just because I listen to them . . . Then I get grief from EMO kids who think MCR sucks and aren't "Real Emo" . . . There is no winning for MCR where I live . . . But my best friend likes them, and I sport MCR shirts at least 3 out of 7 days of the week . . . I've gotten one awesome comment from this Hardcore Metal guy at Guitar Center . . . He told me how different the Lead Guitarist is, and how he does something no one else would have ever thought of.[91]

Note how the approval of a "Hardcore Metal guy at Guitar Center" is important to forlornangel in validating her fandom. This "guy" bears all the signifiers of cock rock masculinity, via his implied appearance and his job. Moreover, his praise for the technical skills and innovation of Ray Toro, MCR's "Lead Guitarist" (note the capitals), is in keeping with the theme that instrumentalism is the highest value in music. Overall, though, the "emo" label was pulled in three main directions:

1. as something ridiculous and derogatory, which entails denying that the bands in question are;
2. as referring to emotion and thus applicable to most/all music;
3. as a legitimate genre/subculture that is applicable to the bands in question.

Some comments seem to waver between two definitions: "Ever noticed a lot of the new emo trends actually came from what a lot of people saw in

MCR?? I.e., black and red, thick rimmed glasses, suits with red ties, gerard-style hairstyles . . . it gets so silly. What happened to the old school emos?? They were actually quite cool."[92]

It is unclear whether the "old school emos" this user misses are those imitating MCR and that have now apparently stopped, or whether she is claiming that emo used to mean something superior to what it does now. In either case, this is one of the earlier connections of the word to the Trinity bands, in essentially approving terms (definition 3). But there are also items denying this explicitly (definition 1). User sunnydlita complains that "MCR deserves for the general public to stop pigeonholing them as the 'goth emo' band,"[93] and sorrowful_eagle hopes that "with this album they're going to kick the 'emo' tag square in the balls and send it crying into a corner >:)."[94] This item imagines a violent expurgation of the feminized label with the text-speak imitation of a face smiling savagely (the greater-than symbol depicts eyebrows drawn inward). I'm not sure how accurate it is to say that MCR were being pigeonholed in the later 2000s, but the point here is the fans' perception. Similarly lord_spamulon, another male-presenting fan who has been invested in the community since the beginning, quotes a (formerly linked but deleted) article with disdain, which claims that MCR's next album will have:

"NO MORE angst. No more whingeing. No more playing the victim etc" [end article quotation].

Goddammit. They were never really like this, they weren't emo, blah blah blah, so tired of seeing this/making this argument.[95]

Meanwhile, other users deny that the term is necessarily insulting but define it a very general sense (definition 2):

EMO DOES NOT MEAN DEPRESSED MEN WEARING EYELINER SCREAMING INTO A MICROPHONE. at least that's what my friends think.
emo=emotional music. which means almost any kind of genre of music is emotional music.[96]

Clearly, though, this conception is far too wide and nonspecific when compared to the shaping work fandom has performed up to this point, even before we are in a position to pin the label down. The specificities of "emo" will become more visible in the coming chapters, but already, there is a set of statements that begin to defend the concept and attach it to the Trinity bands: "I've always considered Panic! to be 'emo', but, then, I think 'emo' is stereotyped as something to be ashamed of (unless you're of the black-nailpolish-eyeliner-woe-is-me club), and I'm not ashamed that I love 'emo' music."[97]

Finally, the term starts to be used self-referentially for self-mocking effect. Commenting on the end of a longtime friendship between Gerard Way and The Used's frontman Bert McKracken, user charlizard comments that the separation "makes [her] little emo heart cry because those two together were magical."[98] If genre affiliation is an important marker of identity, the fact that fans are starting to claim it here, even in jest, suggests the spreading influence of identity constructions that challenge the traditional gendering of music and its listeners.

I have established then, that the fan communities that formed on LiveJournal for MCR, FOB, and Panic! do significant work to prepare the ground for fandom's construction of emo. LiveJournal links these bands together intratextually in a consistent manner. The discourse forms four streams that have not yet cohered into a construction but have begun the work we will see consolidated (and much changed) by modern fandom. Retrospectively, this is what we know:

1. The new shape of emo will cohere around the three bands in question.

2. The cultural heritage of masculinity in music makes a significant impact on emo. Traditional masculinities are disavowed, but emo will be in constant struggle with the specter of femininity.

3. Emo will valorize "authenticity," in negotiation with the feminization of commercial culture.

4. Relatedly, intimacy or the appearance of intimacy between fans and bands will be expected.

5. Emo will negotiate a genre hierarchy with rock at the top and pop at the bottom.

6. Emo will become a means of self-construction and identity.

What we have not yet seen is the fulfilment of the playful, humorous, and irreverent context that structures contemporary emo fandom. There are jokes—usually based around gender—but the overall impression from

MySpace to LiveJournal is that fandom and music are quite serious business. Part of this is due to the thread format of html journals serving relatively closed communities. These affordances encourage discussion and direct address and support text with less input from the user than graphics require, but equally, web culture in the early 2000s was less sophisticated, less reflexive and ironic than it is now. When we turn to the next chapter, comparing fan and official YouTube output to the pastiched surfaces of Tumblr, we will observe a consolidation in the meanings of emo and the unpredictable shaping force of the much-expanded, highly pervasive, uber-reflexive digital fan culture of the present.

# 3

## CONTEMPORARY EMO ONLINE

### FANDOM FROM YOUTUBE TO TUMBLR

On January 10, 2018, a music video for the single "Wilson (Expensive Mistakes)" was posted to the official Fall Out Boy YouTube channel. To anyone unfamiliar with fandom and digital culture, this video seems incomprehensible. Its format imitates a home shopping network such as QVC, wherein the band members, their instruments, and objects from previous videos are being sold for hundreds to thousands of dollars. The band as an object is billed "The Fallout Boys," a contraction of various misnomers attributed to them by journalists over the years, and pop-up bullet points describe them as "beautiful boys" who are "made of real skin" and "eat food." A pair of overly cheerful presenters in matching khakis and polo shirts help the band display items ranging from a stuffed sheep with wings, which was pictured on the cover of their 2009 album *Infinity on High*, to the life-size llama-like puppets that feature on their 2018 record *MANIA*, to completely random items like "crap in glass" (a few sticks in a drinking glass) and "Holy Miracle Water" (an ordinary bottle of water, originally priced $899.99 but reduced to $56.99 plus shipping). Pop-up boxes, text, and a running footer describe the items and their prices in shopping channel jargon, and the rest of the text is either a reference to a song or event in the band's earlier career or a paraphrase of trends and expressions from fandom. As the sheep is displayed, a text box urges "Take Franklin home. He's just a small boy." Referring to someone or something as a "small boy" is a fannish meme to describe anything cute or appealing. As one commenter puts it (and receives two thousand likes), "this whole video is a meme."[1]

How has this become possible? How do these items not only communicate but communicate clearly and broadly enough to make a video? The degree of referentiality and synecdoche on display is only possible in a clearly defined group or subculture. To a knowledgeable fan, everything in the video makes sense: everyone knows (to return to Greenwald) "what it is." As I will demonstrate, emo fandom has become intensely reflexive and self-definitional via the affordances of YouTube and Tumblr, in looking backward to LiveJournal and MySpace to create its genealogy and define what has come before it. Although YouTube (est. 2005) is the older site, I will discuss Tumblr (est. 2007) first, because it seems from the data that most of the contemporary fan discourse shaping emo comes from Tumblr, where it exists in porous proximity with all the other fandoms Tumblr supports, and then spreads into YouTube, undermining and blurring the boundaries of gender and genre we observed in the previous chapter. The "small boy" item, for instance, definitely did not start in emo fandom, but because of Tumblr's reliance on reblogging, it has spread frictionlessly across that platform and beyond. Moreover, because YouTube remains the most popular site for hosting video, Tumblrs often embed YouTube videos in their posts, which create a literal link from Tumblr to YouTube and sets the items into a different lexia.[2] Here is a key illustration of Hills's point regarding the demise of textual boundaries: if a video is uploaded to YouTube by an official channel, even with a description guiding interpretation, the affordances of YouTube make it automatically copy-and-pasteable into Tumblrs with their own agendas and perspectives. Obviously, this is not the only way items "move" across the websites—a user's personal activity can function as a link, as practices and vocabulary learned from Tumblr are applied elsewhere—but it provides a good example of how programming channels and shapes the movement of online discourse.

For this chapter, I used the app TumblRipper to download each band's official Tumblr account, in addition to the most popular fan accounts for each. I also downloaded and coded the top five Tumblrs tagged with "emo" and followed all of these accounts with a Tumblr blog I made for this purpose, so new data would arrive on my dashboard daily. On YouTube, I performed the analysis on all the official music videos by Fall Out Boy (FOB), My Chemical Romance (MCR), and Panic! at the Disco and coded the top 500 comments for each. I entered the search terms "band name + fanvid," "band name + fan edit," and "band name + crack" and analyzed the five most popular results for each, before coding the top 500 comments.

In the previous chapter, I identified four streams of items feeding to the construction of emo, which I labeled gender, genre, authenticity, and fandom. The YouTube and Tumblr material continued to contribute to these sets, but less as separate streams and more gathered together under the named discourse of "emo," demonstrating how the solidity of the construct has increased over time. They also introduced the significant theme of nostalgia, a thread that ran through all sets of items. Nostalgia is often a theme in emo lyrics, but as utilized here, its function is not so much to recall the past as to actively frame and define it, and this is a crucial element in fandom's construction of emo. On these sites, the term "emo" is suddenly much more common—although it can have a slightly ironic inflection, fans on these sites seem much readier to identify with the word and use it to frame their music. Moreover, I found that the borders of the discursive constructions on these sides were much more porous than those on MySpace and Live-Journal.[3] Memes and other items from web culture more broadly intersect with the construction of emo much more frequently, and the borders of the subculture are less rigidly policed. This aligns with Stein's argument that "fan culture and millennial mainstream digital cultures are, to a degree, discursive fictions" and demonstrates their potential for mutual influence.[4]

Tumblr is often thought of as the site where anarchic, playful fandom humor dominates.[5] Launched in 2007, it allows users to post short, rebloggable text, photographs, links, audio and video clips, and quotations. The use of animated GIFs to express an opinion or reaction is particularly popular. A Tumblr account thus becomes a sort of scrapbook, usually built around a theme. Posts are tagged, and users can either "follow" a tag, causing relevant posts to appear on their homepage (dashboard) or use the tag to search the site. Despite Tumblr's popularity, it presents several barriers to researchers.

The difficulties of studying it in any consistent way have been well document-ed. First, its search function can be unreliable, and the algorithm by which results are presented is frustratingly opaque. Second, as Attu and Terras note, there are "few technological approaches to analysing Tumblr content by automation or scale," which poses a significant challenge to quantitative researchers or, indeed, those seeking representative samples.[6] The "permanent state of flux" of the site and a lack of metadata are also significant barriers to research.[7] One can analyze the items at a particular point in time, observe their flow over a period, and draw inferences from this about their broader application, but it is difficult to present reliable overviews or make generalized statements about the site as a whole. As a result, researchers have tended to be vague on their methods of data collection and analysis when it comes to Tumblr. Attu and Terras note that "researchers rarely talk about the size and scope of their data sets."[8] "In collecting examples for this analysis," writes Newman in his study of *Pulp Fiction* fandom, "I have often searched Tumblr by tag."[9] But which tags? Why? How far can results of his analysis be generalized, when we cannot judge the relationship between the posts his searches found and the broader context of *Pulp Fiction* fandom on the site?

Although this study cannot answer all these questions in full, I have taken several measures to ensure the sample of posts I analyzed was as represent-ative of emo on Tumblr as possible. Using the freeware app TumblRipper, I downloaded the full archives of the following microblogs:

1.  The official Tumblr account for each band, which in the case of FOB and MCR also serve as the bands' official sites now. This heightens interaction and intertextuality between the bands' official presence, industry discourse, and fandom.
2.  The first fan account returned by each search for a band that did not have a narrow specialty remit (e.g., devoted to one band member).
3.  The first five search results returned for the hashtag "emo."
4.  The first five search results for the hashtag "emo trinity."

Tumblr's search algorithm is private, but given that the first results had so many more notes and reblogs than those further down the list, we must conclude that it measures popularity by logical scale. It is safe to say the items hosted on them make significant impact on fan discourse. I followed these tags and blogs with a Tumblr account I made specifically for this purpose, meaning their new posts would show up on my dashboard. Then I performed a multimedia discourse analysis on this material, adding to the set as my dashboard provided more items. Having these posts show up on my dashboard provided a more naturalistic impression of Tumblr, while coding the past entries gave a broader overview of posts. The majority of posts fell into five categories:

1. Official promotion, such as tour dates. These posts typically started on the bands' official accounts, then were recirculated through the fandom after the "emo" tag is attached.

2. Scanned or embedded items of old media related to the bands, such as magazines from the early 2000s or video clips, tagged "emo" and "emo trinity." This is a key example of Booth's intratextuality and narractivity—fans are creating the "text" of emo, often retrospectively.

3. Memes, either specific to the fandom or adapted from broader web culture. The most circulated items in this category were embedded reaction videos by YouTube personality Frank Gioia, known by his username CrankThatFrank.

4. Aesthetic posts: images of young people dressed in band T-shirts and skinny jeans, hair often teased into androgynous styles.

5. LGBT-positive notes and images.

The fact that the items were tagged #emo or #emo trinity made them available for the search crawl, which picks them out and recirculates them to display on the dashboard of users following that tag. These will appear juxtaposed with items from the searcher's other interests. The flatness of the medium makes them equally influential in the way they appear on dashboards. This is an example of Booth's intratextuality, but unlike blog templates that provide a space for the main text followed by comments underneath it, all Tumblr posts appear on the same surface, creating a parity of impact. The first category originates on the bands' official Tumblrs, from where they spread, ending up side-by-side from the fan posts with no clear distinction. So there might appear in no particular order, the following series of typical posts (see figure 9).

In figure 9, we observe a meme based on *Tom and Jerry*, whereby Tom pushing a rifle labeled "turning shuffle on" into a mousehole causes the end of the gun labeled "The Light Behind Your Eyes" (a sad MCR song) to emerge

FIGURE 9: Tumblr posts.

aimed at his own head. Many of the memes imply that listening to emo hurts the user in some way, but they are presented with humor. So the stereotype of emo kids being depressed and self-destructive is in a sense upheld but inflected with self-conscious humor. Next we see an item that contributes to an aesthetic that has not changed much since MySpace: a black and red backpack, black guitar, and customized Converse sneakers, but here it is explicitly tagged "emo." It has something in common with goth, but could be read as softer and more feminine, thanks to the prevalence of cute and colorful accessories combined with black and a lack of metal and studs. Relatedly, the popular Tumblr blog emo-church re-creates the backdrop of an early 2000s MySpace account, with the header "wow it really wasn't 'just a phase.'" The subheader reads, "Just a guy who repressed his emo phase in middle school and now it's coming back to haunt him. Welcome to the 2000s."[10] Along with band pictures, this Tumblr posts frequent pictures of outfits in that aesthetic, consolidating it as the visual representation of emo. The next picture is of Gerard Way on stage in front of a fire effect and is tagged "arriving from hell like." The final post is from a FOB fan account but is not specifically related to the band. It discusses the difficult relationship some LGBT teenagers who are also Christian have with their religious communities. The fact this appears in a FOB fan blog consolidates the idea of emo as an LGBT-positive space: this is much more emphatic and explicit than it was on MySpace or LiveJournal. We find none of the gendered insults those communities used so casually.

Still, many more posts were dedicated to uploading media featuring the Emo Trinity bands from the past fifteen years, organizing and categorizing, a form of narractivity that contributes to the construction of a community conceptual archive.[11] Old media that called the bands "emo" is prioritized, including magazine photographs. Other times, pictures will be spliced together and labeled "emo" or "emo trinity" by the user. The other favored category is media where band members discuss gender and sexuality, which lends legitimacy to the multiple posts promoting LGBT equality. They might initially have appeared side by side with an image or sound bite from one of the bands expressing support for LGBT causes, but because of the Tumblr format, they can reappear in other places detached from them. These posts rarely have any explicit link to music, suggesting their place in emo as a subculture is now taken for granted. Again, this is a form of narractivity that works to construct emo retrospectively as a queer space.

Finally, one also finds deliberate absurdities called "shitposting," like the Pepe meme in figure 3, and the poor-quality photoshops of Stump, Way, and Urie's faces onto Christian iconography. The provenance of the term "shitposting" is unknown, but it may have originated on 4chan before gaining popularity on Tumblr and spreading to other sites. Much shitposting makes use of what Nick Douglas calls "internet ugly," which he describes as a "a definable aesthetic running through meme culture, a celebration of the sloppy and the amateurish."[12] Its function is to implode seriousness, to take down anything too self-important, to "emphasize human messiness" in contrast with the smooth efficiency of technology. Internet ugly is "supposed to look like shit."[13] Emo crack roundly punctures the seriousness of the feeling/thinking male subject, even in its emotional investment.

As we might expect, there were a few gatekeeping posts and linked discussion of genre, but the frequency and intensity of these discussions has decreased. The standard response from blog owners was that genre is no longer important and that one can include the agency of the end user in constructing the meaning of new media.[14] They define one's preferences how one wishes. This illustrates De Kosnik's point regarding archives as categorization. The emo-church blog also features pictures of contemporary rappers who use a sensitive, depressed aesthetic, such as the "goth boi clique" collective, whose output concerns emotion, self-destructive habits, and doomed love. Their aesthetic is similar to traditional emo but may include more jewelry, facial tattoos, and a predilection for cigarettes and prescription drugs. These rappers are still a minority in Tumblr's construction of emo, but as they work their way in, their presence definitely expands the boundaries of the discourse, for the first time questioning the necessity of instrumentation. I explore this fully in chapter 5.

One cannot get far into emo fandom on Tumblr before encountering reblogs of video posts by Frank Gioia, known as CrankThatFrank, who maintains a Tumblr of the same name to update his followers about his new videos. Referred to by fans as "emo father," Gioia has more or less created a career out of his fandom, having close to 700,000 subscribers and using advertising and merchandise sales to monetize his work. Branding himself as a "repressed emo," Gioia publishes a variety of discussion videos related to FOB, MCR, and Panic! in addition to Twenty One Pilots and various related bands. He uses the word "emo" extensively in his branding, featuring it in most video titles and descriptions. His most popular output is a long-running series of

FIGURE 10: A comment Patrick Stump left on a girl's LiveJournal in 2002, about Pete Wentz cock blocking him.

reaction videos to "emo crack compilations" (standing at sixty-seven episodes as of April 2020).

"Crack" is a difficult phenomenon to describe verbally, being an intensely visual form of humor. It is essentially composed of short videos that splice together clips from music videos, interviews, and candid sources with sounds and images from popular texts such as *SpongeBob SquarePants* and *Shrek*, broadly used memes, Vines (short videos), and more to humorous effect. For example, one popular clip plays Panic! at the Disco's "This Is Gospel" over a home video in which a child's flying fairy toy flies directly into an open fire, incinerating at the lyric refrain "if you love me let me go." Another popular format is to freeze band interviews at moments displaying unfortunate facial expressions, zoom in dramatically, and play a comedic sound bite over the top. These items undermine the discursive pretensions to authority, authenticity, and seriousness we've been observing since the MySpace entries, yet they are not insults. They are presented and received with affection among a community of self-confessed "emos"—it is not the value of the bands or their music that is deconstructed but the value of constructs like authenticity and authority. As we have seen, these values are strongly associated with masculinity in the history of music. On Tumblr, we observe the bands appreciated through a different discourse, which uses terms like "cute," "adorable," and even "soft." For example, a Tumblr blog happyfalloutboys (with the plural) exclusively reblogs and archives pictures of the members Fall Out Boy smiling and laughing.

There is also a trend of featuring and revaluing much older content, such as posts and comments from then-teenaged band members made on LiveJournal in the early 2000s. Fan-made Tumblr accounts have a particular habit of "bringing back" such items: one rapidly spreading item with 734 reblogs (as of February 26, 2019) was a LiveJournal comment from FOB frontman Patrick Stump, then aged seventeen, documenting an unsuccessful attempt at flirting before being "cock block[ed]" by Pete Wentz. The fan-made Tumblr uploading it notes: "I felt it was my duty to share this with everyone" (see figure 10).

**Transcription:**
**it's the thought that counts**
**2002-03-12 07:43pm UTC**

> You made the attempt to go to the show . . . and you drank a bunch afterwards, and you know, it was more fun dancing with you than it was getting ground into a couple making out in the corner by the percolating ass of one Chris Deadstop.[15] You were also my only dance that evening as all the rest of the girls there were noticeably too much older (and pretentious . . . ironic considering how pretentious I am myself) to bother with little sober me. That and the girl I was most interested in stumbled by making out with another girl.
>
> Did you hear about Pete's cock block in Orland Park?
>
> So I'm talking to this girl (gorgeous) after the show. I pointed to her a bunch while I sang and now she seems genuinely interested in me. I'm pleased with myself. I'm usually shy, but there I am: approaching a girl who, by the looks of things is WAY out of my league and engaging her in conversation. We're talking; she's decently articulate, really cute, my age, and Pete walks up in a baseball cap (bad news) he's all, "How old do you think this kid is?" She looks me over and goes "19." I'm thinking, okay, I'll take that. Then he goes, "What about me?" she's like "Oh you're 16." He's like "Yeah of course I am!" [He would have been twenty-two.] and he makes an ass of himself which is no problem with me. Then we continue talking and Pete interrupts with "Seniors RULE!!!" and he runs away.

So we're talking some more. This time Pete and Joe check me into the wall in mid-sentence, then they pile on me . . . them and everybody in all the other bands. Now I'm the butt of some joke I haven't been let in on in front of some girl I'm trying to impress in the middle of bloody nowhere. Rad. So anyway, I get up and I say my goodbyes, and we head for the party. Before I leave she grabs me (wow) and hugs me (wow) and whispers in my ear: "Tell your bassist he's cute."

And that's why the highlight of my evening is currently a toss-up between dancing with you and talking to the dude from Tom Sawyer about shows.

-patrick

As the self-described "butt of some joke I haven't been let in on in front of some girl I'm trying to impress," Stump's persona as shy, awkward, and overshadowed by his charismatic friend is received as "adorable," "cute," and so on in the user notes. This undermines the construction of serious musicianship and authority that we observed in previous chapters but hooks into the construct of geek or nerd masculinity, which was just beginning its revaluation at that time. This accords with Sam de Boise's point that dominant masculinities are not a monolith, and historically, the figure of the "sensitive man" has been used to justify and uphold male privilege, just as the "macho" one has. On one hand, this is a story about male failures and insecurity. On the other hand, it continues the theme of emo as a boys' club, where boys' voices are perceived and valued in the communal archive. In this world, girls exist to let boys have feelings.[16] Moreover, although not a form of relational communication (because it was appropriated and not addressed thereto), recirculating these items consolidates the aspect of the authenticity construct that positions emo bands as very similar to their listeners.

Because Tumblr posts often embed YouTube videos, including music videos, interviews, and fan vids, the platform provides a strong link between the construction of emo on YouTube and Tumblr. You can play the videos on Tumblr or follow them to YouTube to read comments and view related videos. The flow is two-way: images flow from YouTube to Tumblr, and as we will observe, there is a verbal influence as linguistic memes and trends travel backward from Tumblr to YouTube. YouTube also supports the bands' professional channels to host their videos and attracts a wider range of commenters than the relatively fandom- and youth-oriented Tumblr. This means that the now well-developed reflexive discourse of fandom collides with items from music culture more generally and even casual listeners. We turn now to examine the bands' presence on YouTube, in addition to the most popular fan vids and comments uploaded by fans and viewers.

In reviewing the videos of singles, one becomes increasingly aware that all the members of all the bands are male. Of course, I already knew this, but watching the videos side by side drives home the solidity of the construct—women really are very excluded as performers. They appear in crowd shots, but nowhere near as frequently as they do at real concerts. Since the early 2000s I have seen all three of the Emo Trinity bands live multiple times, in venues ranging from small clubs to stadiums: the male/female distribution of the audiences is usually about one in four, maybe one in three for MCR. This is certainly not the impression constructed by the videos, reminding us that male viewership is more valuable: according to the authenticity construct, girls may be at shows for the "wrong" reasons, such as sexual attraction, but male appreciation validates the music's value. Given emo's roots in punk, it isn't surprising that the early, lower-budget videos tend to evoke the aesthetic of hardcore shows—especially in the case of FOB. The videos for their earliest singles, such as "Saturday" (2004), are composed of candid clips of touring and performance. The audience shown is primarily young, male, and white, dressed in jeans, shirts, and hoodies. Comments make the visual items explicit:

So many white boys in the concert![17]

———

Literally only white teenage boys at that concert.[18]

———

'member when fob fans weren't just cringy 13 year old girls? I member.[19]

Nostalgia is at work already: "cringy 13 year old girls" are framed as an intrusion that has interrupted a superior masculine domain. Joseph Lyle's comment is a reference to season 20 of the long-running animated satire show *South Park*. This episode, which was broadcast during Donald Trump's successful campaign for presidency of the United States in 2016, concerns a plague of so-called member berries: animated talking fruits that constantly ask if listeners "[re]member" cultural texts or events, such as scenes from

*Star Wars*, before sliding seamlessly into loaded rhetoric like "'member when there weren't so many Mexicans?"[20] Interdiscursively, Lyle's statement contains its own ironic critique against romanticizing the past as some sort of white-washed haven of authenticity. Even the highly stylized videos that come later (the elaborate dreamscape of MCR's "Welcome to the Black Parade"; the absurdist, disjointed narrative about celebrity that makes up Fall Out Boy's "This Ain't a Scene It's an Arms Race"; or the black-and-white idyll of Panic!'s "Northern Downpour") put a heavy emphasis on performance and playing, careful to construct the bands as instrumentalists first and foremost, in keeping with the valorization of technicality.

So men are the active subjects of emo music videos—as performers, narrative focalizers, or both. Women and girls in the videos fall into one of three categories: members of an audience, love interests, or antagonists. We generally don't find the mass objectification and sexualization of women common to rock and hip-hop: there is some, for example, in where the camera pans over dancers' bodies in Panic!'s burlesque-themed video for "But It's Better If You Do," but compared with the broader norms of music videos, it's minimal. More common is for women to appear as the cause of male emotional suffering, like the dead ballerina who is mourned in MCR's "Helena," or the unfaithful bride motif that appears in several Panic! videos. Elsewhere, women feature as the prize in wish-fulfilment narratives, such as where an unlikely nerdy hero gets the girl in FOB's "Grand Theft Autumn" and "Sugar We're Going Down." Again, de Boise has discussed emo's problematic obsession with this trope, and its implicit notions of certain men "deserving" women. Given that YouTube is a platform where media narratives meet direct user feedback, there was surprisingly little critique of the trope in the comments. User slim shady notes, "remember kids, all of your problems will be solved if you make out with your stalker,"[21] under FOB's video for "Grand Theft Autumn," but this was the exception, not the rule. The response to female guest performers is lukewarm and meets with gatekeeping from fans, shoring up the discursive lines that exclude women from subjectivity. FOB's *The Young Blood Chronicles* (*TYBC*) is a series of eleven videos, the visual companion to their 2013 album *Save Rock and Roll*. *TYBC* is a fantastical story concerning a cult that attempts to banish music, and the band is entrusted to save a briefcase that symbolically contains (presumably) rock and roll. The cult members are beautiful, sinister, and violent women known as "vixens." The female-threat-to-male-virtue story is literalized as frontman Patrick Stump gets kidnapped and brainwashed to serve the cult's purposes. The cult leader is played by singer-songwriter Courtney Love. Love is a guest vocalist and cowriter for the track "Rat a Tat" and features heavily in the video. Love has been a frequent target of misogyny for many years, first for being a woman in punk, and also for the fact that she was married to Nirvana frontman Kurt Cobain at the time of his death in 1994. I knew what the top comments would say before I read them, and sure enough, the highest-rated comment chain on the video is:

Courtney absolutely kills this (159 likes).[22]

————

You mean the same way she killed Kurt Cobain?[23]

————

she kills a lot of things.[24]

————

@pixel even her husband.[25]

Framing women as men's literal destruction crosses the metatextual boundary out of the videos and into the construction of reality. Cobain's death was ruled an unambiguous suicide, but rumors of Love's direct or indirect responsibility have been circulating ever since. User crunchy makes an all-caps claim that FOB "FEATURED THE WOMAN WHO KILLED THE MAN THAT FOUNDED THE GENRE OF THE MUSIC THEY PLAY,"[26] which is almost mythologizing in tone—it is empirically dubious that FOB's music should share a genre with Nirvana. There are also some comments defending Love, but any feature of a female performer is met with at least some degree of resistance. One version of FOB's "Irresistible" features pop-rock singer Demi Lovato, and while one comment approves her as "a perfect fit,"[27] the majority are dismissive or derisive. User Soboleva describes her as "just unnecessary."[28] Commenter H3rO 142 claims, "The Woman ruins the song, it's there for decoration," explicitly associating femininity with passivity and men with subjectivity.[29] While the nonhuman pronoun is probably a translation error, its effect is to minimize the female performer's subjectivity. There are many comments of this type, and a few that are more ambiguous. User Anne Rosario comments that "Demi looks like a legit fall out boy member,"[30] to which the first response is, oddly, "Bless."[31] "Bless" is an indulgence, an extension of tolerance to a female performer on masculine territory. User Spongebob ROUNDpants makes the spatial metaphor of contamination explicit, observing that "teens are so edgy and unappreciative that they don't want Demi mixing in with the band."[32]

We observed in previous chapters that emo girls sought to set themselves apart from behaviors and identities framed as feminine excess. Interestingly, in the context of YouTube, such attempts are called out and mocked. On MCR's video for "Helena," user Sophia Hay claims, "the girls in my class are afraid of me because they can hear mcr from my headphones :),"[33] to which the top responses are "I'm not like other girls!!!! Xdee!!!"[34] and "how edgy."[35] Here again we see the interdiscursive influence of broader web culture and the more porous boundaries of fan discourse on YouTube. A range of popular sites including Thought Catalog, The Odyssey, and TV Tropes have discussed the inherent sexism of the "not like other girls" trope, and Reddit hosts a community devoted to mocking it.[36] I did not find this sort of reflexivity in the earlier emo communities, which tended to denigrate femininity unproblematically. This was especially true on MCR pages. One YouTube commenter writes on the MCR documentary video: "other girls spend two hours learning the steps to the kpop dances. i spend two hours watching a band that broke up four years ago talking about how imperfect they are."[37] This received 308 likes, and four people comment "same." But user Kawaii Punk, whose username juxtaposes the Japanese term for (roughly) "cuteness" with the connotations of punk, responds "HAHAHAHAHA I do both."[38] User rainetheawesome claims, "I'm both that kpop fangirl, and the girl in tears over watching this video."[39] These comments deny the absolute binary between masculinity and femininity, rock and pop, authenticity and inauthenticity, staking out a space for the properties that were devalued in the communities. This may be another influence that has worked its way back from the patchwork Tumblr format that allows culturally masculine and culturally feminine items to mingle nonhierarchically. It may also be that the younger generation of fans is becoming more feminist and more open-minded, challenging the gendered boundary policing of earlier sites, or an effect of the looser boundaries of YouTube attracting a wider range of viewers, including casual ones. However, it is notable that the two commenters deprecating "other girls" were the ones with "emo" in their usernames.

So femininity and the role of women remain problematic, though commenters are starting to critique the tropes we found in earlier communities.

Moreover, the attachment of femininity to men meets a lot less resistance than it did on LiveJournal and MySpace. One of the top-rated comments on MCR's early video for "Honey This Mirror Isn't Big Enough for the Two of Us," reads "Gerard is really pretty."[40] Where the earlier communities tended to police such statements with at least some reprimand for fangirlishness, but here the responses are:

Yes. Yes he is.[41]

———

Gerard is prettier than me.[42]

———

julia villarreal ikr like why can't I b as boobyful as him?[43]

And so on. In fact, statements that would have been dismissed elsewhere as fangirling are generally approved on YouTube. Commenter princess nicole writes on FOB's "Just One Yesterday":

[Gets arrested]

Officer: You have the right to remain silent, anything you say can and will be used against you-

Me: PATRICK STUMP!!!!!!!!!!!!!

Officer: I'm so sick of these bloody fangirls.[44]

This item received 358 likes and no backlash. Indeed, the top reply is: "Hell, I would say it to the officer and I'm a male."[45] Compare: "I'm a 50 year old hetero man and when I saw that haircut, that jawline . . . man I feel all funny . . ."[46] and "I just came here to listen to my favorite song, what are these comments? Hot or not? (Even though I am the male gender and attracted to the female gender, I do agree they always look hot)."[47]

There were no comparable expressions of sexual interest from self-professed heterosexual men in the MySpace and LiveJournal communities. This may be dismissed as a matter of time—it is now more generally acceptable to express homosexual feelings in Western countries than it was even five or ten years ago. But my argument is that the development of emo as a subculture is a both a cause and an effect of this shift, because texts and cultures are mutually constitutive and enmeshed. It could also relate to the fact that YouTube's medium is visual, focused on bodies moving through space, while LiveJournal is primarily textual and thus one level further removed from physical, embodied experience.

Just like on Tumblr, YouTube commenters are firm in their assertions that emo is queer-positive. When a commenter claims to "hate LGBT stuff,"[48] she is told to "get out of our emo community" and informed that "people who hate LGBT aren't allowed to listen to mcr."[49] She is reminded of Gerard Way and Frank Iero's penchant for stage-gay, to which she has no response. Moreover, fans use the Barthesian technique of linguistically anchoring visual items, narrowing down and fixing the meanings of multivalent images. At the opening of this book, I discussed Panic!'s 2009 video for the single "Girls/Girls/Boys." The song is a celebration of female bisexuality, wherein the object of the narrator's affection is attracted to another woman over him. The video features frontman Brendon Urie against a black background, wearing no visible clothes and giving the impression he is naked, as the camera stops panning at his pelvis. The director's cut includes scenes of two women in nude-tone underwear, kissing and caressing each other as they ignore Urie. As I noted, it could be argued that only lesbian relationships are affirmed here, and moreover that sex acts between conventionally attractive young women are being fetishized by the heterosexual male gaze. But commenters choose to repeat the lyrics that claim one cannot choose whom one loves, often in capital letters, and commenter Gloupyli asserts that "live performances as well as the clip abundantly proved it was for LGBT+ (I saw that form as well) support."[50] Given the wider range of commenters one finds on YouTube, perhaps it is unsurprising that one comment dismisses the video as "propaganda from the left," but it receives zero likes and is rapidly buried, whereas the gay-positive ones typically have like counts in the double digits. That said, LGBT causes are considered fair game for mockery. In Panic!'s 2018 video for "Don't Threaten Me with a Good Time," a shape-shifting monster takes the form of a beautiful woman to seduce Brendon Urie at a bar before eating him, assuming his appearance, and heading out the next night to repeat the cycle. In the top-rated comment, user OneLoneVoice comments:

Wow what an LGBT+ supportive video.
The monster is bi (1.2K likes).[51]

Historically, shape-shifting monsters have often been coded queerly on screen, but this joke functions by assuming a context wherein most people support bisexuality—it obviously isn't really supportive to conflate bisexuality with eating humans. The top response, from user ZanktheGreat, is "are you assuming its gender? This is 2017" (276 likes).[52] User Sandy Jones responds, "please tell me you are being ironic."[53] Here the broad range of users and looser boundaries of the discourse has rendered the joke less intelligible than it would be in the more tightly bounded LiveJournal communities. Sandy Jones's comment indicates that she thinks ZanktheGreat is joking, invoking the meme of assigning ever-more outlandish gender identities to everything from fictional characters to inanimate objects—but she cannot be sure. This meme is essentially conservative, being a backlash against gender self-identification that stretches the argument to absurdity. Another conservative meme that pops up in the comment sections is the phrase "BEGONE THOT" usually in all caps. THOT is an acronym for "that ho over there," and it is used in response to videos that feature women doing, well, anything—but particularly attempting to interact with band members. Although the tone is humorous, the accumulation of these items continue the objectification of women as opposed to the male subjects.

Commenters had surprisingly little to say on the subject of stage-gay—indeed, considering the attention academics have paid to it, this holds true across all the sites. The fact that this kind of performativity comes in for so little comment reminds us that what strikes scholars as important may not be so notable to fans. It could also indicate that queer performativity between men is becoming more unremarkable. Much more prominent was the feminizing frame of "cuteness," which we first observed on Tumblr, is imposed across all the videos, but especially older ones. These are recent comments on a low-budget short film Fall Out Boy made near at the start of their career, originally distributed on CD as a B-side in 2004:

My babies grew up so fast.[54]

———

I FEEL LIKE I'M AN OLD PERSON WATCHING A BUNCH OF OLD HOME MOVIES OF MY KIDS AHHHHH.[55]

———

Patrick with a buzz cut is so adorable.[56]

The term "adorable" was used six times in the top 500 comments on this video, all from commenters with female usernames. Commenters presenting themselves as male, conversely, were more likely to identify with band members in failing at hegemonic masculinity, performing gendered self-effacement. The following comments are on Fall Out Boy's video for "Dance, Dance," in which they simultaneously play as the band at a high school prom and play themselves as unpopular, nerdy high school students in attendance.

Patrick is me when i think my dance is good.[57]

———

Same.[58]

———

I'm Andy, just reading quietly.[59]

It seems on the surface of things that fans have become more critical and self-conscious regarding gender, readier to critique constructs of masculinity and display feminine characteristics.

Does this carry through to the discussion of genre? I found this was an area of explicit tension—there was a lot of boundary policing and a lot of deconstruction of those boundaries. YouTubers spend more time discussing and categorizing genre than Tumblr users, which makes sense considering that YouTube displays one video and one set of comments per lexia and offers videos that the algorithm considers similar, as opposed to the multiple items displayed simultaneously on Tumblr. Again, displaying Tumblr influence, YouTube commenters frequently referred to themselves, each other, and the bands as "emo," far more frequently than on LiveJournal:

I Love all You Emo MotherFuckers, stay bitter.[60]

———

Chantel Robert I will I will be emo forever ♥.[61]

———

Proud to be an og [original gangster] emo.[62]

I also found several uses of the phrase "Holy Emo Trinity" here, having worked its way from Tumblr to YouTube. This phrase seems to have originated in a relatively niche context on Tumblr. It's exposed and spreads to a wider audience here: wide enough to have made its way to urbandictionary.com. Notably, however, it was much more common for commenters with feminine usernames to identify themselves or the bands/songs as "emo," while those with masculine usernames still preferred "rock" or "punk." That gendered hierarchy of genres seems to be extremely deep-rooted in our culture, to the point that users presenting as male find it difficult to identify with anything outside the rock/punk/metal triad. It is fascinating that in the same comment, user Johnx reinforces this binary in stating that MCR would have made an excellent hardcore punk band, then describes the song as "cumworthy."[63] The homoerotic overtone is apparently less threatening to the masculine/ feminine binary than the threat of contamination by a feminine-coded genre. On the other hand, comments are alert to emo's critique of rock and punk, possibly because they are immediate responses to videos explicitly making that critique. For example, the 2009 video for Fall Out Boy's single "I Don't Care" contains a preamble unavailable in recordings. An older man bearing all the semantic hallmarks of a 1970s cock-rocker is shown lounging backstage at a music venue. He has long hair, a moustache, and a goatee; he wears a blue denim jacket, blue jeans, and sunglasses indoors; and he has a lurid red electric guitar slung across his lap. A crowd cheers in the background, and the members of Fall Out Boy enter from what is presumably a stage door. The rocker eyes them with disdain, then sneers to his friend: "What the *hell* happened to rock and roll? [.] *Eye*liner? [.] Energy drinks? And no guitar solos? [laughing] I've taken shits with bigger rock stars in them!" The band looks disconcerted, and the rest of the video depicts them attempting to cause chaos in a stereotypical "rock star" manner, but failing ineptly at it. User TJ Williams comments:

> "What the hell happened to rock & roll?"
> It's 2018. DEAL WITH IT![64]

This framing of the present as preferable to a regressive past exists in tension with a strong current of nostalgia, which frames the past as more authentic:

> I feel like FOB has become less hard core? punk? idk but does anyone else notice that their style has changed? Well I guess that's what happens when you no longer live in 2003 XD.[65]

> ———

> I feel sorry for their early fans who had to watch them grow into the pop band they are now instead of the decent punk/Emo band they were.[66]

> ———

they arent pop.[67]

_____

+sophia craig well theyre not punk anyway. ●[68]

This exchange is interesting because emo is aligned with punk as a highly valued "authentic" genre opposed to superficial pop, removing any mocking or derisive connotation from "emo." Indeed, some degree of gatekeeping seems to have emerged around claiming "emo" as identity. Few people want to admit to pop fandom. Justin Yee takes another commenter to task for "say[ing] shes emo" while using "a fucking gay kpop profile picture."[69] Notice how the use of "gay" as an insult, so often attached to emo bands in the past, has moved to the contemporary genre of K-pop (Korean pop). This illustrates how the item "gay" has no signification with regard to music (could any genres be audibly more different than emo and K-pop?): its meaning depends completely on the positive-masculine/negative-feminine binary by which music's authenticity is culturally constructed.

Fans have also developed a sort of shorthand around these videos, sourced in fan culture and used for comedic effect. Consider this series of top-rated comments on Panic!'s video for "Lying Is the Most Fun a Girl Can Have Without Taking Her Clothes Off":

that's a nice bath tub Ryan.[70]

_____

Trinity Urie [previous user] o no you didn't.[71]

_____

Better stay on that side of the street [previous user]. Oh yeah i did (also love the name ♥♥♥). [72]

_____

Trinity Urie hehe ty! ♥ 👅[73]

To an outsider, these items make no sense, but they are densely referential. "Better stay on that side of the street" is a reference to the 2006 MCR documentary _Life on the Murder Scene_. Herein Gerard Way relates how he walked out of the band's tour bus one morning still wearing stage makeup to be greeted by a "guy outside in front of a crackhouse," who warned him that he'd "better stay on that side of the street, motherfucker. I'll knock you *out*."[74] The full documentary has been uploaded to YouTube by a fan, as have all the band's backstage stories. This clip features regularly in "crack" compilations. The "bath tub" refers to an extremely notorious piece of slash fan fiction known as "the milk fic," featuring band members Ryan Ross and Brendon Urie, a bathtub, and some dubious usage of milk. It has become a fandom in-joke to react with horror whenever someone mentions milk or a bathtub. This is partly mimetic—the fic isn't actually *that* extreme, by the standards of what can be found on the internet—but its notoriety is increased because several band members have read it and mentioned it on social media. In 2016, Gerard Way live-tweeted his reading of it, professing to find it "well written" and (as was my reaction) rather less shocking than reputed.[75] Brendon Urie made a parody song about it on the now-defunct video platform Vine (see the YouTube channel Brendon Urie Vines for a fan-made archive). Sexual humor, homoeroticism, and parody might be considered an extreme expression of the gendered self-mockery we observed in previous chapters, but the key developments here are the high degree of interactivity between fans and band members and the degree of shorthand and in-group language. We have already discussed the popularity of "crack videos" that dominate the user-generated content around these bands. User Night Senpai comments on a crack video: "That moment when you are so well versed in emo memes you understand the whole video but yet somehow feel the same as when you first became a yeemo (AKA shook, listening to angels, and in tears)."[76]

"Yeemo" is a contraction of "yee" and "emo": "yee" refers to a meme in which a cartoon utters this noise, made popular by CrankthatFrank. His influence over the discourse doesn't stop at his own videos: his comments on the bands' more recent videos almost automatically become the top-rated and most visible. This sort of humor and referentiality has been picked up in the "Wilson" video described at the start of this chapter. The top comment, posted by Gioia almost as soon as it premiered, is "MEMEIA DELIVERING US THE BEST MEMES. IT'S MEME SEASON BOIS."[77] It had 3,200 likes at the start of 2019 and more than 131 responses. "Memeia" is a play on *MANIA*, the album from which the song is taken, implying that it is constructed entirely of memes. Strikingly, Gioia's comments sometimes receive more likes than comments from the actual band that uploads the video, as acknowledged by user brooke on a Panic!'s video: "YOUR COMMENT HAS MORE LIKES THAN THE OFFICIAL COMMENT BY ACTUAL PANIC HOW DO YOU FEEL."[78]

Here is clear evidence that fandom is actively shaping what emo means and is aware of it. YouTube, then, seems to serve as a meeting point between older forms and styles of fan participations, such as the arguments over gender, genre, and authenticity, with expressions of the playful internet that puncture the seriousness of those categories.

Finally, there were a handful of fan vids devoted to "shipping" band members. "Shipping" is the fandom term for imagining or wishing characters to be in a relationship, and the definition of "character" was broadened to include the media persona of famous people very early in the genre's popularity.[79] Obviously, fandom didn't invent this—incorporating real people, dead or alive, into fiction, has always been a common practice for authors. Nonetheless it is met with a fair amount of resistance and discomfort in many fandoms, with some finding it disrespectful or inappropriate. True to this trend, there were only a handful of shipping videos popular enough to turn up in the YouTube searches, and these received no more than ten comments and fewer than 150 views. Although surprising, this correlates with the lack of attention to stage-gay I noted earlier. Indeed, when user Jo Zhang creates a montage retelling FOB video series "The Young Blood Chronicles", s/he notes, "Sorry for scenes can be viewed as peterick [the compound name for shipping Pete Wentz with Patrick Stump] but 99% concert videos I hoarded is peterick."[80] Thanks to FOB's penchant for stage-gay, it seems the sources were queerer than the fan work! Nor is Tumblr, a current hub of shipping in all fandoms, particularly enthused by it, as the most popular fan Tumblr hosts profess not to read fan fic or enjoy shipping. On the contrary, when band members express discomfort with feminized forms of appreciation, such as fandom of themselves rather than fandom of their music, they are roundly supported by fans. In 2013, FOB's lead guitarist Joe Trohman wrote a long text post on his Tumblr, expressing disappointment with some fans' expectations that they should necessarily get to meet, talk, and spend time with the band after a show: a physical, in-person form of that emotional labor that Baym believes is now routinely expected of musicians. Carefully titling it "This Is Meant Out of Respect and Love, Not Disregard," Trohman goes on:

> There has been a considerable amount of chatter lately from some Fall Out Boy fans in regard to what we, as a band, do with our time after we play a show for you guys . . . What is expected out of us, past a great rock show, seems to perplex me. [He describes seeing shows as a

teenager, and his appreciation of live experience] We're back. We made a new record, for you. And now we're on tour. [He describes some of the work involved in a tour] We do this ALL for you guys. To see that, for some of you, it isn't enough is . . . well . . . it's kind of sad. Listen, I understand wanting to meet the members of a band you really, truly love. I appreciate it too. But is that the whole reason you came to see us? Would it be better if we didn't play and we just did a really long meet and greet? Is that really the point of it all? . . . Again, we love you guys. We appreciate you guys . . . We respect you guys. I think, perhaps, we could use a little bit of reciprocation at times.

Thanks for reading this.

Joe[81]

Baym suggests that where musicians choose to engage with fans in the participatory strategies emo bands favor, this "can leave musicians with social obligations that would not be there were the transactions clearly bounded by market economics": thus Trohman's uncertainty, in other words, "what is expected out of us."[82] This post has been reblogged over 2,700 times, and appreciative notes have been added, shoring up the construction that the proper way to appreciate music is cognitively and rationally, with attraction and emotion relegated to the denigrated feminine. So it seems less likely that the broader YouTube audience has limited the "shipping" items than that they aren't a significant aspect of emo fandom outside sites specifically devoted to fic. As a researcher, I was surprised by this, and it reinforced the importance of a rigorous methodology in moving beyond one's personal perspective in fandom to perceive larger patterns.

In this chapter, then, I established that by the time we arrive at the Tumblr/ YouTube interchange, the shape of emo is fairly clear. The central place of the Emo Trinity in defining its sound has been consolidated, with a few other bands (such as twenty one pilots) closer to the outskirts of the discourse. It is LGBT-positive and fairly gender critical, but retains real subjectivity for men and relegates women to supporting roles or props. It relies on a high degree of referentiality and shorthand between fans and bands and is self-conscious, humorous, and capable of incorporating an aesthetic of "cuteness" and "softness" alien to punk and hardcore. The fan practices of Tumblr and the connectivity by which Tumblr embeds items from YouTube seem to have allowed this aesthetic easy passage from the relatively niche, fan-focused Tumblr context to the broader concept of YouTube. There is some degree of gatekeeping around genre, and male fans especially can struggle with the idea of emo being in any way related to pop, retreating to the cultural strongholds of punk and rock to ward against this idea. Moreover, the intricate associations between fans and bands has led to humorous incorporation of meme culture into actual music videos, including expressions of softness and cuteness.

How will these statements play out once we leave the Tumblr/YouTube pathways, and turn to UGC-based sites more associated with masculinity—indeed, even with toxic masculinity and aggression? The next chapter is focused on fan content and addresses Reddit and 4chan, before we turn back to professional media's incorporation of this shaping process.

# THE TROUBLE WITH GATEKEEPING

## EMO IN MASCULINE SPACES

The sites I have explored so far might be some of the first that we consider when we think of fandom—and for those of us who grew up on them, when we think of emo. But it is a mistake to let our own history in fandom dominate our whole perspective—not because of some pretense of objectivity but to admit and confront our biases and prevent us from holding up a piece or aspect as a false representation of a whole. In the interest of a balanced assessment, we must expose ourselves to areas of fandom we are unfamiliar with and even uncomfortable about. The websites Reddit and 4chan were never part of my fan experience, but they have active fan communities discussing all kinds of music, video games, and films. Given the sites' differing norms and reputations when it comes to gender online, and the fact that they also hosted contributions to the construction of emo, it is only fair to compare and contrast them to Tumblr, LiveJournal, and MySpace.

Reddit is a website originally intended to be a news aggregator, launched by Steve Huffman and Alexis Ohanian in 2005. It was later acquired by Condé Nast.[1] The site is divided into boards called subreddits (subs), which are devoted to an enormous range of subjects, from headline news in India, to obscure anime franchises, to pictures of pet dachshunds. These subreddits currently number about 1.2 million (as of April 2020) and are moderated by one or more volunteer users. Users, known as Redditors, would submit links to news stories or other events for fellow Redditors to comment and vote on, though the practice quickly expanded to include submission of original content like pictures, GIFs, or short written pieces. The highest-rated submissions rise to the tops of subreddits, though they can also be sorted by "new" or other algorithms ("hot," "controversial") and filtered by date of posting. Comments can also be voted on and replied to, and these lexia are sorted so that the highest-rated comment rises to the top of the post. Upvotes earn the submitters "karma"; while downvotes remove it. Comments with the most downvotes disappear, although they can still be viewed by clicking on "load more comments" in comment threads. One can sign up for Reddit anonymously and as many times as one wishes. As Bergstrom has demonstrated, Reddit displays a communal norm valuing "authenticity."[2] Its "About" pages describe the site as a place for "authentic human connection," and moderators are advised that "healthy communities are those where participants engage in good faith, and with an assumption of good faith for their co-collaborators."[3] This means that with the exception of certain specific subs, posts appearing to be truthful, honest, and linked to a recognizable posting history tend to be favored and upvoted, whereas those suspected to be fabricated are downvoted. Reddit has a strong reputation for culturally masculine norms: aside from authenticity, rationality and logic are valued, provision of evidence and the display of knowledge are respected. Its logocentric format contributes to the promotion of reasoned debate, using plain white backgrounds, collapsible comment threads built into larger discussions, and prioritization of writing. Photos and videos are generally only used to start discussions—although it is technically possible to upload an image to a comment thread, it is against site social norms and hardly ever done. While I have been familiar with Reddit for some time, I was unaware before this project that it contains subreddits devoted to emo as a genre, plus subreddits for each of the Emo Trinity bands.

If Reddit has a reputation for one set of masculine forms, 4chan has a reputation for what has lately been called toxic masculinity. Associated with trolling, bullying, aggression, doxing, profanity, and pornography, 4chan is nonetheless a vast hub of unregulated creativity and humor and the breeding ground of some of the internet's most well-known memes. Lolcats come from 4chan, as does Anonymous, the hacker vigilante group that Gabriella Coleman has described as both "agent of chaos" and "seeker of justice."[4] Anonymous's projects range from hacking the websites of oppressive governments and doxing pedophiles to bullying posturing preteens off the internet. 4chan is variously described by media outlets as "brilliant, ridiculous and alarming" to the "lawless Wild West of the Web, a place of uninhibited bawdiness and verbal violence."[5] Site discourse is abrupt, offensive, rude, mocking and self-mocking, scathing of political correctness, and punitive of sensitivity and weakness. Though the notorious general board /b/ may be the most "habitually unpleasant," abrasion and rudeness is the norm even on "safe for work" boards.[6] Contrary to popular belief, not all of 4chan is obscene or pornographic. There are plenty of boards devoted to everyday topics like films and video games, and on those that are tagged "safe for work," explicitly offensive or illegal content should be deleted by moderators. But antagonistic norms of speech pervade these boards, too, and insults are common. Phillips, Coleman, and Knuttila have all commented on the widespread casual use of "fag" on 4chan, particularly as a suffix.[7] Knuttila writes:

> While there is of course no divorcing such terms from their offensive usage and associations, it's worth noting that on 4chan, the term "fag," at least, is used so often and in such a cavalier manner so as to seem less of a homophobic slur and more of a generally offensive suffix to refer to users of varying interests, hobbies, professions . . . Hence, on 4chan, a user who posts original artwork is considered an "artfag," whereas a "newfag" is a new user not yet familiar with the culture of the site or a specific board. The co-opting of "fag" and the insistence on its non-offensive nature fits with 4chan's general ethos of hostility toward any practice seen by its users as even remotely gesturing toward sensitivity or political correctness.[8]

I agree that opposing political correctness is the primary function of the item, but I still argue that the intertextual echo of homophobia reinforces an environment that prizes the culturally masculine qualities of toughness and lack of sensitivity. To be hurt, to take offense, carries feminized stigma. 4chan has a penchant for casual use of specifically taboo insults, including "retard(ed)" and "autist(ic)." According to Trammell, the terms "autism/autistic" "are often used to describe any type of post or behaviour that a user deems to be obsessive, overly analytical, or lacking in broader social awareness."[9] On the other hand, users habitually describe 4chan's whole userbase as autistic, presumably including themselves: hacking and doxing missions are described as "weaponized autism." Reddit does technically allow slurs at site level, leaving moderation up to individual communities, but the usual norms of speech are much more standard. The vast majority of 4chan postings are made under "the site's default identity, 'Anonymous,'" and because 4chan has no long-term storage capacity, old messages are deleted when the database is full. According to Knuttila, this format makes the 4chan experience one of contingency, ephemerality, and disavowal of responsibility. She is correct in the sense that posted items are not tied to particular identities. However, I found the discursive construction of emo on 4chan to be much more enduring than the presence of the individual users, its borders surprisingly firm. Indeed, despite Reddit's reputation for civility, valorization of knowledge, and rational discussion, the construction of emo across these two sites was similar. Both were earnestly and urgently concerned with its definitions and positioned themselves as gatekeepers in opposition to incorrect ideas of what emo means, implicitly and explicitly constructing themselves as the corrective to other sites. The forums' functions as gatekeepers were metatextually discussed at many points:

> Honestly though listen to whatever you want and think its whatever genre you want. Nobody really gives a shit, this sub just loves to gate-keep the genre.[10]

———

> I try not to be a gatekeeper for the genre, and I fucking LOVE this album with a passion, but as far as I know this is, was, and always will be pop-punk.[11]

———

**Anonymous:** Don't tell me you are a gatekeeper

**Anonymous:**
>people still defend crap music
>people still defend garbage style pizza
You're god damn right I keep that gate.

**Anonymous:** Just stop. There's objectively nothing wrong with gate-keeping. When other forms of media have stopped gatekeeping it all becomes bland trash.

**Anonymous:** Legitimate question: when did people start spewing this "gatekeeping" bullshit? It's got to be one of the dumbest arguments ever. I started seeing this shit on /tg/ and the fact that people actually believe that shit is fucking terrifying as a hobbyist.[12]

Despite their reputations, then, the discourse constructions on Reddit and 4chan were similar in many ways—4chan was far more brash, rude, and politically incorrect, but the shared preoccupation with defining "real" emo as an objective phenomenon, that exists outside of and in opposition to what 4chan would call "plebeian" misunderstandings, was notable and persistent. Moreover, both sites were invested in the masculine-coded display of knowledge, taste, and debating skills, while retaining a tendency to self-mockery and understanding that their practices may be seen as pretentious. As an image board supporting a variety of media brought together in close range, the codes of 4chan encourage an atmosphere that at first appears anarchic but is actually quite tightly regulated: the use of shorthand, memes, and reaction GIFs as responses requires a high degree of in-group understanding.

In this chapter, I will demonstrate that these sites seek to shape and police a definition of emo grounded in the masculinist histories of "real music" observed in the introduction, bolstered by a masculinist model of good fanship as authoritative, highly knowledgeable, rational, and utilizing a classist conception of "good taste." This model of the Good Fan, as opposed to the irrational, feminized, hysterical and uncritical Bad Other, is well established by now.[13] Gatekeeping, however, proved to be a fraught enterprise on these sites. I suggest that the increasingly osmotic and connected internet is making it progressively harder for communities such as 4chan and Reddit to define their fannish objects in isolation, and users are uneasily aware of this. Users move back and forth among sites via hyperlinks, lists of recommendations, and embedded objects. Tumblr is arguably the primary site for fandom online today, while YouTube dominates the video uploads that all sites refer to. Occasionally, Reddit and 4chan mentioned Tumblr explicitly, either disparagingly or neutrally, but the anxiety around osmosis from Tumblr and LiveJournal was evident throughout the whole discourse. In attempting to gatekeep the genre, Reddit and 4chan seek to protect masculine space and masculine fan identities against the feminizing influence of other fan sites. But the process is riddled with cracks, self-consciousness, anxieties, and even self-mockery. There was also a counterdiscourse in evidence on 4chan, which posited emo as hopelessly feminized, the bands and the fans worthy of mockery.

To gather material for this chapter, I searched Reddit subs by search terms "emo," "Fall Out Boy," "Panic! at the Disco," "Panic at the Disco," and "My Chemical Romance." I found a subreddit for each band, one for emo as a genre, and a joke/meme subreddit called r/emojerk.[14] I saved the top ten threads on each subreddit and coded them; then searched "r/emo" and "r/emojerk" for the bands' names and the band subreddits for the term "emo" and coded those results. 4chan does not have a searchable database, so I used the customized search engine 4chansearch.org to search "emo" and the band names across all boards. Each search turned up 200 threads (the maximum stored by the site). The majority were from the board /mu/ (music), with substantial minorities from /v/ (video games) and /fa/ (fashion), a few from pornography boards, and a few from miscellaneous boards such as /r9k/, which is for telling personal anecdotes. I searched within results for key terms if whole threads were not relevant and coded either the relevant section or the whole thread if applicable.

The items generally fell into five categories, very similar to the other sites. The first, as we have noted, is concerned with the definition of emo as a genre that objectively exists regardless of what people say or believe about it, either represented or misrepresented by the Emo Trinity bands. Both sites acknowledge that MCR, FOB, and Panic! are called the "Emo Holy Trinity," but contra the principles of discourse analysis, usually maintain a belief in some essential, prelinguistic genre definition with objective boundaries. This set of items could be both serious or ironic—I did consider whether "serious" and "ironic" should be discussed as separate sets, but there is less a clear division between them than a spectrum of stances, and some items fulfill multiple roles, so I have kept them together. Second, there is set of items concerned with fandom and the meaning of being a fan; third, there is a set concerned with gender. This set is more concerned with guarding and gatekeeping masculinity and masculine fan identity than with femininity and queerness, but because the latter themes do appear and are involved through the masculine/feminine definitional binary, "gender" remains the appropriate title for the set. Finally, there is a set of items framing emo as a subculture, style, and identity rather than a music genre, a theme that has not come to such prominence before.

Subreddits are free to customize how their membership numbers and online users are displayed in side panels. Because anyone familiar with Reddit can tell what the numbers represent by their position on the webpage, some moderators choose words that would be incomprehensible in another context. This is an example of in-group shorthand, demonstrating on-site knowledge and experience valued within subreddits, and acting as a barrier to entrance for outsiders. The subreddit r/emo's panel reads: "39.5k [total members] arguing what emo is and is not" and "119 [online now] listening to REAL REAL EMO."[15] Thus it is established from the outset, with a humorous note, that the definition of emo is more contentious than other genres and fans are invested in the idea of a "REAL REAL EMO," a genre that authentically and objectively exists, regardless of people's opinions. In keeping with Reddit's valuation of encyclopedic knowledge, the subreddit has a wiki page charting emo's development from the 1980s to the present day. It concurs with Greenwald that "Emocore began in the mid-80's as an emotionally charged and politically progressive form of hardcore punk, centred in Washington, DC, as a response to the machismo of the larger hardcore scene."[16] Taking a journalistic tone, it documents a variety of subgenres and their development over time, including Midwest Emo, and emo pop, in which it includes the Trinity bands. This "brief history" is expanded in a series of long posts by moderator Sarcastasaurus. They argue that "Fall Out Boy are the most notable beneficiary of the emo pop explosion" and credit them with bringing emo to the relative mainstream, as "2005's major label debut From Under the Cork Tree virtually blew any concept of an underground emo scene to smithereens."[17]

These posts, which serve as a semi-official reference work for the sub, rate Fall Out Boy highly, praising their "polished and soulful vocals, and blackly comic lyricism," before moving on to acknowledge My Chemical Romance and Panic! at the Disco in briefer nods of inclusion. Even as the author praises the band, there is an undercurrent of equivocation in the claims that their singles "wreaked havoc on mainstream perception of emo" and, having acknowledged a range of "pop-punk and alternative rock bands that were influenced by or somehow affiliated with Fall Out Boy rose to prominence and success," observes that "the market was over-saturating, and as always happened, was leading to a crash."[18] To "wreak havoc" on a "perception" suggests something illegitimate about FOB's ascension, implying that they and the other Trinity bands somehow misled public perception of what "real real emo" is. This trend continues on both sites, with frequent questions like:

> Now, I understand that the mid 2000's gave birth to a massive misconception about what emo is, but I'm still stuck wondering where MCR fits into all of this.

> I can totally hear emo influences in the other "emo" bands like Fall Out Boy and Panic! At The Disco (early on both accounts), but for some reason MCR eludes me . . . Do you, denizens of /r/emo, consider My Chemical Romance to be emo, and if not, what caused them to be the essential public image for what many people see the scene to be?[19]

User toke81 responds:

> No I don't and I just wrote three paragraphs on the reasons and then I pressed back on my phone.

> Basically the lack of real emo music in the mid 2000s mixed with the emergence of the highly visible mallcore bands led to it. They had emotional lyrics, right, but that's as far as the similarities went. But when you have all these bands preening with their eyeliner singing about cutting wrists and stuff, it's easy to see how the general public could conflate the two genres, especially when "real emo" wasn't even a factor in the industry at that time.[20]

This item consolidates the attribution of illegitimacy to the Trinity bands, which are constantly linked together on both Reddit and 4chan. The Trinity is acknowledged as a finished discursive concept now, one that originated elsewhere, possibly on other, less knowledgeable fan sites. The coinage "mallcore" has connotations of commercialism, implying that MCR is aimed at shallower consumers (teens, or more likely, girls who "hang out" at large modern shopping centers). "Preening" is a pointed verb choice, with its connotations of femininity and artificiality. Exactly why eyeliner is a problem is unclear, except for its associations with femininity and performance. User 2relad claims that the early to mid-2000s saw a "bastardization of the term of 'emo.'"[21] Similarly, user Rentington contends that "A lot of people don't realize what 'emo' is . . . [They think] Emo is Panic at the Disco and . . . that hot-topic commercial post-goth thing from 2005ish."[22] Yet imposing quotation marks around "emo" or "real emo," as these commenters tend to do, creates a tension in this attempt to divide emo into genuine and artificial. Quotation marks signify the speech of another person, real or hypothetical, positioning their content at one remove from the subject position of the comment. The writer, it is implied, is not quite willing to use the designation and make the judgment—it is something other people say. Compare the humorous repetition of "real real emo" in the sidebar, which frames the category as problematic from the outset.

Relatedly, all three bands are described across the sites as having been better at some earlier stage, either before their major record deals or before a personnel change:

> Anonymous: Ryan Ross + Jon Walker era Panic was GOAT [greatest of all time].

> When they left and it was just Brendon and Spencer it was meh. Now they're shit.[23]

> ———

> Anonymous: My girlfriend still likes [MCR]. I discovered them at KROQ Weenie Roast back in 2012, but once they turned Hot Topic I ditched that shit faster than these guys can slit their wrists.[24]

Hot Topic is a chain retailer of music, film, and TV merchandise and clothes, which regularly stocks MCR, FOB, and Panic! T-shirts and posters. Commercialism is linked to one particularly pathologized act of self-harm. The implication seems to be of weakness: that a person of what 4chan calls "plebeian" taste is a follower, lacking authenticity and fortitude, thus resorting to a self-harm behavior that, regardless of the facts, is commonly associated with melodrama and thus femininity. The verb choice in the phrase "turned Hot Topic" claims that the band changed in order to appear on Hot Topic merchandise, rather than simply becoming more well known, thus preserving the "patrician" taste of the writer who formerly liked them. "Patrician" is 4chan's opposing modifier to "plebeian": a noteworthy choice, given that it shares a lexical field with "patriarch" and "patriarchy." Again, we observe the lexical slide Coates established between high art, nobility, rarity, sophistication, and the masculine versus commerciality, commonness, plebeian, and the feminine. "Good" taste in music is "patrician" on 4chan—a position of cultured authority.

On the other hand, one can also find assertions that the Trinity bands (or at least some of their work) are both the definition of the genre and significant to self-identification as an emo fan. "If early fall out boy isn't emo, I'm not either," writes Reddit user twavisdegwet.[25] "Around 2001 is when emo gets big," writes a 4chan user: "Bands like fall out boy, panic at the disco, my chemical romance."[26] In response to the question of whether MCR is emo, user kage6613 replies, "Wdym? [What do you mean?] They're part of the holy emo trinity. Their debut album, The Black Parade, is an emo classic up there with The Used self-titled, which is arguably the genesis of what we call screamo today (2018)."[27] However, this item is complicated by its obviously incorrect statement (The Black Parade is MCR's third album) and by its author function. Discourse analysis is not concerned with the meaning or intention behind text, nor the biography and opinions of the writer, but with its impact, meaning, and function in its published context. However, part of that impact and meaning is determined by the reputation and image of its writer, which is popularly used as a lens for interpretation. Kage6613 is known across the Reddit communities as "the legend behind the REAL REAL EMO copypasta."[28] "Copypasta," derived from "copy and paste," is slang for a block of text that is frequently copied and pasted in different places in one or more online communities. The "REAL REAL EMO" copypasta appears several times across the subreddits:

> "Real Emo" only consists of the dc Emotional Hardcore scene and the late 90's Screamo scene. What is known by "Midwest Emo" is nothing but Alternative Rock with questionable real emo influence. When people try to argue that bands like My Chemical Romance are not real emo, while saying that Sunny Day Real Estate is, I can't help not to cringe because they are just as fake emo as My Chemical Romance (plus the pretentiousness). Real emo sounds ENERGETIC, POWERFUL and somewhat HATEFUL. Fake emo is weak, self pity and a failed attempt to direct energy and emotion into music. Some examples of REAL EMO are Pg 99, Rites of Spring, Cap n Jazz (the only real emo band from the midwest scene) and Loma Prieta. Some examples of FAKE EMO are American Football, My Chemical Romance and Mineral

EMO BELONGS TO HARDCORE NOT TO INDIE, POP PUNK, ALT
ROCK OR ANY OTHER MAINSTREAM GENRE.

This was indeed originally authored by user Kage6613, who uses the flair
"resident elitist elitist." A Reddit flair is a short phrase attached to a person's
username wherever it displays, thus serving as a sort of signature or personal
identifier. The copypasta is so accurate in its parody of gatekeeping that it
sometimes gets taken at face value: "Why are you so pretentious?" asks
a commenter whose username was deleted in response.[29] Yet in the very
same thread as they are praised for creating the copypasta, Kage6613 adopts
another parodic stance toward definition, claiming, "All sad music is emo in
spirit uwu!! All emo means is emotional, and all music is emotional!!!!1"[30] The
lexeme "uwu," associated with Tumblr, depicts a face smiling sleepily and/
or smugly, and the excess of exclamation points ending in a "1" implies that
an overexcited typist used the wrong key function. Both are associated with
Tumblr, excess, and fangirls, with the image of the feminized Bad Fan that is
scorned across these sites. This tendency to parody elitism and gatekeeping
on one hand and poorly informed emotional excess on the other means that
it is difficult to take any statement from this user at face value, and to some
extent this is true across the sites. "The only difference between r/emo and r/
emojerk is one layer of meta," observes user Giga_Alex.[31] User Wulcan_WTF
responds, "Wrong. They are literally identical subs."[32] Sometimes one will find
earnest attempts to modify the discourse of gatekeeping: "I've always had
a middle-of-the-road mindset about what is and isn't 'real emo,'" says user
EET FUK. "Like, why can't it all be considered emo? Where MCR, FOB . . .
etc could be labeled 'Mainstream Emo' or 'Emo pop' . . . And A[merican ]
F[ootball], M[odern] B[aseball], Front Bottoms, Tigers Jaw etc could be
considered what they already are, which is 'Midwest Emo' or even 'Classical
Emo'. And we can all cry at 3 O'clock in the morning together and live in
harmony."[33] This last line self-effacingly admits a kind of feminized stigma
to all emo, in keeping with Greenwald's claims that the term has always been
slightly derisive. Continuing the trend of self-reflection, user in_san1ty asks,

Are we an elists [sic]?
This question appeared in my mind since I've been called an elite for
saying that bands like these are not emo. For example, if we correct
someone that Panic! At The Disco isn't emo and we showed him/her
the emo bands like pageninetynine, Rites of Spring, Embrace, Thurs-

day. Does that count we are being an elists or just fighting for the true emo genre?[34]

Hotdogtacos187 responds with the assertion that "it's not being elitist to defend the genre from bands that gave emo a dirty name and warped people's perception of it."[35] The metaphor of contagion, first encountered in the LiveJournal anxiety over emo bands appearing on or near pop texts, spreads to implicate the Trinity bands as "dirty" (perhaps as a result of that same contagion-by-pop, just further along in the process). Both Reddit and 4chan display a fairly equal split between items that would dismiss the Trinity bands entirely and items professing to enjoy—even love—them, but question or qualify their status in emo. A 4chan discussion from the music board asks users to post their guilty pleasures, the original poster starting the thread off with FOB's album *Take This To Your Grave*. The first response tells the poster not to feel guilty for this, praising the quality of the album. The second reads simply, "Hey OP," with an attached image file called Consider_the_rope.jpg, showing an image of a man staring contemplatively at a noose.[36]

The theme of uneasy gatekeeping extends into the set of items constructing fandom. As the reader may have predicted, the majority of these items were concerned with being the right sort of fan, where right is a gendered category. Parodic constructions of Bad Fans fell into three overlapping categories: the excessive, hypersexual Tumblr girl; the oversensitive, feminized male fan; and the immature, melodramatic MySpace teen. Elements of the Tumblr and MySpace figures are evident in user Duodecim's caps-locked post titled "BEST eMO ALBUMS OF ALL TIME," who's opening blurb reads: "THIS ARE THE BEST ALBUMS OF EMO OF ALL FUCKING TIME BECAUSE I SAY SO AND FUCK YOU IF YOU DISAGREE YOU ARE DUM AND DON'T UNDERSTAND ANYTHING BECAUSE NO ONE UNDERSTANDS ME."[37] List entries take the form of slightly incorrect album titles: "10. PANIC! AT THE DISCO-A FEVER YOU CAN'T SWEAT," and justifications like "OKAY SO I LIKE THIS RECORD CUZ THE LYRICS ARE FUN, IT'S SO IRONIC, LIKE ME, I'M SO SAD EVERYTHING'S IRONIC TO ME AND OH MY GOSH THE SINGER IS SO CUTE AND HIS MAKE UP SOOOOOOO EMO" or simply "PETE WENTZ IS SOOOOOOOOOOOOO HOT." The "writer" includes unnecessary asides like "(they [the band Hawthorne Heights, listed at 5] are ugly as fuck so they are not higher)" and admits to having never heard the album placed at number one, but "A FRIEND OF MINE WHO WORKS IN

PITCHFORK (aka best music site ever) TOLD ME YOU ALWAYS HAVE TO SAY THAT THIS IS THE BEST." The post is very well received, as are most of this type. The humor depends on constructing female sexuality as absurd, excessive, and a detriment to the kind of rational, informed debate Reddit prioritizes. Sexual attraction is looked down on—anyone admitting attraction to a band member is immediately accused of being a fake or shallow fan. "I remember hearing 'Three Cheers for Sweet Revenge' when it came out in 2004, I was a just a kid," writes user GroundbreakingWest7 in the My Chemical Romance subreddit: "The original fanbase were rockers, and at least the older emo subculture. The new fanbase seems to be these teen girls who care more about Gerard Way's looks . . . Kid you not, some of these fans I've met didn't even know 'I Brought You My Bullets, You Brought Me Your Love' was a thing!"[38] Note how seamlessly the accusation of valuing "looks" slides into the claim that such fans lack empirical knowledge of the band. Building up these declarative sentences side by side creates the impression that one follows logically from another—when of course, there is no reason that finding an artist attractive should lessen one's knowledge of their catalog.

The feminized male fan represents the second kind of Bad Fandom. We have already observed that self-harm is consistently linked to a failure of masculinity—compare user Wulcan_WTF's question: "who were even the original fans of the emo genre? I'm willing to bet like $5 that it's not guyliner slit wrist scenefolks . . ."[39] This is the second time that self-injury is derided as a marker of weakness. Fan failures of masculinity are mocked in the meme known as "emo guy," which appeared on both sites: a flannel-wearing guitarist who cries his way through multiple activities and enjoys taking pictures of screenshots of pictures for his Tumblr (see figure 11).

Unsurprisingly, 4chan is particularly scathing regarding feminized forms of fandom. On this site, the greater-than symbol > is commonly used to depict actions or instructions. In response to a male user seeking advice on an androgynous emo aesthetic, a reply suggests:

**Anonymous:** >>O[riginal] P[oster]
>grow hair out
>straighten it
>push fringe across
>buy black skinny jeans and band T-Shirt

50's hair

not too much beard

flanel shirt

khaki shorts

anchor tat from the pop-punk phase

sup im emo guy. i love american football, brand new, moose blood and american football. i also like some new pop-punk bands like modern baseball and major league but just cause their sport-like names reminds me of american football. i used to listen pop-punk but i grew out of it, it's all too happy. emo is a gang. my hobbies are writing songs while crying, watching american beauty while crying, stage diving while crying, basically everything that involves crying. that's why i'm emo. i cry cause i have no girl to listen american football with, and even if i do find one i'd cry with her while listening to american football. but there will never be a girl with my patrician and exclusive music taste. why does my house have a flat roof. why i dont' have a polaroid. did you just call me faggot? go listen to your kid rock metallica confederate flag dad butt rock you fucking privileged alpha patriotic straight edge piece of shit. american football. hey guys i just found this picture of an empty street during the   sunset on tumblr. i'll make a screenshot, take a picture of the screenshot, take a picture of the photo of the screenshot with a polaroid and then take a picture of the polaroid picture of the photo of the screenshot. it will be a perfect cover for our album. shut up i'm not a hipster, i'm emo. theres a difference. i hate fighting with the plebeian conception of emo. brb going to cry, my balance and composure limited edition vinyls got only 16 reblogs on tumblr, a whole paycheck down the drain. american football.

FIGURE 11: The "emo guy" meme.

> take up light self harm
> delve deeper into self harm
> realize that you've ruined your body
> kill yourself.[40]

Likewise, tastes attributed to young girls are derided. When a commenter defends his love of MCR against a detractor by stating, "they're fantastic bands, pussy,"[41] a third commenter replies: "Not for nothing, you could listen to whatever you want but calling people pussies while listening to something a 14 year old girl listens to is just weak bait."[42] This is consolidated with another commenter's mocking impression of the politically correct culture 4chan hates: "Calling my favorite band shit means you're spreading your toxic masculinity on me. PUSSY!"[43] But at once, a fellow 4chan user impersonates the impersonator:

> g-guys look at how much testosterone I have! I am a fat virgin on 4chan . . . but I don't listen to MCR!
> *flex*[44]

It is notable how often this charge of "fatness" comes up as an accusation in being the wrong type of fan. I have not seen this in other fandoms. "The truth is all the fans of MCR, fall out boy, and shit like that were fat teen girls who wrote bad fan fiction," writes a 4chan user.[45] Being a teenage girl and writing fan fiction are commonly pathologized categories, but why is fatness grouped with them? One reason might be a shared perception that the emo aesthetic looks better on thin bodies (see chapter 5). One 4chan user admits that he "was a bit of an emo kid growing up but I could never really get into the fashion aspect of it because I was fking [sic] fat and looked like shit in it."[46] Usually, fatness is perceived as a feminine quality—a counter to the hard-and-defined ideal Dyer recognized as a marker of hegemonic white masculinity. But emo kids don't like hegemonic masculinity—so why is "fatness" added to the usual derisive epithets of teenage, girl, hysterical, and so on? My theory is that fatness is perceived as obscuring the desired aesthetic of androgyny, further illustrating how critiques of traditional masculinity can still pathologize the feminine simultaneously.[47]

On 4chan, the very state of being female opens one to the charge of inauthenticity. "What do girls listen to?," asks a user in the music forum. Panic! and FOB are both suggested, followed by "Whatever fits the image they want to achieve" and "it's not about the music, when I was in college I heard girls talking about the attractiveness of certain band members which is what dictated what they listened to."[48] Fear of being the "wrong kind" of fan is also evident on the subreddits devoted to particular bands: users take each other to task for focusing too much on the bands' appearances and reflect with proclaimed embarrassment on their own "excessive" phases of fandom. Norabedamned admits in the Panic! subreddit, "I was in the 'fandom' for the release of DOAB.[49] I was REALLY cringey, like, I was the epitome of gross 12 year old. In late 2016 I grew out of that phase of my life."[50] It seems that even in a subreddit devoted to fandom of a particular band, the rational norms of Reddit frame excessive investment as undesirable: as "cringey." MySpace are Tumblr is associated with irrational and excessive forms of fandom: the MCR subreddit even lists "No Tumblr blogs" as its second rule—no explanation is given, and apparently none is necessary. When a user asks around for MCR fans on 4chan, someone replies, "Quiet you might attract the tumblrinas."[51] "The self cringe is real though," reflects a 4chan user: "I don't want to remember my edgy teen days."[52] User A_Good_Kitty's post crystallizes some of these anxieties, asking the community "how far is too far?" in terms of dress and behavior at concerts:

Asking for an autograph or a pic . . . is pretty common, duh, but how about holding signs? . . . Basically, do you think there is a limit of how far you go to show your love at a Panic! concert, should it be normal clothes and normal responses, or is dressing like the emo king himself and talking about those goddam doors being a bit too far? Tldr [too long didn't read, online acronym meaning "abbreviated version follows"]: How far can a fan go (Dressing like Brendon in Mona Lisa, etc) before it's too far? Or, is it even possible to go too far, as long as it's all in the name of fun?[53]

Although some responders admitted to long-distance travel for a show, the comments on concert etiquette were surprisingly conservative:

Maybe I'm petty, but I can't stand signs/flags. I feel like they ignore/ruin the view of literally everyone around them.[54]

———

I completely agree and am SO thankful so many venues ban them. Can you imagine paying $50+ for a seat and you get blocked by a huge sign?? So rude.[55]

———

The only flag I, personally, would bring to a show is a LGBT pride flag, but that is just for
Girls/Girls/Boys.[56]

———

I had a spastic 14 year old girl next to me at the Pittsburgh show with a pride flag and she was whipping it everywhere . . . during every song . . . and nailing me in the head and eyes with the metal grommets on it.[57]

Physical displays of enthusiasm were framed as problematic, in line with the elevation of thought and reason common on Reddit. Using that maligned figure of the excessive teenage fangirl, this last comments hooks into the mental/masculine bodily/feminine binary we noted in the introduction. Excessive, out of control ("spastic") physicality is the problem, associated here with femininity and queerness. Being the "right" kind of fan, then, seems to be a tenuous business on Reddit and 4chan. One must be highly knowledgeable, but not express that knowledge in a way suggesting pedantism. One must be emotionally involved but not too emotional: hysteria must be avoided at all costs.

The denigration of femininity we've seen thus far was predictably disappointing and demonstrates how very solid the discourse of male superiority in music is. But the discussion of masculinity and other kinds of gender and sexuality are more interesting and constitute some of the most sophisticated discussion of gender I found in any emo web space. As we have noted, 4chan's use of "fag" is multifaceted, functioning like an endlessly adaptable pronoun to refer to both self and others. Its work depends strongly on context. For instance, the porn board regularly featured "emo guys" for blatant homosexual appreciation, and the term "fag(s)" featured heavily as a reclaimed badge of identity. Even outside this niche, the boards were less homophobic than I thought they would be. A user posts in the fashion threads: "why are scene boys so cool n sexy, nohomo," with an accompanying picture. I agree with Joshua Brown that the phrase "no homo" shouldn't be assumed as automatically and exclusively homophobic but an indicator of the complexity of gender identity filtered through situational social norms.[58] Here it indicates sexual desire for an aesthetic—an androgynous one to be sure, and thus it diverges and critiques from hegemonic masculinity without necessarily constructing a sexual identity for the writer. "Scene" is sometimes used interchangeably with "emo," and sometimes denotes a related club culture that is more focused on style than music and uses more color and neon than emo. The boy in the attached picture is dressed in a stereotypically emo style, mostly black with straightened black hair with an angled fringe, plus heavy eyeliner. Rather than immediately castigating the poster for expressing a homosexual impulse, responders mock him for the object of his desire: "because you had an absent father and bad taste."[59] The "absent father" charge may imply that the OP is lacking in masculine role models, but his sexuality is not insulted. One does find predictably flat declaratives like "Emo is gay shit for fags"[60] and "fallout boy is for faggots,"[61] but again, while the words carry the echo of homophobia from their discursive history, in the context of 4chan these statements do little more than express dislike. More curious is the attachment of memes like "no homo" to posts that blatantly do express homosexual desire. "Would it be gay to get a blowjob from an emo male who looks like this?" one user asks of a feminine-looking emo boy pictured.[62] A brief stated denial obviously doesn't negate the entire discourse of homosexuality to which these items belong; thus their function reads primarily as humor, an obvious delusion on behalf of the writer, whether genuine or tongue-in-cheek.

Sex and sexual conquest is a dominant theme on 4chan:

Sooo many scene bitches hitting me up purely because I had emo kid hair. good times.[63]

———

Tfw [that feeling when] you'll never go back and bang one of those big titted emo girls who were so obviously up for it in hindsight but you were shy and never bothered to try.[64]

In the midst of one such discussion, a user confesses: "The 00s were weird man. I sucked a dudes dick at a sleepover once to impress the girls that were watching."[65] No one mocks or castigates the user for admitting this. 4chan's conception of emo, then, actually has quite a lot of room for male queerness—much more than it has for women.

Second, when Reddit and 4chan users reflect on their own "emo phases," this entails performance and parody of softer masculinities. We noted that some construct their past selves as bad or excessive fans, in contrast to a more dignified present. But not all the recollections were constructed as embarrassments. Male-presenting users on Reddit talked frequently about feeling, sentiment, and interpersonal relationships experienced while listening to emo. User bastardjames posts a photo with the title "We randomly got each other the same album . . . and of course, it was Best Buds."[66] The image is of two teenage boys holding copies of the album with their arms around each other, smiling at the camera. The top comment, with ninety-eight upvotes, reads: "This is so wholesome. Thank you for this. Enjoy the album, guys."[67] The adjective "wholesome" is an interesting choice, repeated twice more in the comments. Given its connotations of purity and innocence, it contributes to a dislike of physical sexuality in this subreddit, idealizing male platonic bonds instead. By contrast, user mlb3621 teases, "now u guys have to listen to it together and cradle each other as you cry about ex girlfriends."[68] The response is not censured, but it receives no reply and only 19 upvotes where the prior reply had 101. This indicates that the subject of male bonding is being taken relatively seriously, but with some discomfort navigating physicality.

The construction of gender on Reddit is generally measured and reflexive, aware of the histories of misogyny in popular music. For example, the emo subreddit rules state on the homepage that misogyny, homophobia, and transphobia are banned. This doesn't mean they don't occur, but it positions emo as a better and fairer subculture compared with classic punk and cock-rock. The moderators must be quite efficient at removing it, as I found no openly offensive comments nor use of slurs. Users are perceptively aware of what de Boise would call beta-male misogyny, though they don't use the term:

> I think certain emo bands like to create a sort of high school jock-vs-nerd fantasy so they can position themselves as the downtrodden Nice Guy™ in their music. Sports imagery brings to mind the teen movie trope of the hyper-masculine preppy dude that your crush likes instead of you.[69]

> It generally represents women as an "other." It's basis champions male emotion as if it's something unique or commendable simply because it's male. The gist of most songs is that women are incapable of being rational or kind and the men are always victims.

> The important thing is the supposed danger of misogynistic tendencies in emo. Like rock in general, emo is written mostly by men.

> I think there is at least an unintentional tendency in emo to have lyrics that portray women as being hurtful, with "us" (men) as victims . . . Your Favorite Weapon is a fun album to jam out to, but damn if it's not borderline misogynistic, if not that. So much angst and hostility against a woman/women.[70]

Users presenting themselves as female and/or feminists generally minimize this, claiming they would "rather music honestly reflect what the artist was feeling at the time, than see some sanitised piece where the artist has tried to pander to everyone and make them happy."[71] They tend to deny that the problem is specific to emo but is "a lack of women in music overall. We'd hear more balanced views if there were more balanced representation. Beside a preference for male vocals, would anybody here really not listen to a woman singing about being hurt by a man just because it's a woman?"[72] No one answers the hypothetical question. It appears that the commenter is implying "no" (i.e., that we the listeners in this community would indeed listen to songs from female perspectives), but given the denigration of femininity across the sites and the fact that male performers are given more respect and opportunities generally (see chapter 1), this is a questionable point. The gatekeeping tendency around taste enters here, with user 2relad

claiming that "The emo scenes I have been involved with have been explicitly and openly anti-sexist. The problem is that the public doesn't know
these scenes . . . There is lots of stuff to criticize about mall emo culture . . .
[implied, as opposed to "real" emo] and latent misogyny is surely among
it."[73] Thus the wrong kind of emo is positioned as blameworthy. Reddit user
GoodMoleManToYou complains:

> I kind of hate Saves The Day, the Get Up Kids and a few others (not
> really but sort of really) for unwittingly giving birth to friendzonecore.
> It's the bands that nursed at their teat that thought writing sad bastard
> breakup songs was somehow innovative. Mall emo took it and ran, as
> you and others have noted, leading many people to either think emo is
> all sexually frustrated boys and/or self-mutilating semi-goths. I'd expect
> better, though, from a dude ostensibly steeped in independent music.[74]

There is much to unpack in this item. First, it may well be a no-true-Scotsman
effect: gatekeeping operates by asserting that real emo is not sexist, therefore
whatever is sexist is not emo. Of course, this is a paradox: it simply shifts the
goalposts of the definition by excluding examples that counter its premise.
"Friendzonecore" seems to be a term for music that bemoans men being
seen as friends by women they are attracted to (adding the "-core" suffix to
unexpected words is a meme on this subreddit). The "friendzone" is typically
associated with "sexually frustrated boys," with an inherent misogynistic
suggestion that said men and boys are owed romantic/sexual relationships,
which women and girls are denying them. It tends to be associated with
the "nice guy" figure, unfairly denied his implicit right to sex, which he is
entitled to for not being outwardly abusive. This phrase "mall emo" was used
on both sites as a shorthand for a commercialized and debased form of the
genre, here attached to a devalued kind of masculinity, depicted as pathetic
and weak. Conversely, the metaphors associated with the band he considers
superior are absolutely feminine, based in birth and nursing. This metaphor
of art-as-birth has a loaded genealogy and was especially common in the
Romantic period, but is actually traceable to ancient Greece.[75] These images
typically rely on a separation of body and spirit, as art is the product of the
brain or mind, thus the art-as-child trope "imagines the male self-sufficiency,
and thus the perfection, of such activity."[76] But GoodMoleManToYou's imagery of "birth[ing]" and "suckl[ing]" is so explicitly physical that the ideal
of sole-male creativity is stretched almost to breaking in this item. Indeed,

metaphors of bodily extremity or injury as a threat to the masculine can be traced throughout the Reddit forums. "I must say that Something to Write Home About by The Get Up Kids changed my life," notes unicornurine: "It was my first taste of 'emo' music. You basically just kicked me in the dick by comparing them to Fall Out Boy."[77] The masculine/mind/positive versus feminine/body/negative binary is so strong in the discursive management of musical value that a perceived insult to the user's taste is taken as a painful physical assault on his masculinity.

Finally, there is a set of items constructing emo as an aesthetic and/or marker of identity. Given the queer semiotics and borderline flamboyancy associated with emo, I was initially surprised to find that the concept of emo as an identity was much more popular on 4chan than on Reddit. On reflection, though, I should not have been surprised: 4chan had already proved rather queerer than I expected, and the Reddit norms that privileged knowledge and rational debate as models of good fandom leave less room for queer performativity than does 4chan's jumble of visual items, even when 4chan is blatantly misogynist or homophobic. Whereas Reddit users recalled their past display of fandom as "cringey," a surprising number of 4chan users looked back fondly on a time when they displayed a queer emo aesthetic: "I remember going full emo in high school, black nail polish, eyeliner, checkered belts, endless supply of black band t-shirts . . . I don't miss how I dressed but I do miss how much fun I had with the music. Seeing MCR in concert back then was probably the best thing teenage me experienced."[78] The verb choice "going" identifies emo as a state one can enter, a way of being. By contrast, a new user asks on a Reddit forum whether it is reasonable that her friends "consider themselves emo and call me emo too."[79] The omitted verb form is "to be," as the rather cool responses make clear:

> You can't really *be* emo in a meaningful sense of the word, emo is a genre of music, not exclusively a sense fashion or appearance.[80]

———

> Lurk more.[81]

"Lurk more," or its variant "lurk moar," is a derogatory item that has been used since at least the early 2000s to imply that the original poster is too inexperienced to contribute, is writing in a way that is naive or inappropriate, and should study the community in silence for longer to properly observe its norms. The implication one can "be emo" is worthy of mild derision on Reddit, but 4chan users are much more invested in emo as an identity and aesthetic code. One user writes: "Emo was the last real subculture we had. Hipsters were basically a parody of subculture and now that they're gone, subcultures in the sense we used the word in the 20th century don't really exist anymore."[82] This provocative item is not developed or responded to, but the construction of emo as a distinct and recognizable scene of the mid-2000s is prevalent across the forums. Again, definition works retrospectively: we observed in chapter 2 that LiveJournal and MySpace users in the mid-2000s didn't necessarily identify themselves and their scene as emo, but those semiotics are clearly what 4chan users are describing. Some even repost their MySpace pictures from that time. The tone of discussion was surprisingly sentimental, with several observations on how emo music is relatable to struggling adolescents. FOB, MCR, and Panic are consistently brought up in these discussions, sometimes by indirect reference such as typing a line of lyrics in caps lock. There is frequent use of a meme known as "that feeling when" (TFW), which assumes the reader will empathize with the writer via similar experience:

**Anonymous:** >>OP
>tfw mum wouldn't let me get snakebits [*sic*]
>tfw hair could never get quite long enough because it was so damaged
>tfw will never be able to look at my school photos without cringing.[83]

This shorthand constructs emo as a cohesive, well-understood scene, whose signifiers are understood by all participants in the discussion. Indeed, one user suggests that "/fa/ [fashion board] is were former emo kids come during their quarter year crisis," positing that everyone in the forum was an emo kid in the 2000s, now in their mid-twenties. Conversely, Reddit users struggle with the conception of emo as a community or even an aesthetic code:

The "emo" community is just a bunch of teenagers who dress in a certain way to make themselves seem dark and edgy, and are a terrible representation of the emo genre.[84]

———

If you're referring to emo as in people who call themselves "emo," wear black for the sole purpose of being "emo" . . . then you'd be surprised that is pretty much nobody here.[85]

> What makes a band emo is having emo music. What makes a band
> """"emo"""" (aka the clueless stereotype) is purely based on the fans and
> how the band members look.[86]

The quotation marks are doing a lot of work here, visually cutting off the impostor versions of emo and attributing their declaration to some misguided outsider. Not everyone is convinced, though. Without using the technical terms, users saintoillie and BlueElectivire argue from the perspective of discourse analysis. saintoillie claims it doesn't matter "exactly what [MCR and Panic!] play" but that how bands are described by "the people that listen to them" comes to be their definition.[87] BlueElectivire adds that "it is the public that makes labels, not labels that make the public."[88] User -y-y-y goes as far to say that "what makes a band emo is more the fan base than the music."[89] Cleave Warsaw suggests that the fact "the fandoms overlap so much" is what groups MCR, FOB, and Panic! together as the "holy emo trinity."[90] Others disagree that culture and aesthetics can be separated so neatly from sound:

> [MCR] aren't *musically* emo, but you can't act like they (along with
> FOB and Panic) weren't ever a major part of modern emo culture.
> Their aesthetics and attitudes resonated with that scene even if the
> music sounded different.[91]

> Since people began to group scenes on appearance rather than musical
> content, [MCR] was ingested into what is considered modern emo.[92]

"Ingested" is a fascinating choice of verb, framing the retrospective process of definition I have been arguing as an almost monstrous process, indiscriminately absorbing whatever is in its path.

Gatekeeping attempts to impose order—but the proliferation of meaning gets out of control, threatening the orderly knowledge base and categorizations of its users. There is a strong parallel in the subreddit's written account of emo's development in the later 2000s. This guide, which is featured in the sidebar, breaks down into a series of short declaratives, with no punctuation as it approaches the present time, visually reflecting the rapid expansion in definitions:

IMPORTANT DEVELOPMENTS [in the mid-late 2000s]:
kids at the mall start calling themselves "emo"
bands start "selling out" left and right
clean singing!/SCREAMED CHORUS/breakdown
it becomes okay for "normal" kids to be into this type of music
all the kids start dressing scene
every popular "post-hardcore" band from here on out
bands that SUPERFICIALLY look and sound similar to emo pop bands,
but have zero connection to the original scene, start fucking flooding
the place
everyone starts superficially ripping off At the Drive-In, Thursday,
and Poison the Well
everyone starts ripping off everyone, becoming incestuous and bizarre
in a way that isolates the scene from its hardcore, DIY-oriented roots
ESSENTIAL RECORDS:
. . .
From Under the Cork Tree - Fall Out Boy
I Brought You My Bullets . . . - My Chemical Romance.[93]

The FOB and MCR albums are mentioned under "essential records," but without description—were they a cause of this sort of explosion in definition? A result? The verbs have negative connotations: "ripping off," "fucking flooding," yet both *Cork Tree* and *Bullets* are extremely well liked on the sub, and there's something almost carnivalesque about this entry, as though the concepts of authenticity and the work of gatekeeping are just becoming too absurd, failing to hold all these elements together, and there is a note of celebration in their demise. The final section in this long post is subheaded "Part VI: Tumblrcore and Where We Are Now," recognizing the inextricability of Tumblr to contemporary emo on this subreddit and elsewhere. Now "fucking everything has at least superficial influences from 90s emo," and the carnivalesque note becomes more prominent, as "fashion-conscious hardcore homoeroticism and expression of sexuality in hardcore attractive girls coming to shows." The commenters seem to take it in that spirit, too: "It was fucking hilarious reading through this. Thanks for the nostalgia and laughs."[94]

Ultimately, then, the enterprise of gatekeeping breaks down, pulled apart by the tensions of competing fan sites, popularity, and yes, commercialism. In this chapter, we observed how Reddit and 4chan demonstrate the anxieties and tensions involved in attempting to maintain a discourse that privileges masculinity, noncommercialism, and authenticity in some sort of "pure" state, while an increasingly osmotic and interconnected fandom websphere compromises the construct from every direction. Attempts to separate "good" and "bad" fandom are caught between the traditional disavowal of excess, hysteria, and fangirlishness and the acknowledgment of charges of pretentiousness and elitism. The influence of Tumblr as a shaping force in fandom is necessarily acknowledged, and as the new fans of emo exert their influence and opinion, the question of who defines a genre cannot be avoided. The bands that everyone acknowledges are called the Emo Trinity are sometimes framed as a misrepresentation of the genre, a bastardization or unwarranted invasion of commercialism into what should be a DIY scene. Yet if these bands are what are called emo now—if "kids at the mall are calling themselves emo"—the construct of an exclusive, pure, and noncommercial "real real emo" collapses under its own weight. "Don't take the 'emo' so literally," user alineinasong advises a fellow FOB fan struggling with the term. "It's been a long time since it has been used exclusively for the bands that are actually responsible for creating the genre."[95]

In the final chapter, I return to professional media to analyze how the discourse of "emo" has developed mutually with fandom's work of categorization and definition, and how in a process that seems unique to this genre, industry figures and publications have actually taken up and reauthorized fandom's usage of "emo" as a fairly settled definition in the late 2010s. From the MySpace days onward, emo kids have had an unusually close relationship with industry figures, as we observed in the shared space of LiveJournal and YouTube forums. With particular attention to the so-called moral panic that developed around emo in the mid-2000s, I ask: what has been the impact of the fandom's extremely active and ongoing work of defining the meanings of emo, and how has this played out in official publications? Finally, I look at some more recent developments fusing emo with hip-hop, rap, or similar, asking what this may mean in the future.

# 5

## FULL CiRCLE

### EMO IN THE MUSIC PRESS, EMO IN THE FUTURE

In November 2017, the major American music magazine *Alternative Press* ran a cover story titled "The Ultimate Guide to Emo: Past, Present and Future." Despite the title, the lead story is rather more past-focused than anything else, an attempt to "connect emo's various roots, branches, and virulent strains" into a coherent narrative account.[1] Likewise, when UK periodical *Kerrang!* ran a cover story on emo in 2012, it took the form of a retrospective, a discussion of "The War on Emo . . . Half a Decade On."[2] The cover featured the frontmen of MCR, FOB, and Panic!, which is important, because when those bands first came to media attention, it certainly wasn't a given that those magazines would refer to them as "emo." As I write this in late 2019, clicking on the "emo" tags at either magazine's website brings up a string of articles about these bands, in addition to some stories on the current emo-rap movement that has developed from the music distribution website SoundCloud. In this final chapter, I bring my argument full circle by assessing how the music press constructs the concept of emo in the present, with attention to the nostalgic lens through which it is constantly framed. Then I compare some early appearances of the Emo Trinity bands in magazines, observing the degree of hedging and evasion around the word "emo," before going on to discuss the documentation of fandom activity in the media. As the *Kerrang!* headline suggests, a significant event here is retrospectively named "war on emo," a bizarre if short-lived moral panic sparked by a surreally inaccurate *Daily Mail* story, warning parents against the "sinister cult" of emo that apparently encourages teenagers to self-harm and commit suicide. I compare some more recent articles on the Trinity bands, again with attention to fandom influence, before discussing press predictions on developments of emo in the future.

As I will demonstrate, the solidity and unity of the emo construct and its application to the Trinity bands increases greatly between the early 2000s and the late 2010s. Here we observe that the discursive work of fandom gets taken up and reauthorized by the music industry. In researching this chapter, I am indebted to the archival work of emo fans on LiveJournal, Tumblr, and Reddit. In addition to searching the websites of major music magazines by tag (primarily *Alternative Press*, *Kerrang!*, *NME*, and *Rolling Stone*) I have collected and studied features on the Trinity Bands in physical copies and scanned and uploaded versions posted by fans over the past twenty years. The collection for My Chemical Romance is particularly exhaustive, with hundreds of interviews and features archived at a specialized site (to which I do not link for the sake of respecting a fan space that may be judged as copyright infringement). This site provides a key example of Booth's narractivity, as a database through which we can charts the band's discursive construction in the trade press. Although the aim is comprehensiveness, it is also an example of De Kosnik's community archiving, as magazine texts traditionally treated as disposable are saved, revalued, and shared in a fan community. Scans of FOB and Panic! were not as comprehensively collected but are still readily available on Tumblr and LiveJournal.

Jesse Richman writes in *Alternative Press* that while "all of us have heard, embraced, quoted and lived by the music . . . nobody has really nailed down a die-hard definition of 'emo'. UNTIL NOW."[3] His article adheres pretty closely to the schema set out by Andy Greenwald in *Nothing Feels Good*, citing the US hardcore punk scene as emo's progenitor and proposing a "general consensus that the 'emo' begins with the formation in 1984 of Rites Of Spring." Richman disputes the notion that "being underground" is a necessary component of emo, framing it as a mainstream phenomenon by the early 2000s, "whether the purists like it or not." He cites MCR and FOB as examples of mainstream emo, arguing that while their sonic qualities may differ widely, "Each generation of emo takes something from the last. In 2005, it's the bright hooks, the gray poses and (especially) the jet black hair and eyeliner. Spread via the internet, the suburban 'mall-punk' look becomes as part-and-parcel to emo as its heartrending poses."[4]

This is telling: what Richman is constructing is less a genre, strictly speaking, than a subculture, community, and aesthetic, which accords with AP's frequent reporting of the event "Emo Nite" as a "celebration of a culture."[5] Emo Nite began as a monthly club party founded by three now-adult fans, Babs Szabo, T. J. Petracca, and Morgan Freed. The fact that these former scene kids have grown up to become gatekeepers is a key illustration of fandom's definitional work. Emo Nite has become successful enough that the major music magazines regularly report on its events, solidifying its definitions through their cultural capital. The parties are explicitly nostalgic and explicitly communal: "'Emo, to me, are these bands that you listen to through sad times and happy times and kind of [are] there for you no matter what,' founder Szabo says . . . A genre of music that was once mocked (if someone called you 'emo' in middle school, it was usually an insult) is now celebrated. It fostered a bonding experience for people who once felt isolated and angry at the world—and still does, if Emo Nite is any indication."[6] Szabo says that the organizers "encourage people to come on stage . . . We always let the venues know that we don't want a barricade so that there's no wall between an artist and the fans."[7] This is another reason we should oppose the more simplistic idea that fans reinterpret industry discourse: new media culture and skills and the relationships between fans and bands mean that more young fans are growing up to secure positions in or adjacent to the music industry.

According to Szabo, "Emo Nite started out as an event in Los Angeles where we invited people to come out to a bar and listen to our favorite emo and pop punk songs. In the past 2 and a half years, the event has expanded to about 25 cities. We also have a clothing line that started as a single t-shirt and has expanded to about 20 pieces, including shirts, sweaters, hats, pins and jackets."[8] The events now regularly attract present and former band members as performers or guests. In this context, MCR's bassist Mikey Way described the term "emo" as "aging nicely," quoted in a *Rolling Stone* retrospective called "How Emo Night Vindicated the Scene." There is thus a strong sense in the music press that emo is something that happened: a movement, a sensibility, a moment in time defined by fan culture, defined as much by its participants as by the music industry, which grown-up fans can now frame on their own terms. The Emo Nite founders thus stress emo's capacity for a "celebration of a culture . . . that many of us have probably moved on from, some of us probably still thoroughly enjoy, but both alike can come together and celebrate the hard work of amazing musicians that changed the world with their music."[9]

Only now, the late 2010s, is the press explicitly comfortable in naming emo. Richman asserts that "by 2005, emo was a commercial force," citing the popular The Bamboozle festival, which all three Emo Trinity bands have headlined, as evidence. Yet none of those bands were unproblematically called emo at the time. Nor were they calling themselves emo.

Articles tagged with "emo" on the magazines' websites are frequently nostalgic. When the music streaming site Spotify introduced a feature called Time Capsule in 2017, *Alternative Press* ran a feature on emo's dominance of its staff lists. Time Capsule extrapolates from the user's present tastes and current age to infer what the user was listening to as a teenager and presents corresponding playlists. Again, given that the emo kids of the 2000s were in their late twenties to early thirties in 2017, it is perhaps not too surprising that "AP Staff Share Their Spotify Time Capsule Playlists and There's a Lot of Emo."[10] The article praises the algorithm as "unbelievably accurate" and foregrounds old pictures of My Chemical Romance and Panic!'s first lineup in addition to some related bands on their record labels. The reader is invited to create their own Time Capsule from their Spotify account in pursuit of the ultimate #TBT (throw-back Thursday). My list was harder and less melodic than I thought it would be—I had forgotten how angry I was, in a culture that polices biracial girls' anger so intensely. It's correct, though—after all, in my experience, starving oneself to the point of forced hospitalization takes enormous reserves of silent rage: channeled rage, if you like, rage disciplined. I had also forgotten my investment in Welsh post-hardcore bands like Funeral for a Friend and Feeder, which I could see regularly and locally—I grew up in Cardiff, which I presume Spotify gleaned from my Facebook profile.

South Wales has a distinguished history of alternative music, and crucial as the internet has been to music since the early 2000s, this fact reminded me that we shouldn't lose sight of locality—there is definitely more work to be done on emo and identity as related to place, possibly starting in the cities that pioneered it.

AP's invocation of the #TBT hashtag connects to the broader usage of social media as cultural memory, as storage of personal histories with shared cultural significance. The articles made frequent reference to LiveJournal and MySpace, appealing to a mingled sense of fondness and cringe: "MySpace has long since gone and passed, and maybe that was for the better," writes Devon Hannan in a feature called "If You Remember These 10 Emo Memes, You Deserve a Senior Discount": "Before we became socially conscious, us emo kids were running amuck on Reddit and Omegle, starting YouTube channels and running MCR fanfic blogs. Since those deep web days, most of us tried to repress any vague memory of our former internet presence."[11] It is notable that emo is relegated to a time before being "socially conscious," as though there is something intrinsically problematic about it and/or it simply belongs to a different period, a less sophisticated time. Visual semiotics and descriptions of sound mesh together seamlessly in descriptions of the past:

> As huge bands made their emotionally-honest music more pop-oriented and radio-friendly, plenty of newcomers adopted the genre for its catchiest tunes alone. Skinny jeans, lip rings, and baring your soul became par for the course.[12]

> ———

> While the heart and soul of Emo Nite is in the music, it's about so much more. It seeks to embody a culture that we still hold so dear to our hearts, and that includes the style. So squeeze into that pair of skinny jeans that are a little bit tighter than you remember, clip those Hot Topic extensions in your hair and paint your eyes as black as your tortured teenage soul, because this time it's not a death wish, it's a fashion statement.[13]

The last two phrases are an inversion of an MCR song from their second album, titled "It's Not a Fashion Statement It's a Fucking Death Wish."[14] The reference is an in-group signifier—this article, this event, is for a specific type of person, those of us who remember a painfully intense sincere connection with that album and that scene and are now old enough to smile wryly at the intensity of our teenage feeling, even as we appreciate their importance. Occasionally there's some acknowledgment that "When this style of music was first coming out, 'emo' was saddled with a handful of negative connotations,"[15] but not usually—the past few years' output on emo in the major magazines generally creates the impression that Panic!, FOB, and MCR have always and unambiguously been called emo. But this isn't so. When the Trinity bands first appeared in the press in the early 2000s, they were framed quite differently. MCR's first appearance in *Alternative Press* was in April 2003, a half-page feature under the subheader "Low Profile" and credited to writer "Lycia Shrum." It introduced them as a "post-everything quintet" from New Jersey playing "melodic hardcore injected with a healthy dose of punk-driven energy," and devoted most of its column space to describing Thursday frontman Geoff Rickly's role in producing their album, probably their biggest selling point at that moment.[16] *Rolling Stone*'s first feature called MCR's music a "weirdly catchy hybrid of goth, glam, metal and punk."[17] Indeed, "punk" is probably the most used genre term for MCR and FOB in their early appearances, with MCR's first major cover (*Kerrang!* in February 2005) billing them as "punk's new superstars."[18] FOB's cover (*Alternative Press* in August 2004) was captioned "Save pop punk? I'd rather shoot it in the head," though of course, the article went on to situate them as a pop punk band, albeit a highly disruptive one.[19]

When "emo" appears in early MCR and FOB features, it is used half-jokingly or mockingly, such as in a "hot new band" report in a 2004 issue of *NME* (*New Musical Express*). Describing an MCR set in a small club in Manchester—which it referred to as "Sadchester" for some stretched comparisons to Morrissey—the reviewer described MCR's budding fanbase as "fiercely serious backpacked and bespectacled emo souls." The write-up is grudgingly complimentary, acknowledging the show's energy and Gerard Way's charisma (though the author can't resist the gendered snub "pretty-boy singer"), and notes the "adoration of the emo geeks" in the crowd.[20] The adjective was consistently applied to the fans before the bands, largely because of how they dressed and behaved at shows. Journalists would hedge the term in their descriptions: *Rolling Stone* described MCR's sound as "scary-sad punk that lives up to emo's unspoken promise: that sometimes the most miserable songs are also the easiest ones to sing along to."[21] "Punk" is the only term applied to MCR's sound as a noun; emo is suggested by association. By the time Panic! started getting magazine covers, the term "emo" was starting to gain more currency: magazines would hedge the term by calling them post-emo or a "new breed of emo."[22] Given that Panic! were always acknowledged as FOB's protegés, thanks to the story of their discovery via LiveJournal,[23] the term "emo" starts attaching to Fall Out Boy more regularly in the late 2000s. *SPIN* magazine gave them a cover feature in 2007 with the subheading "emo heroes grow up in public";[24] *Rolling Stone* ran a story the same year that negotiated carefully with the term. Though the headline billed them (dubiously) as "rock's hottest band," the story introduces "de facto frontman" Pete Wentz as a "MySpace hero to a legion of eyeliner-hoarding emo kids."[25] Notice again how the term is attributed to the fans first. Similarly, *SPIN* writer Brian Rafferty describes the FOB fanbase as having evolved from "a legion of barely legal emo kids" to a "grown up kiss army."[26] Both articles are important to the gendered construction of emo in official terms, although *Rolling Stone* carries greater cultural capital and may thus be considered more influential. The themes of fandom, credibility, and Wentz's status as an alternative sex symbol intersect, highlighting how female enthusiasm for rock bands is always framed as something slightly problematic, slightly compromising to credibility. The *Rolling Stone* opening paragraph is a neat condensation of these frames:

> Pete Wentz plays bass in Fall Out Boy, but his real instrument of choice is a Sidekick smart phone—a device he employs to write lyrics, manage a business empire, argue with girls, check fan sites and take the occasional glamour shot of his dick. He never stops his virtuoso thumb-typing, even when he's rehearsing for a Letterman appearance: As the rest of the band—singer Patrick Stump, lead guitarist Joe Trohman and drummer Andy Hurley—fools around with a tricky riff from Steely Dan's "Reeling in the Years" on the Ed Sullivan Theater's fabled stage, Wentz ignores the black-and-red bass guitar hanging at his tiny waist and texts away instead.[27]

Both articles manage to slide in a mocking reference to the leaked-nudes incident (see chapter 2): Rafferty imagines an interlocutor asking "haven't I seen his wiener on the internet?" as a measure of FOB's increasing visibility to the general public.[28] Wentz's appearance is described in explicitly gendered terms. Developing the waist size comment, *Rolling Stone* writer Brian Hiatt observes that Wentz is thin enough "to fit comfortably in the girls' jeans that he's helped popularize for guys—a style choice . . . so popular that the emo masses are all but starving themselves to squeeze in."[29] The attribution of dieting/restricting behaviors to boys reinforces the construct of emo as androgynous-leaning-feminine. Hiatt uses the term "pretty" to compare Patrick Stump's voice and Pete Wentz's "bone structure," which was much quoted with amusement in the LiveJournal communities.

Both articles depict the band members as geeky and unlike rock stars: though Hiatt's writing includes an interview at 3:30 a.m., he is clear that the cause is Wentz's lifelong insomnia rather than partying, depicting him as articulate and sensitive as they discuss anxieties and childhood bullying from much tougher boys. Despite the writers' tendency to frame the photo leak with crude humor, Rafferty also quotes Patrick Stump as stating that he felt "miserable for [Wentz] . . . because it was so invasive and so crude and so unreasonable."[30] The majority of discussion concerning leaks in the press have concerned female celebrities, who typically express dismay and anger in terms similar to Stump's initial statement. But because the broader cultural discourse constructing male bodies is different—specifically, that they be sources of either pride or indifference—he defaults to humor again, citing the incident as motivation that "if [we] write a good enough album, no-one's going to remember Pete's dick."[31] The construction of male bodies is thus in extreme tension throughout the articles. In *Rolling Stone*, Stump rejects derisive comparisons of FOB to a boy band by exclaiming, "Boy band? I'm fat! If we were a boy band, I'd look good, I'd dance and I'd be charming—so what the fuck are you talking about? I write songs, that's all I do."[32] On one hand, privileging the mental over the physical (composition rather than dancing) aligns with the discourse of male creativity; on the other hand, the claimed incompatibility of being "fat" with looking good introduces an insecurity that men rarely expressed in 2007 in the rock press.

Both articles stress the band's interaction with fans, with the *SPIN* journalist claiming that FOB "seem at times less like a band and more like a user-friendly wiki . . . the quintessential 21st century band." He claims that "fans don't just purchase their records and attend their shows, they become proxy board members, helping to steer the group's decisions and spread the word."[33] This may be an exaggeration, but it does bear witness to the influence of those "eyeliner-hoarding emo kids" on MySpace and LiveJournal. Both articles identify the fan websphere as a shaping force. *SPIN* describes Wentz's blogs (plural) as intensely revealing, to the point they may "seem cloying rather than charming" to "those who didn't grow up on emo."[34] Once again, emo is framed a culture rather than exclusively a genre.

We can see that the influence of fandom in shaping emo has always been acknowledged to some extent. However, its importance becomes clearest in response to a 2006 article by *Daily Mail* journalist Sarah Sands, titled "EMO Cult Warning for Parents" (caps in original, inexplicably). Sands describes a "dangerous teenage cult" distinguished by a "celebration of self harm," claiming that "emos exchange competitive messages on their teenage websites about the scars on their wrists and how best to display them."[35] She attributes emo's embrace of androgyny to her claim that "teenage girls are frightened of manliness: they like boys who look like girls," oddly omitting any motivation of the boys who initiated the style. In addition to the lazy stereotyping, Sands made a few claims that are just factually wrong and leave one confused as to where she gathered her information, such as that emos ride Vespa scooters. Although most of the piece makes no reference to music, Sands did name My Chemical Romance as an example of an emo band, and in 2008, the *Daily Mail* explicitly linked the suicide of a thirteen-year-old girl to the fact that "two weeks before her death, she had started following U.S. band My Chemical Romance." The article detailed her suicide in grossly exploitative style, claiming that she took her life "after becoming an Emo, whose followers wear dark clothes, practice self-harm and listen to 'suicide cult' rock band."[36]

Phillipov claims that emo was an unusual moral panic, reflecting an anxiety around youth generally more than the creation of a distinct threat, due to the absence of either a "clear group of participants" ready to self-identify as emo or cultural spokespeople willing to defend and define them.[37] This is incorrect: these statements provoked an intense reaction from fandom, and the music press in turn framed the controversy as a "war on emo," a phrase used by both *NME* and *Kerrang!* for covers.[38] As Thornton noted, tabloid outrage has a legitimating and a framing effect on youth subcultures: offending the sensationalist right-wing tabloids is a mark of authenticity and mitigates charges of "selling out."[39] It also disseminates and recirculates labels: *NME* and *Kerrang!* both covered the "emo protest" organized by MCR fans on May 31, 2008, outside the *Daily Mail* offices in London. *Kerrang!* featured the photographs and comments of a range of teenagers on how MCR and fandom have been positive influences, many going as far as to state that they "saved their life." Fans writing in on the subject extended their objections to the treatment of emo kids more generally: "This is just another example of the false stereotypes emo fans confront everyday. Even the metallers at Download Festival this year were terrorising emo kids, ruining the atmosphere."[40]

Some of these letters grouped MCR, FOB, and Panic! together as examples of emo, though the term "Emo Trinity" has never to my knowledge made it into the magazines. The *Observer Music Monthly* ran a feature on emo kids as a misunderstood subculture. The article opens with a description of the time MCR was bottled at Reading Festival, adding that "for the outnumbered fans of the emo group, it seemed as if the everyday ridicule and disdain which they feel they experience was being made real."[41] The report similarly focuses on the voices of teenagers and how MCR fandom has helped them, but it also interviews Paul Brannigan, then the editor of *Kerrang!* "Emo fans are the whipping boys of the moment," he stated perceptively: "there's a misogynistic air to it. A lot of the credible metal bands have got an older, very metal following and they see teenage girls getting into bands like MCR and think they've not earned the right to be called a rock fan."[42] Older rock and metal fans would dismiss emo as insufficiently credible, insufficiently subcultural, but as Hill writes, this was largely a form of sophistry attempting to maintain the "boys' club" masculinity of those genres:

> Because anything which is associated with women or with femininity, for instance via its large female fanbase, is positioned as mainstream, emo, with its large female following and its rejection of many of the masculinist tropes of rock, presents a significant danger to the ideology of metal as different and authentic, the risk being that metal will become "mainstream" . . . However, this fear of the mainstream is a subterfuge driven by the desire to maintain metal's masculine exclusivity whilst retaining the myth of equality.[43]

The discursive sleight-of-hand makes sexism harder to identify, and Brannigan's position as editor of *Kerrang!* makes his public recognition of it significant. More problematically, he claims that MCR's fanbase is "far too smart and stylish to be self-harming," as though intelligence and fashion sense were somehow protective factors. Indeed, these defense-of-emo stories depend on seeing the fans' experience as overwhelmingly affirmative and celebratory. There is little room for expressing pain or anxiety. The teenage girls profiled are framed as well adjusted, academic, social, and successful: "so much for the stereotype." The piece ends as the girls emerge from Brixton Academy in

London "flushed and jubilant" from having just seeing MCR live: "'It made me feel proud to be an MCR fan,' Stacey says, neatly summing up what is so exciting about being a young rock fan. 'To know that there are so many other people out there who like them and go to the gigs makes you feel like you're part of something bigger.'"[44] It is striking that in the last sentences, the descriptor reverts to "rock." Of course, "rock" is an all-encompassing term, of which emo is technically a subgenre, but notably this work of validation invokes the more traditionally credible term to close.

The "war" coverage serves as a tipping point: from hereon, the term "emo" is routinely used to describe MCR, FOB, and Panic! *NME* in 2010 cited the three bands as the center of "the great emo boom of 2006."[45] The term still suffers a slight credibility problem, with positive reviews of particular albums seeking to portray them as somehow better than or transcendent of other emo bands: *NME*'s Dan Martin called MCR's *The Black Parade* "crisp, vast and fiercely melodic stadium punk that's barely emo in this slightest."[46] Martin stresses the album's humor, praising its "understand[ing] that real tragedy is inherently a bit funny, and vice versa," connecting this to the odd claim, "it's that fact which sees them leave the jibbering bodies of a thousand emo jessies in their wake." "Jessie" is British slang for an effeminate or weak man, a less sexual synonym of "pussy." It is ironic that one of the magazines reporting on the mistreatment of emo kids is now resorting to gendered insults. But fandom's claim of the term has outlasted this: in 2017, *Alternative Press* ran a retrospective "My Chemical Romance Saved My Life" story, recalling those war on emo statements from the mid-2000s, except that this is written from the perspective of a now-adult Luke Dean, himself a professional musician, reflecting on the band's impact on his early adolescence. He begins: "If you were an 'emo kid' in the 2000s, there's a solid chance that you saw someone post on Myspace or write on a T-shirt the sentence 'My Chemical Romance saved my life.' Maybe that sounds like hyperbole to you, and maybe it was, in some cases. For me, that sentence feels like a pretty accurate description of what happened in my life as an early adolescent."[47] Dean reflects that when he was experiencing suicidal tendencies, he was comforted and encouraged by the MCR documentary in which Gerard Way discussed depression and his own past suicidal feelings:

I didn't want to admit to everyone that I didn't want to exist anymore; that I didn't see a point in carrying on; that I didn't want to live in a world that rejected me because of the situations that life had thrown at me. In that documentary, Gerard said something that has stuck with me to this day, at 21 years old: "It's okay to be messed up, because there's five dudes that are just as messed up as you, and we've overcome that to do what we do." That's what I wanted to do: I wanted to overcome. I felt so fucked up inside and hated myself so much that hearing that from one of my heroes helped change my perspective.[48]

Dean describes how he would dress in clothes associated with emo, down to "sharpied black nails and ripped up black jeans" because it felt "representative of who [he] was" and let him "feel as close to comfortable in [his] skin as [he] could get while being bullied, assaulted and called a 'f*ggot' on the grounds of [his] Christian school." Searching the "emo" tag at *Alternative Press* and *Kerrang!*'s sites now, we see that overwhelmingly stories like these have survived, as misogyny and homophobia become less and less openly tolerated. Statements like Martin's seem increasingly to belong to a bygone era, when machismo was less questionable and the voices of girls and unmasculine boys more discountable.

Contemporary pieces on MCR, Panic!, and FOB always acknowledge that they are categorized as emo, even "represent" it, whether or not that label should strictly apply to their sound. Yet searching the "emo" tag also turns up another set of articles, more various and forward-looking than the retrospectives. Most of these are tagged "emo-rap" or "emo revival" and focus on the SoundCloud-based movement, which has seen young hip-hop artists remix samples from older emo bands with stripped-down percussion, heavy bass, and electronic sounds. Its themes include subjects previously foreign to mainstream hip-hop, such as mental illness, male vulnerability, and insecurity. Although the fusion might at first seem unlikely, emo has some precedent for connection with hip-hop: FOB in particular have sampled rappers, blues, and soul sounds in their albums since at least *Infinity On High* (2007). *Kerrang!*'s Marianne Eloise asserted that "In 2017, emo and rap are well and truly intertwined" and went on to discuss the popularity of Gustav Åhr, known professionally as Lil Peep, who in 2017 was frequently described as "the future of emo."[49] Although Åhr died at the end of that year, aged just twenty-one, his output has remained influential on a range of associated musicians sometimes referred to as "SoundCloud rappers," because of their early distribution on that platform. The "emo" in emo rap refers specifically to Trinity bands and similar acts that were popular in the early 2000s. Eloise writes: "Today's emerging generation of young rappers were teenagers when emo and pop-punk were hitting the mainstream. That, combined with the redundancy of older-fashioned and more easily definable genres, means that once-unlikely influences can seep, naturally, into their work."[50]

Rapper Lil West likewise comments that "this generation is full of kids that grew up on this type [of] shit and are finding new ways to not just rap and sing over trap beats, but are smart enough to blend what they grew up on with trendy trap shit in today's rap."[51] Since Åhr's death, his friend and collaborator ILoveMakonnen arranged to feature Fall Out Boy on a new version of a song they had made together, noting that FOB were some of Åhr's "musical heroes."[52] *Alternative Press* and *Kerrang!* regularly feature emo rappers discussing MCR, FOB, and Panic! as influences, with pop-up videos urging readers to "Watch rapper Post Malone playing Welcome to the Black Parade at Emo Nite."[53] Naturally, this new phase of the genre has instigated a fresh wave of gatekeeping: "Tbh half the people that go to emo nite look like they bullied emo kids in high school," comments user Good S U C C on the video.[54] "Or like they're using the 'emo' trend to gain popularity," agrees Destiny Lawson.[55]

Before I began this project, and started looking at gatekeeping objectively, I felt similarly hostile toward the whole concept of "emo rap," a feeling ultimately grounded in my unacknowledged class and generational prejudices. I resented the appropriation of what I considered "real" musicianship into a genre and set of norms I didn't particularly value, especially those of electronica. This is because I have internalized discourse that defines authenticity as poetic lyricism combined with technical accomplishment on instruments I consider "real." I think of myself as a good writer and a mediocre guitarist, and I am filled with admiration at displays of technical prowess and speed (despite my teacher's insistence that "faster does not equal better!"). As Rosemary Hill writes, all her interviewees shared this conception despite the fact there is no real a priori reason for these value judgments. Why should we consider it more meritorious to play a physical drum kit well than to program a synthesizer?[56] The answer is probably class-based, as traditional musical capabilities are a middle-class mark of distinction. I also found the fashion for face tattoos and multicolored accessories vaguely ridiculous, and the praise of wealth and braggadocio tropes inherited from the hip-hop side of the fusion to be distasteful. I still have the instinctive response upon hearing emo rap that it isn't "true emo"—but, of course, as this whole project has established, "true emo" is a red herring. Emo is the ultimate illustration of a genre molded by new media fandom, but the music press has started to address this artificiality of genre boundaries generally, often in humorous pieces, acknowledging the rise of Spotify and other streaming services as changing habits of reception. An *Alternative Press* quiz challenging the reader to "guess which lyrics belong to your beloved emos and which lyrics are home to hip-hop bops" opens with the assertion that "it's 2018, folks. If you can't handle our Spotify playlist jumping from Kendrick Lamar to Hawthorne Heights, you can't sit with us."[57] In the late 2010s, genre and subculture boundaries are far less distinct than they were the early 2000s, when teenagers purchased physical CDs with cover art as discrete units.

Similarly, *Alternative Press* reported on a study by journalist Matt Daniels that "ranks songs by how emo the lyrics are," inspired by his observation that contemporary rapper Juice Wrld reminded him of a "hip-hop Dashboard Confessional."[58] By calculating the "percent of each song's words associated with sadness or fear," Daniels established a somewhat tongue-in-cheek chart measuring "emo rap and other hip hop" against "emo bands and other rock" on a scale of least to most emo.[59] Unsurprisingly, My Chemical Romance ranked highest, but Juice Wrld ranked above Fall Out Boy and Panic!, with Kanye West somewhere between the latter two. The definition of emo is what the fans and industry call emo, and now that includes Lil Peep, Post Malone, and their contemporaries. Thirty-somethings like me will just have to deal with it.

What does this latest incarnation of emo mean in terms of gender construction? On one hand, mainstream hip-hop and rap has a similar legacy of toxic masculinity to the hardcore punk the first emo bands were rebelling against. Resistance to authority via hardness, violence, and machismo were shared themes, with the discrepancy that hip-hop tended to valorize the capitalist wealth accumulation punk critiqued. Emo rap has changed this, indisputably. As Lindsay Zoladz writes, "it does feel genuinely progressive for so many male artists to be expressing and embracing sadness—it is, of course, often difficult for men to express emotion without being labeled 'soft.'"[60] Yet in illustration of that persistence of masculinism that accommodates change and variation in masculinities, this is only half the story. In much the same way as 2000s emo, emo rap remains largely a boys' club. There are female artists, but they are massively outnumbered, underexposed, and underpromoted compared with their male peers. The depiction of women in emo rap is at least as problematic as it was in the early 2000s, and some find it worse. Zoladz goes on: "The steely armor of Auto-Tune, the company of their mostly male cliques, and the welcoming codes of a shared aesthetic have all recently made a certain kind of 'sad boy' attitude not only acceptable, but au courant. And yet, while these artists are revising and often expanding stereotypes about masculinity, their attitudes about women are old-fashioned, objectifying, and often plain antagonistic."[61]

Writing for Stereogum, Tom Breihan notes that rather than "treating women as objects," emo rappers are "treating them as actively hostile forces. Every broken heart, every wounded feeling, is the fault of some conniving, disloyal, unfaithful, manipulative woman. It's a whole new generation of male rappers embracing their own victimhood."[62] Breihan acknowledges Jessica Hopper's 2003 essay "Emo: Where the Girls Aren't" as establishing emo's problematic heritage, but then he seems to imply—somewhat unfairly—that emo rap is worse because it "exists within a musical tradition where ferocious misogyny has long been the rule, rather than the exception" (as though punk and hardcore didn't?). The word "bitch," with all its loaded genealogy, is a regular feature in emo rap, not necessarily as an insult but a general term for the female population. This simply didn't happen in 2000s emo, whether or not one can objectively claim that emo rap is more or less misogynistic. Early Panic! and FOB in particular had no shortage of misogynistic lyrics, but as Sam de Boise recognized, classism and educational privilege means that sharp poetic turns and clever similes and metaphors are much less vulnerable to accusations of misogyny than the flat repetition of "bitches," "THOTs," and "hos" common to emo rap.[63] Whether they are actually less misogynistic is another question. Similarly, "faggot" still appears in emo rap, including from queer-identifying artists like Tyler, the Creator, who also released an album titled *Flower Boy*, who frequently expresses his attraction to the young Leonardo DiCaprio and collaborates with openly gay singer-songwriter Frank Ocean. Discourse analysts believe that words can change in meaning, and thus Tyler's claim that "faggot" is just an insult and doesn't mean gay anymore is not impossible.[64] But we must also recognize the loaded interdiscursive histories words bring with them: the marks of all the millions of times they've been used before, in this case, in a context of violence. "Faggot" can't just shed its whole genealogy in a couple of years because a user specifies how they "mean" it. Words do things on their own, regardless of speaker intentions. So although we cannot claim that emo rap is antihomophobic, it is definitely increasing the range of expressions and identities, including gender identities, available to boys in hip-hop culture. And perhaps beyond—*Alternative Press* reported that "emo rap" was the fastest growing genre on Spotify in 2018, and genre boundaries are far less rigid now because of a combination of technological and social changes.

In the introduction to this book, I proposed that we needed to start looking beyond a "resistant reading" model of fandom, or considering texts as provided by the media industry and transformed by subcultures of reception. Emo has long been associated with digital media, and online communities were considered a site that shaped it. But as this book has demonstrated, that is not quite accurate. No one agrees on the definitional boundaries of emo, but that doesn't negate the point—indeed, as Hills recognized, the idea of a bounded text is rapidly becoming insupportable. What matters is that before the development of online fan cultures from MySpace to LiveJournal to Tumblr, the term "emo" didn't have anything like the coherent set of referent points it does today, and this process was enacted by fandom. Messy, sprawling, self-contradictory, and fiercely antagonistic, we have nevertheless established a process of narrativity that pins together a set of ideas regarding sound, music, musicianship, authenticity, and their relation to gender—not to mention their relation to fandom—which is solid and coherent enough to support its own shorthand and a wealth of memes and finally be reuptaken and authorized the music press. The effect then becomes circular—once authorized by magazines, websites, and the bands, the definition of the genre takes on the impression of having always existed. A great deal of construction thus occurs retrospectively, in fan culture and later in industry material. Moreover, the increasingly close relationship between fan cultures and the music press, which necessarily maintains a strong online presence, now makes recirculation and consolidation of material easy.

This process poses a challenge to how fan studies has traditionally viewed the relationship between fandom, texts, and the media industries. Some academics have discussed this in regard to texts that are almost entirely fandom-created, such as the texts-inside-texts we mentioned in the introduction.[65] But if Hills is correct, we are increasingly going to have to adapt our ways of thinking to account for UGC and fandom's contribution to the meaning and definition of all sorts of texts, with music genres being just one example. Emo is an easy choice to illustrate this process because of its particular unusual history in online spaces and uneasy relationship with traditional gatekeepers, but as new processes of musical consumption continue to challenge the concept of genres as objective categories, it will become increasingly important to consider how fandom constructs and defines a whole range of music in the future. This is not to say that fandoms have abandoned the process of boundary demarcation: on the contrary, gatekeeping has remained a theme throughout this project. But as the process of gatekeeping is played out, fans display self-aware and critical recognition of gatekeeping as a contingent process, relating it to the gendered history of music that informs the construction of genres.

Indeed, while online fandoms have traditionally been celebrated as progressive arenas of contemporary gender, we have discovered that in confrontation with emo's checkered history of gender construction, the process is not so simple. Denigration of feminine properties and properties associated with "Bad Fandom" remained consistent across the early sites from MySpace to LiveJournal. Moreover, any good-faith attempt to discuss "online fandom" needs to account for the spaces less comfortable and palatable to our preconceptions: Reddit forums, for example, where despite a high degree of skepticism and reflection on the processes of gatekeeping, I still found many earnest attempts to preserve emo as some sort of "pure" masculine space (where masculine is taken as the fully human subject). Tumblr provided some of my most interesting findings, in keeping with Booth's "philosophy of playfulness": the pastiche format's challenge to authority and authenticity claims, the use of crack humor as a challenge to self-important and overly serious rock, and the revaluation of cute/soft aesthetics all pose a real challenge to the masculinist hegemony of punk rock histories. Moreover, we saw that via a process of osmosis, these constructions are spreading to YouTube, a huge site with a wide and varied audience. Even the official music press is beginning to pick up Tumblrisms, with its embrace of memes. But for all this revaluation of feminine properties, the influence and experience of real women and girls continues to be elided and effaced. The construction of emo has challenged and widened the ways it is possible to be man and for qualities expressed by men to be valued. As Zoladz wrote, tracing these influences into emo rap, this is probably a good thing. In the most generous interpretation, we could suggest that gender is increasingly becoming irrelevant—that these processes are breaking it down, a sort of post–third wave revolution, the end of which is that all of us should feel free to feel the range of our emotions, forgoing masculinity and femininity in the discovery of being human. Yet, as the final chapter in returning to the industry makes evident, the construction of emo is still seen as a male artform. Men dominate the bands. The stories concern male feelings. If fandom—a web of narractivity and intradiscursivity that we have observed defines the shape and structure of the genre—is, if not female dominated, then at least populated by a high proportion of women and girls, why is it that the voices of girls' experiences, with music, in fandom, are still uncomfortably so quiet?

# NOTES

## INTRODUCTION

1. Magdelena Red, "Who Are the 'Emos' Anyway? Youth Violence in Mexico City and the Myth of the Revolution," *Journal of Popular Music Studies* 26, no. 1 (March 2014): 101–20, 102.

2. Andy Greenwald, *Nothing Feels Good: Punk Rock, Teenagers, and Emo* (New York: St. Martin's Press, 2012), 8–55.

3. Ibid., 2.

4. Mavis Bayton, "How Women Become Musicians," in *On Record: Rock, Pop and the Written Word*, ed. Simon Frith and Andrew Goodwin (London: Routledge, 2006), 201–19; Susan McClary, *Feminine Endings: Music, Gender, and Sexuality* (Minneapolis: University of Minnesota Press, 1991); Pirkko Moisala and Beverly Diamond, eds., *Music and Gender* (Champaign: University of Illinois Press, 2000); Ian Biddle and Kirsten Gibson, eds., *Masculinity and Western Musical Practice* (Farnham, Surrey: Ashgate, 2009).

5. Sarah Williams, "'A Walking Open Wound': Emo Rock and the 'Crisis' of Masculinity in America," in *Oh Boy!: Masculinities and Popular Music*, ed. Freja Jarmen-Ivens (London: Routledge, 2007), 145–60; Brian M. Peters, "Emo Gay Boys and Subculture: Postpunk Queer Youth and (Re) thinking Images of Masculinity," *Journal of LGBT Youth* 7, no. 2 (2010): 129–46; Matthew Carrillo-Vincent, "Wallflower Masculinities and the Peripheral Politics of Emo," *Social Text* 31, no. 3 (2013): 35–55; Emily Ryalls, "Emo Angst, Masochism, and Masculinity in Crisis," *Text and*

*Performance Quarterly* 33, no. 2 (2013): 83–97; Sam de Boise, "Cheer Up Emo Kid: Rethinking the 'Crisis of Masculinity' in Emo," *Popular Music* 33, no. 2 (2014): 225–42; Sam de Boise, *Men, Masculinity, Music and Emotions* (London: Palgrave Macmillan, 2015).

6. Red, "Who Are the 'Emos' Anyway?"; Achim Rohde, "Gays, Cross-Dressers and Emos: Non-Normative Masculinity in Militarized Iraq," *Journal of Middle Eastern Women's Studies* 12, no. 3 (2016): 433–49.

7. Greenwald, *Nothing Feels Good*, 1–2.

8. Fabian Holt, *Genre in Popular Music* (Chicago: University of Chicago Press, 2007), 4, 14.

9. Ernesto Laclau and Chantal Mouffe, *Hegemony and Socialist Strategy: Towards a Radical Democratic Politics* (London: Verso, 1985).

10. Oliver Marchart, "Bridging the Micro-Macro Gap: Is There Such a Thing as a Post-Subcultural Politics?," in *The Post-Subcultures Reader*, ed. David Muggleton and Rupert Weinzierl (Oxford: Berg, 2004), 83–97.

11. Angela McRobbie, "Settling Accounts with Subculture: A Feminist Critique," *Screen Education* 34 (1980): 37–49.

12. Judith Fathallah, *Fanfiction and the Author: How Fanfic Changes Popular Cultural Texts* (Amsterdam: Amsterdam University Press, 2017).

13. Holt, *Genre in Popular Music*, 21.

14. Ibid., 29.

15. Greenwald, *Nothing Feels Good*, 56.

16. Paul Booth, *Playing Fans: Negotiating Fandom and Media in the Digital Age* (Iowa City: University of Iowa Press, 2015).

17. Paul Booth, *Digital Fandom 2.0* (New York: Peter Lang, 2017), 221–49; Louisa Stein, *Millennial Fandom: Television Audiences in the Transmedia Age* (Iowa City: University of Iowa Press, 2015), 154–59.

18. Stein, *Millennial Fandom 2.0*, 10.

19. Ibid.

20. Booth, *Digital Fandom*, 8.

21. Stein, *Millennial Fandom*, 15.

22. Booth, *Playing Fans*, 1, 4.

23. Henry Jenkins, *Textual Poachers: Television Fans and Participatory Culture* (London: Routledge, 1992); Camille Bacon-Smith, *Enterprising Women: Television Fandom and the Creation of Popular Myth* (Philadelphia: University of Pennsylvania Press, 1992); Dick Hebdidge, *Subculture: The Meaning of Style* (London: Routledge, 1979); John Fiske, *Understanding*

*Popular Culture* (London: Routledge, 1989).

24. Booth, *Playing Fans*, 19.

25. Linda Hutcheon, *A Theory of Parody* (Urbana: University of Illinois Press, 2002).

26. Fathallah, *Fanfiction and the Author*.

27. Hutcheon, *A Theory of Parody*, 26.

28. Matt Hills, "Review of *Fans: The Mirror of Consumption*, by Cornel Sandvoss, and *Media Audiences and Identity: Self-Construction and the Fan Experience*, by Steve Bailey," *Popular Communication* 5, no. 2 (2007): 149–54, 53.

29. Booth, *Playing Fans*; Paul Booth, *Crossing Fandoms: SuperWhoLock and the Contemporary Fan Audience* (London: Palgrave Macmillan, 2016); Booth, *Digital Fandom 2.0*; Rebecca Williams, *Post-Object Fandom: Television, Identity and Self-Narrative* (New York: Bloomsbury, 2015); Stein, *Millennial Fandom*.

30. Matt Hills, "Foreword," in Paul Booth, *Digital Fandom 2.0* (New York: Peter Lang, 2017), i–xxiii, xii.

31. Booth, *Digital Fandom 2.0*.

32. Ibid., 11.

33. Ibid., 2.

34. *Rolling Stone*, "My Chemical Romance's Gerard Way Taps Another Nail into 'Emo' Coffin," September 20, 2007, https://www.rollingstone.com/music/music-news/my-chemical-romances-gerard-way-taps-another-nail-into-emo-coffin-101867/.

35. Robert J. C. Young, *Postcolonialism: An Historical Introduction* (Oxford: Blackwell, 2001), 402. See also Michel Foucault, *The Archaeology of Knowledge*, trans. A. M. Sheridan Smith (London: Routledge, 1989), 28.

36. Booth, *Digital Fandom 2.0*, 85. See also Paul Booth, "Narractivity and the Narrative Database," *Narrative Inquiry* 19, no. 2 (2009): 372–92.

37. Booth, *Digital Fandom 2.0*, 11.

38. Abigail De Kosnik, *Rogue Archives: Digital Cultural Memory and Media Fandom* (Cambridge, MA: MIT Press, 2006).

39. Ibid., 273.

40. Ibid.

41. Ibid., 66.

42. Booth, *Crossing Fandoms*, 5.

43. Ibid., 13.

44. Williams, *Post-Object Fandoms*.

45. Gerard Way, "A Vigil, On Birds and Glass," Twitter, March 25, 2013; archived at Twitlonger, http://www.twitlonger.com/show/n_1rjdh4f.

46. Williams, *Post-Object Fandoms*, 15.

47. Ibid., 29.

48. Greenwald, *Nothing Feels Good*, 279.

49. Angela McRobbie and Jenny Garber, "Girls and Subcultures," in *Feminism and Youth Culture*, 2nd ed., ed. Angela McRobbie (Basingstoke: Macmillan, 2000), 12–25.

50. Jean Burgess and Jonathan Green, *YouTube: Online Video and Participatory Culture* (Cambridge: Polity, 2009), 26.

51. Ibid., 47.

52. Barbara Ehrenreich, Elizabeth Hess, and Gloria Jacobs, "Beatlemania: Girls Just Want to Have Fun," in *The Adoring Audience: Fan Culture and Popular Media*, ed. Lisa A. Lewis (London: Routledge, 1992), 84–105.

## CHAPTER 1

1. Chris Azzopardi, "Panic! Frontman on Being a Little Gay, Bisexual Anthem & Getting Naked," PrideSource, November 6, 2013, https://pridesource.com/article/63018-2/.

2. Ryalls, "Emo Angst"; De Boise, "Cheer Up Emo Kid."

3. Norman Fairclough, *Discourse and Social Change* (London: Polity, 1993).

4. McClary, *Feminine Endings*, 9.

5. Ibid., 8.

6. Lucy Nicholas and Christine Agius, *The Persistence of Global Masculinism: Discourse, Gender and Neo-Colonial Re-Articulations of Violence* (Cham, Switzerland: Palgrave Macmillan, 2018).

7. Simon Frith and Angela McRobbie, "Rock and Sexuality," in *On Record: Rock, Pop and the Written Word*, ed. Simon Frith and Andrew Goodwin (London: Routledge, 2006), 317–32, 317.

8. Ibid., 318.

9. Ibid., 320.

10. Norma Coates, "(R)Evolution Now? Rock and the Political Potential of Gender," in *Sexing the Groove*, ed. Sheila Whitely (New York: Routledge,

1997), 50–64, 52.

11. Rosemary Hill, "Is Emo Metal? Gendered Boundaries and New Horizons in the Metal Community," *Journal for Cultural Research* 15, no. 3 (2011): 297–313, 297.

12. Lawrence Grossberg, "Is There Rock after Punk?," *Critical Studies in Mass Communication* 3 (1986): 50–74, 61.

13. Bayton, "How Women Become Musicians."

14. Ibid., 201–5.

15. Ibid., 205.

16. Siri C. Brockmeier, "'Not Just Boys' Fun?': The Gendered Experience of American Hardcore," MA thesis, Universitet I Oslo, 2009, 66.

17. Ibid. There is no intrinsic reason that bass is an easier instrument than a standard guitar, but it is fair to say that in Western popular music, basslines are usually simpler than the melody and rhythm parts.

18. Helen Reddington, "Lady Punks in Bands: A Subculturette?," in *Cultural Study of Music: A Critical Introduction*, ed. Martin Clayton, Thomas Herbert, and Richard Middleton (New York: Routledge, 2003), 239–51, 239.

19. Ibid.

20. Brockmeier, "'Not Just Boys' Fun?,'" 11, 19, 49.

21. Carrillo-Vincent, "Wallflower Masculinities"; Rosemary Overell, "Emo Online: Networks of Sociality/Networks of Exclusion," *Perfect Beat* 11, no. 2 (2010), https://journals.equinoxpub.com/index.php/PB/article/view/7483.

22. Brockmeier, "'Not Just Boys' Fun?,'" 33–35, 39.

23. Ben Welch, *Fall Out Boy: Our Lawyer Made Us Change the Name of This Book so We Wouldn't Get Sued. The Biography* (London: Music Print Press, 2016), 14–18.

24. myxinfinitexromance, "Gerard and Frank POP Interview," YouTube, 2011, https://www.youtube.com/watch?v=hNUs43Yxme.

25. Maria Raha, *Cinderella's Big Score: Women of the Punk and Indie Underground* (Emeryville, CA: Seal Press, 2005).

26. Brockmeier, "'Not Just Boys' Fun?,'" 37.

27. Ibid., 65.

28. Aaron Robert Furguson, "Surfing for Punks: The Internet and the Punk Subculture in New Jersey," PhD diss., Rutgers State University of New Jersey, 2008, 77.

29. Paul Hodkinson, "'Net.Goth': Internet Communication and (Sub) Cultural Boundaries," in *The Post-Subcultures Reader*, ed. David Muggleton and Rupert Weinzierl (Oxford: Berg, 2004), 285–98, 286.

30. Overell, "Emo Online," 142.

31. Brittany Spanos, "Mark Hoppus, Chris Carrabba on How Emo Night Vindicated the Scene," *Rolling Stone*, November 23, 2015, http://www .rollingstone.com/music/features/mark-hoppus-chris-carrabba-on-how -emo-night-vindicated-the-scene-20151123.

32. Ibid.

33. Ibid.

34. See Fathallah, *Fanfiction and the Author*.

35. *Rolling Stone*, "My Chemical Romance's."

36. Gerard Way, "I actually knocked and Pete's door and said 'Do you wanna take a legends of emo selfie,'" Twitter, April 14, 2015, https:// twitter.com/gerardway/status/588026811000426497.

37. Tom Bryant, *The True Lives of My Chemical Romance: The Definitive Biography* (Basingstoke: Sidgwick and Jackson, 2014), 60.

38. Fueled by Ramen, "Cobra Starship: Send My Love to the Dancefloor . . . [OFFICIAL VIDEO]," YouTube, May 18, 2007, https://www.youtube .com/watch?v=84saYemcJQY.

39. Greenwald, *Nothing Feels Good*, 2.

40. Ibid., 3.

41. Ibid., 14.

42. Matthew J. Aslaksen, "Middle Class Music in Suburban Nowhere Land: Emo and the Performance of Masculinity," MA thesis, Bowling Green State University, 2006, 8.

43. Michelle Phillipov, "'Generic Misery Music': Emo and the Problem of Contemporary Youth Culture," *Media International Australia Incorporating Culture and Policy* 136 (2010): 60.

44. Scuzz TV, "Scuzz Meets Fall Out Boy," YouTube, 2013, https://www .youtube.com/watch?v=L85yQhIOkB8&t=484s7.

45. De Boise, "Cheer Up Emo Kid," 227.

46. Aslaksen, "Middle Class Music."

47. Williams, "'A Walking Open Wound,'" 153; see De Boise, "Cheer Up Emo Kid," 227.

48. Ryan Mack, "Fluid Bodies: Masculinity in Emo Music," MA thesis, Carleton University, 2014, 11.

49. Williams, "'A Walking Open Wound,'" 146.

50. Ibid.

51. Greenwald, *Nothing Feels Good*, 140–41.

52. Ibid., 166.

53. Ibid., 182.

54. Aslaksen, "Middle Class Music," ii.

55. Ibid., 15.

56. Mack, "Fluid Bodies," 136.

57. Ibid., 2.

58. Ibid., 30, 29n.

59. Ibid., 6; emphasis added.

60. Quoted in ibid., 87.

61. Ibid., 13.

62. De Boise, "Cheer Up Emo Kid," 225.

63. Ibid.

64. Carrillo-Vincent, "Wallflower Masculinities," 36.

65. De Boise, "Cheer Up Emo Kid," 238.

66. McClary, *Feminine Endings*, 55.

67. De Boise, "Cheer Up Emo Kid," 235.

68. Ibid., 235–36.

69. Aslaksen, "Middle Class Music," 106.

70. Peters, "Emo Gay Boys," 130.

71. Ibid., 137.

72. Ibid.; Carillo-Vincent, "Wallflower Masculinities"; Rosemary Hill, "Emo Saved My Life: Challenging the Mainstream Discourse of Mental Illness around My Chemical Romance," in *Can I Play with Madness? Metal, Dissonance, Madness and Alienation*, ed. Colin McKinnon, Niall Scot, and Kirsten Sollee (Oxford: Interdisciplinary Press, 2011), 143–54.

73. Jean Carabine, "Unmarried Motherhood 1830–1990: A Genealogical Analysis," in *Discourse as Data: A Guide for Analysis*, ed. Margaret Wetherell, Stephanie Taylor, and Simeon J. Yates (London: Sage 2001), 267–307, 269.

74. Alexander Doty, *Making Things Perfectly Queer: Interpreting Mass Culture* (Minneapolis: University of Minnesota Press, 1993).

75. I was born in 1987, making me one of Kristoff's "girls who are fifteen" in 2002. My family got dial-up internet in 2000 and broadband in approximately 2003.

76. Greenwald, *Nothing Feels Good*, 276.

77. Ariela Mortara and Simona Ironico, "Deconstructing Emo Lifestyle and Aesthetics: A Netnographic Research," *Young Consumers* 14, no. 4 (2013): 351–59, 351.

78. Ibid.

79. Ibid., 352.

80. Ibid.

81. Michelle Phillipov, "'Just Emotional People'? Emo Culture and the Anxieties of Disclosure," *M/C Journal* 12, no. 5 (2009), http://journal .media-culture.org.au/index.php/mcjournal/article/view/181; Overell, "Emo Online."

82. Overell, "Emo Online," 142.

83. Ibid., 152.

84. Ibid., 151.

85. Ibid., 156.

86. Sarah Thornton, *Club Cultures: Music, Media and Subcultural Capital* (Cambridge: Polity, 1995), 104.

87. Ibid., 158.

88. Rosemary Hill, *Gender, Metal and the Media: Women Fans and the Gendered Experience of Music* (New York: Palgrave Macmillan, 2016), Kindle edition, location 1375. Citations to Thornton 1995 are to Thornton, *Club Cultures*.

89. Overell, "Emo Online," 158.

90. Angela Thomas-Jones, "Emo Is Not the New Black: Current Affairs Journalism and the Marking of Popular Culture," *Metro Magazine: Media & Education Magazine* 156 (2008): 72–77.

91. Hill, "Emo Saved My Life," 145, 147.

92. Michel Foucault, "The Discourse on Language," *Social Science Information* 10, no. 2 (1971): 7–30; Foucault, *Archaeology of Knowledge*; Michel Foucault, *The Will to Knowledge* (London: Penguin, 1998); Michel Foucault, *The Order of Things* (London: Routledge, 2002); John Langshaw Austin, *How to Do Things with Words* (Oxford: Clarendon Press, 1962).

93. Fathallah, *Fanfiction and the Author*.

94. Jackie Marsh, "The Discourses of Celebrity in the Fanvid Economy of Club Penguin Machinima," in *Discourse and Digital Practices: Doing Discourse Analysis in the Digital Age*, ed. Rodney H. Jones, Alice Chik, and Christopher A. Hafner (New York: Routledge, 2015), 192–208, 196.

95. Fairclough, *Discourse and Social Change*; Normal Fairclough, *Analysing Discourse: Textual Analysis for Social Research* (London: Routledge 2003).

96. Laclau and Mouffe, *Hegemony and Socialist Strategy*.

97. Neil Selwyn, "The Discursive Construction of Education in the Digital Age," in *Discourse and Digital Practices: Doing Discourse Analysis in the Digital Age*, ed. Rodney H. Jones, Alice Chik, and Christopher A. Hafner (New York: Routledge, 2015), 225–40, 228.

98. Arthur Kok Kum Chiew, "Multisemiotic Mediation in Hypertext," in *Multimodal Discourse Analysis: Systemic Functional Perspectives*, ed. Kay L. O'Halloran (London: Continuum, 2006), 131–59.

99. Ibid.

100. Judith Butler, *Bodies That Matter: On the Discursive Limits of "Sex"* (London: Routledge, 2014).

101. Kay L. O Halloran, "Introduction," in *Multimodal Discourse Analysis: Systemic Functional Perspectives*, ed. Kay L. O'Halloran (London: Continuum, 2006), 1–10, 1.

102. Arthur P. Baldry, "Phase and Transition, Type and Instance: Patterns in Media Texts as Seen Through a Multimodal Concordancer," in *Multimodal Discourse Analysis: Systemic Functional Perspectives*, ed. Kay L. O'Halloran (London: Continuum, 2006), 83–108, 87.

103. Roland Barthes, "Rhetoric of the Image," in *Image, Music, Text* (London: Fontana Press 1977), 32–51.

104. Chiew, "Multisemiotic Mediation in Hypertext," 132.

105. Ibid., 157.

106. Rodney H. Jones, Alice Chik, and Christopher A. Hafner, "Introduction," in *Discourse and Digital Practices: Doing Discourse Analysis in the Digital Age*, ed. Rodney H. Jones, Alice Chik, and Christopher A. Hafner (New York: Routledge, 2015), 1–16, 4.

107. David Barton, "Tagging on Flickr as a Social Practice," in *Discourse and Digital Practices: Doing Discourse Analysis in the Digital Age*, ed. Rodney H. Jones, Alice Chik, and Christopher A. Hafner (New York: Routledge, 2015), 48–65.

108. Jones, Chik, and Hafner, "Introduction," 6.

109. Ibid.

110. Crack is a multifandom autonym denoting a particular kind of absurdist humor, based on incoherence and randomness.

111. Camilla Vasquez, "Intertextuality and Interdiscursivity in Online Consumer Reviews," in *Discourse and Digital Practices: Doing Discourse Analysis in the Digital Age*, ed. Rodney H. Jones, Alice Chik, and Christopher A. Hafner (New York: Routledge, 2015), 65–80, 65–66.

112. Ibid., quoting Meriel Bloor and Thomas Bloor, *The Practice of Critical Discourse Analysis: An Introduction* (London: Hodder and Arnold, 2007).

113. Phil Benson, "YouTube as Text: Spoken Interaction and Digital Discourse," in *Discourse and Digital Practices: Doing Discourse Analysis in the Digital Age*, ed. Rodney H. Jones, Alice Chik, and Christopher A. Hafner (New York: Routledge, 2015), 80–96, 81.

114. Susan C. Herring, Inna Kouper, John C. Paolillo, Lois Ann Scheidt, Michael Tyworth, Peter Welsch, Elijah Wright, and Ning Yu, "Conversations in the Blogosphere: An Analysis 'From the Bottom Up,'" in *Proceedings of the Thirty-Eighth Hawai'i International Conference on System Sciences* (HICSS-38) (Los Alamitos: IEEE Press, 2005), 1–11, 1.

115. Limor Shiffman, *Memes in Digital Culture* (Cambridge, MA: MIT Press 2014), 8.

116. Ibid., 8, 18, 58.

117. Amber Davisson, "Mashing Up, Remixing, and Contesting the Popular Memory of Hillary Clinton," *Transformative Works and Cultures* 22 (2016), https://journal.transformativeworks.org/index.php/twc/article/view/965, 3.8.

118. Whitney Phillips and Ryan M. Milner, *The Ambivalent Internet: Mischief, Oddity and Antagonism Online* (Cambridge, MA: Polity, 2017), 7.

119. Whitney Phillips, *This Is Why We Can't Have Nice Things: Mapping the Relationship between Online Trolling and Mainstream Culture* (Cambridge, MA: MIT Press, 2015), 123.

120. Zizi Papparchissi, *Affective Publics: Sentiment, Technology and Politics* (Oxford: Oxford University Press, 2015).

121. Phillips and Milner, *The Ambivalent Internet*, 188.

122. Andy Bennett, "Subcultures or Neo-Tribes? Rethinking the Relationship between Youth, Style and Musical Taste," *Sociology* 33, no. 3 (1999): 599–617.

123. Hill, "Emo Saved My Life," 145.

124. "That was our greatest victory as a show . . . We got bottled for being dangerous. We oppose everything that's conventional about

[stadium] rock and roll in this country, our home country, everywhere in the world." Quoted in Reindhart Haydn, *My Chemical Romance: This Band Will Save Your Life* (Plexus: London, 2013), 133.

## CHAPTER 2

1. Nancy Baym, *Playing to the Crowd: Musicians, Audiences, and the Intimate Work of Connection* (New York: New York University Press, 2018), 19.

2. 8_light_minutes, comment on "Beating hearts baby," LiveJournal, May 18, 2005, https://patd.LiveJournal.com/42338.html. When quoting fans, I have usually left the comments as written, for example, uncapitalized acronyms to refer to bands. Minor grammar and typographical errors, such as missing apostrophes, have been corrected for ease of reading.

3. blushandrecover, comment on untitled post, LiveJournal, December 1, 2008, https://chemicalromance.LiveJournal.com/3230231.html.

4. geraldway, comment on "War on emo, eh?," LiveJournal, September 14, 2006, https://chemicalromance.LiveJournal.com/1804083 .html#comments.

5. Fathallah, *Fanfiction and the Author*, 19.

6. Victoria Cann, *Boys Like This, Girls Like That* (London: Tauris, 2018).

7. Pierre Bourdieu, *Distinction: A Social Critique of the Judgement of Taste* (London: Routledge and Kegan Paul, 1984), 6.

8. Baym, *Playing to the Crowd*, 171–72.

9. Rhiannon Bury, "The X-Files, Online Fan Culture, and the David Duchovny Estrogen Brigades," in *The Post-Subcultures Reader*, ed. David Muggleton and Rupert Weinzierl (Oxford: Berg, 2004), 285–96; Rhiannon Bury, *Cyberspaces of Their Own: Female Fandoms Online* (New York: Peter Lang, 2005); Lynn Zubernis and Kathy Larsen, *Fandom at the Crossroads: Celebration, Shame and Fan/Producer Relationships* (Newcastle Upon Tyne: Cambridge Scholars, 2012); Henry Jenkins et al., "When Fan Boys and Fan Girls Meet . . . ," Confessions of an Aca-Fan (blog), May 17, 2007, http:// henryjenkins.org/2007/05/when_fan_boys_and_fan_girls_me.html. All posts mirrored and archived at https://fandebate.LiveJournal.com.

10. truthtruthlie, comment on "March Madness MCR vs P!atD," LiveJournal, March 31, 2010, https://patd.LiveJournal.com/2957522 .html?thread=124018130#t124018130.

11. 555gehenna666, comment on "You can vote MCR 'Most Important Band Of The Decade' over at AP," LiveJournal, October 25, 2009, https://chemicalromance.LiveJournal.com/3270675.html#comments.

12. The Vans Warped tour was a mobile musical festival, which toured annually from 1995 to 2018.

13. electroclash, "An Open Letter to the Warped Tour," LiveJournal, July 11, 2005, https://chemicalromance.LiveJournal.com/1046898.html?page=3.

14. girl_rotten, comment on untitled post, LiveJournal, July 13, 2005, https://chemicalromance.LiveJournal.com/1051141.html.

15. Gerard Way, homepage update to mychemicalromance.com, 2002, accessed via the Internet Archive Wayback Machine.

16. Pete Wentz, homepage update to falloutboyrock.com, 2005, accessed via the Internet Archive Wayback Machine.

17. ritalin_, comment on untitled post, LiveJournal, December 29, 2005, https://chemicalromance.LiveJournal.com/1543247.html.

18. enough_hurt, comment on untitled post, LiveJournal, December 29, 2005, https://chemicalromance.LiveJournal.com/1543247.html.

19. ritalin_, comment on untitled post, LiveJournal, December 29, 2005, https://chemicalromance.LiveJournal.com/1543247.html.

20. wertica, comment on untitled post, LiveJournal, December 29, 2005, https://chemicalromance.LiveJournal.com/1543247.html.

21. ritalin_, comment on untitled post, LiveJournal, December 29, 2005, https://chemicalromance.LiveJournal.com/1543247.html.

22. wertica, comment on untitled post, LiveJournal, December 29, 2005, https://chemicalromance.LiveJournal.com/1543247.html.

23. sgownzme311, comment on untitled post, LiveJournal, December 29, 2005, https://chemicalromance.LiveJournal.com/1543247.html.

24. xpistolax, "I WANNA TAKE YOU TO A GAY BAR," LiveJournal, December 23, 2004, https://patd.LiveJournal.com/8182.html.

25. i_melt_with_u, comment on "I WANNA TAKE YOU TO A GAY BAR," LiveJournal, December 23, 2004, https://patd.LiveJournal.com/8182.html.

26. adiscobloodbath, comment on "I WANNA TAKE YOU TO A GAY BAR," LiveJournal, December 23, 2004, https://patd.LiveJournal.com/8182.html.

27. svkv, comment on "Kerrang Readers Poll 2008," LiveJournal,

November 5, 2008, https://chemicalromance.LiveJournal.com/3225853
.html?page=2.

28. bloodyhands, comment on "Kerrang Readers Poll 2008,"
LiveJournal, November 5, 2008, https://chemicalromance.LiveJournal
.com/3225853.html?page=2.

29. Patentpending, comment on "Kerrang Readers Poll 2008,"
LiveJournal, November 5, 2008, https://chemicalromance.LiveJournal
.com/3225853.html?page=2.

30. scorpy808, comment on "Kerrang Readers Poll 2008," LiveJournal,
November 5, 2008, https://chemicalromance.LiveJournal.com/3225853
.html?page=2.

31. Phillips and Milner, *The Ambivalent Internet*, 188.

32. Jones, Chik, and Hafner, "Introduction," 4.

33. Bryan, comment on the Fall Out Boy MySpace page, September 12,
2008, accessed via the Internet Archive Wayback Machine.

34. ohyoursocool, comment on "Panic mention in Pete Wentz 'Out'
interview," LiveJournal, June 29, 2008, https://patd.LiveJournal
.com/2501773.html?page=2.

35. mandy_croyance, comment on "Panic mention in Pete Wentz 'Out'
interview," LiveJournal, June 29, 2008, https://patd.LiveJournal
.com/2501773.html?page=2.

36. taijutsu_queen, "Mikey is such a blog whore," LiveJournal, March 8,
2006, https://chemicalromance.LiveJournal.com/1609243
.html#comments.

37. x_demolition, comment on "Mikey is such a blog whore,"
LiveJournal, March 8, 2006, https://chemicalromance.LiveJournal
.com/1609243.html#comments.

38. kireina, comment on "Mikey is such a blog whore," LiveJournal,
March 8, 2006, https://chemicalromance.LiveJournal.com/1609243
.html#comments.

39. emokid_wannabe, comment on "Mikey is such a blog whore,"
LiveJournal, March 8, 2006, https://chemicalromance.LiveJournal
.com/1609243.html#comments.

40. fetishism, comment on "Mikey is such a blog whore," LiveJournal,
March 8, 2006, https://chemicalromance.LiveJournal.com/1609243
.html#comments.

41. emokid_wannabe, comment.

42. Matt Hills, *Fan Cultures* (London: Routledge, 2002); Zubernis and Larsen, *Fandom at the Crossroads*; Mel Stanfill, "'They're Losers, But I Know Better': Intra-Fandom Stereotyping and the Normalization of the Fan Subject," *Critical Studies in Media Communication* 30, no. 2 (2013): 117–34; Fathallah, *Fanfiction and the Author.*

43. _operation, comment on "Fangirls ruining it for everyone else?," LiveJournal, September 7, 2006, https://chemicalromance.LiveJournal .com/1780500.html.

44. Anonymous, comment on "Welcome To The Black Parade was just on MTV2 UK!," LiveJournal, Setpember 26, 2006, https:// chemicalromance.LiveJournal.com/1836803.html?page=3.

45. fabledfaith, comment on "Here's a question for you (more for the ladies)," LiveJournal, November 14, 2006, https://patd.LiveJournal .com/1411646.html#comments.

46. dstar_pro, comment on "One chapter ends and another begins . . . ," LiveJournal, March 3, 2010, https://chemicalromance.LiveJournal .com/3278443.html?page=3.

47. mysti112, comment on "Ways To Stop Looking Like A Teenybopper (And Other Such Rants)," LiveJournal, May 28, 2005, https:// chemicalromance.LiveJournal.com/959404.html?page=2.

48. Ibid.

49. Thornton, *Club Cultures*; Hills, *Fan Cultures.*

50. Multiple postings, for example, xxauroraxx, comment on untitled post, LiveJournal, March 5, 2005, https://chemicalromance.LiveJournal .com/597796.html.

51. ex_i_amcland189, untitled post, LiveJournal, November 28, 2004, accessed via the Internet Archive Wayback Machine.

52. ex_i_amcland189, untitled post, LiveJournal, June 21, 2004, https://chemicalromance.LiveJournal.com/96360.html#comments.

53. werenotfussy, comment on untitled post, LiveJournal, August 8, 2009, https://chemicalromance.LiveJournal.com/96360.html#comments.

54. Anonymous, comment on the Fall Out Boy MySpace, 2008, accessed via the Internet Archive Wayback Machine.

55. Baym, *Playing to the Crowd.*

56. Ibid., 16–19.

57. Fall Out Boy, untitled post at falloutboyrock.com, June 13, 2005, accessed via the Internet Archive Wayback Machine. When a musician

has updated using the band's official account and "we" plural pronoun, I have referenced using the band's name. Where they have updated their personal LiveJournal accounts, I referenced their username.

58. how_u_disappear, "I wonder what's the surprise," LiveJournal, August 21, 2005, https://chemicalromance.LiveJournal.com/1218335 .html.

59. Chiew, "Multisemiotic Mediation in Hypertext."

60. _callmeloser, comment on untitled post, LiveJournal, December 23, 2004, https://achemicalromance.LiveJournal.com/329646 .html#comments.

61. totesloveslash, comment on "I wonder what's the surprise," LiveJournal, August 21, 2005, https://chemicalromance.LiveJournal .com/1218335.html.

62. androgynous_ken, comment on "I wonder what's the surprise," LiveJournal, August 21, 2005, https://chemicalromance.LiveJournal .com/1218335.html?page=2.

63. martyrsxhidxme, comment on untitled post, LiveJournal, February 8, 2005, https://chemicalromance.LiveJournal.com/505223 .html#comments.

64. ___starla, comment on untitled post, LiveJournal, February 8, 2005, https://chemicalromance.LiveJournal.com/505223 .html#comments.

65. martyrsxhidxme, comment on untitled post, LiveJournal, February 8, 2005, https://chemicalromance.LiveJournal.com/505223 .html#comments.

66. Jamie, comment on Fall Out Boy's MySpace, June 7, 2004, accessed via the Internet Archive Wayback Machine.

67. The Jo Jo Bean, comment on Fall Out Boy's MySpace, June 8, 2004, accessed via the Internet Archive Wayback Machine.

68. Lovesongwriter, "My Chemical Romance Slam Fame-Hungry Musicians on New Album (Source: Spinner.com)," LiveJournal, December 2, 2009, https://chemicalromance.LiveJournal.com/3273187 .html#comments.

69. innovade, comment on "My Chemical Romance Slam Fame-Hungry Musicians on New Album (Source: Spinner.com)," LiveJournal, December 4, 2009, https://chemicalromance.LiveJournal.com/3273187 .html#comments.

70. Fall Out Boy, untitled post at falloutboyrock.com, July 18, 2005, accessed via the Internet Archive Wayback Machine.

71. Panic! At the Disco, post to panicatthedisco.com, 2006a, accessed via the Internet Archive Wayback Machine.

72. _tune_you_out, untitled post, LiveJournal, December 22, 2004, https://chemicalromance.LiveJournal.com/329646.html#comments.

73. _callmeloser, comment on untitled post, LiveJournal, December 23, 2004, https://chemicalromance.LiveJournal.com/329646 .html#comments.

74. wild_eyed_joker, comment on untitled post, LiveJournal, December 23, 2004, 2018, https://chemicalromance.LiveJournal .com/329646.html#comments.

75. keepmeinmindx, comment on untitled post, LiveJournal, December 23, 2004, https://chemicalromance.LiveJournal.com/329646 .html#comments.

76. fanxx00_0, comment on untitled post, LiveJournal, December 23, 2004, https://chemicalromance.LiveJournal.com/329646 .html#comments.

77. gerards_kitten, comment on untitled post, LiveJournal, February 16, 2005, https://chemicalromance.LiveJournal.com/528083 .html#comments.

78. Panic! at the Disco, post to panicatthedisco.com, October 1, 2006, accessed via the Wayback Machine.

79. untilyoubelieve, comment on "Pop Stars, eh?," LiveJournal, October 18, 2005, https://chemicalromance.LiveJournal.com/1427456 .html#comment.

80. marionnettes, comment on "Pop Stars, eh?," LiveJournal, October 18, 2005, https://chemicalromance.LiveJournal.com/1427456 .html#comments.

81. Hill, *Gender, Metal and the Media*, location 1377.

82. Robster, comment on the Fall Out Boy MySpace, 2005, accessed via the Internet Archive Wayback Machine.

83. galadflower, comment on "War on emo, eh?," LiveJournal, September 14, 2006, https://chemicalromance.LiveJournal.com/1804083 .html.

84. nest_freemark, comment on "War on emo, eh?", LiveJournal, September 14, 2006, https://chemicalromance.LiveJournal.com/1804083.html.

85. flyswatting, comment on untitled post, LiveJournal, October 19, 2006, https://patd.LiveJournal.com/1336782.html?page=3.

86. xstainmybladex, comment on "Number one on TRL. Uh . . . ," LiveJournal, July 13, 2005, https://chemicalromance.LiveJournal .com/1051141.html?page=2.

87. leadtheflock, untitled post, LiveJournal, June 13, 2005, https:// chemicalromance.LiveJournal.com/982420.html.

88. dropthatgun, comment on untitled post, LiveJournal, June 13, 2005, https://chemicalromance.LiveJournal.com/982420.html; lordfuckie, comment on untitled post, LiveJournal, June 13, 2005, https://chemicalromance.LiveJournal.com/982420.html.

89. brndnw22, comment on untitled post, LiveJournal, June 13, 2005, https://chemicalromance.LiveJournal.com/982420.html.

90. leadtheflock, comment on untitled post, LiveJournal, June 13, 2005, https://chemicalromance.LiveJournal.com/982420.html.

91. forlornnangel, comment on untitled post, LiveJournal, August 6, 2005, https://chemicalromance.LiveJournal.com/1143536.html?page=2.

92. melroberts, comment on untitled post, LiveJournal, July 30, 2006, https://chemicalromance.LiveJournal.com/1699243.html.

93. sunnydlita, comment on "New Songs!," LiveJournal, August 1, 2009, https://chemicalromance.LiveJournal.com/3265265.html?page=4.

94. sorrowful_eagle, comment on "New Songs!," LiveJournal, August 1, 2009, https://chemicalromance.LiveJournal.com/3265265.html?page=4.

95. lord_spamulon, comment on "An Article . . . ," LiveJournal, November 26, 2009, https://chemicalromance.LiveJournal.com/3272800 .html#comments.

96. backbones, comment on untitled post, LiveJournal, November 2, 2005, https://chemicalromance.LiveJournal.com/1456090 .html#comments.

97. fortysixthhour, comment on "Spin Reviews Vices and Virtues," LiveJournal, March 7, 2011, https://patd.LiveJournal.com/3024168 .html?thread=125664296#t125664296.

98. charlizard, comment on "BLUNT January '06 Scans," LiveJournal, January 12, 2006, https://chemicalromance.LiveJournal.com/1559129 .html.

## CHAPTER 3

1. poison howlter, comment on Fall Out Boy, "Wilson (Expensive Mistakes)," YouTube, January 10, 2018, https://www.youtube.com/watch?v=wH-by1yd -BTM.

2. Chiew, "Multisemiotic Mediation in Hypertext."

3. See Vasquez, "Intertextuality and Interdiscursivity."

4. Stein, *Millennial Fandom*, 10.

5. See Booth, *Playing Fans*.

6. Rose Attu and Melissa Terras, "What People Study When They Study Tumblr: Classifying Tumblr Related Academic Research," *Journal of Documentation* 73, no. 3 (2017): 528–54, 529.

7. Ibid., 542.

8. Ibid., 543.

9. Michael Z. Newman, "'Say *Pulp Fiction* One More Goddamn Time': Quotation Culture and an Internet-Age Classic," *New Review of Film and Television Studies* 12, no. 2 (2013): 125–42, 128.

10. emo-church, Tumblr, 2018, https://emo-church.tumblr.com/.

11. De Kosnik, *Rogue Archives*.

12. Nick Douglas, "It's Supposed to Look Like Shit: The Internet Ugly Aesthetic," *Journal of Visual Culture* 13, no. 3 (2014): 314–39, 314.

13. Ibid., 327, 314.

14. De Kosnik, *Rogue Archives*, 153.

15. Scene fixture Chris Gutierrez, a writer and photographer from Chicago who was good friends with FOB and MCR and sometimes contributed to fan communities.

16. Compare Gail Simone's description of "women in refrigerators," a comic book/action hero trope wherein a woman's death in the prologue serves as the mechanism for the hero's journey, on her website https://www.lby3.com/wir.

17. Kevin Sherwood, comment on Sail Set, "Fall Out Boy 'The Story' 2004 FULL," YouTube, 2015, https://www.youtube.com /watch?v=z8Z4qbj5B48.

18. Nikita T, comment on Sail Set, "Fall Out Boy 'The Story' 2004 FULL," YouTube, 2015, https://www.youtube.com/watch?v=z8Z4qbj5B48.

19. Joseph Lyle, comment on Fueled by Ramen, "Grand Theft Autumn," YouTube, 2018, https://www.youtube.com/watch?v=GZb_mqH2zJY.

20. *South Park*, "Member Berries," season 20, episode 1, directed by Trey Parker, written by Trey Parker, Comedy Central, September 14, 2016.

21. slim shady, comment on Fueled by Ramen, "Grand Theft Autumn," YouTube, 2018, https://www.youtube.com/watch?v=GZb_mqH2zJY.

22. oysterlovers, comment on Fall Out Boy, "Rat A Tat ft. Courtney Love," YouTube, 2015, https://www.youtube.com/watch?v=MC8nDOXzMYw.

23. tete henkes, comment on Fall Out Boy, "Rat A Tat ft. Courtney Love," YouTube, 2015, https://www.youtube.com/watch?v=MC8nDOXzMYw.

24. pixel, comment on Fall Out Boy, "Rat A Tat ft. Courtney Love," YouTube, 2015, https://www.youtube.com/watch?v=MC8nDOXzMYw.

25. tete henkes, comment on Fall Out Boy, "Rat A Tat ft. Courtney Love," YouTube, 2015, https://www.youtube.com/watch?v=MC8nDOXzMYw.

26. crunchy, comment on Fall Out Boy, "Rat A Tat ft. Courtney Love," YouTube, 2018, https://www.youtube.com/watch?v=MC8nDOXzMYw.

27. chayse choice, comment on Fall Out Boy, "Irresistible ft. Demi Lovato," YouTube, 2018, https://www.youtube.com/watch?v=2Lb2BiUC898.

28. Soboleva, comment on Fall Out Boy, "Irresistible ft. Demi Lovato," YouTube, 2018, https://www.youtube.com/watch?v=2Lb2BiUC898.

29. H3rO 142, comment on Fall Out Boy, "Irresistible ft. Demi Lovato," YouTube, 2018, https://www.youtube.com/watch?v=2Lb2BiUC898.

30. Anne Rosario, comment on Fall Out Boy, "Irresistible ft. Demi Lovato," YouTube, 2018, https://www.youtube.com/watch?v=2Lb2BiUC898.

31. Incredible Shadow, comment on Fall Out Boy, "Irresistible ft. Demi Lovato," YouTube, 2018, https://www.youtube.com/watch?v=2Lb2BiUC898.

32. Spongebob ROUNDpants, comment on Fall Out Boy, "Irresistible ft. Demi Lovato," YouTube, 2018, https://www.youtube.com/watch?v=2Lb2BiUC898.

33. Sophia Hay, comment on My Chemical Romance, "Helena," YouTube, 2018, https://www.youtube.com/watch?v=UCCyoocDxBA.

34. Death Grips, comment on My Chemical Romance, "Helena," YouTube, 2018, https://www.youtube.com/watch?v=UCCyoocDxBA.

35. Aaliyah Kverh, comment on My Chemical Romance, "Helena," YouTube, 2018, https://www.youtube.com/watch?v=UCCyoocDxBA.

36. Emily O'Connell, "I'm Not Like Other Girls, Because 'Other Girls' Don't Exist," Thought Catalog, July 27, 2016, https://thoughtcatalog.com /emily-oconnell/2015/07/im-not-like-other-girls-because-other-girls -dont-exist/; Sallie Bietermen, "'I'm Not Like Other Girls': TheMotivations and Consequences of Saying It," The Odyssey, May 31, 2016, https://www .theodysseyonline.com/not-like-other-girls; TV Tropes, "Not Like Other Girls," n.d., accessed December 10, 2018, https://tvtropes.org/pmwiki /pmwiki.php/Main/NotLikeOtherGirls.

37. emo quartet trash, comment on antonio.gor, "Life on the Murder Scene," YouTube, 2018, https://www.youtube.com/watch?v =-JmsTIJhMOA.

38. Kawaii Punk, comment on antonio.gor, "Life on the Murder Scene," YouTube, 2018, https://www.youtube.com/watch?v=-JmsTIJhMOA.

39. rainetheawesome, comment on antonio.gor, "Life on the Murder Scene," YouTube, 2018, https://www.youtube.com/watch?v =-JmsTIJhMOA.

40. villarreal, julia, comment on @TheBlackP_MCR Channel Twitter, "Honey, This Mirror Isn't Big Enough for the Two of Us," YouTube, 2015, https://www.youtube.com/watch?v=T5_492D-tLA.

41. sneakyMCR Howlter, comment on @TheBlackP_MCR Channel Twitter, "Honey, This Mirror Isn't Big Enough for the Two of Us," YouTube, 2015, https://www.youtube.com/watch?v=T5_492D-tLA.

42. Grace Hannah-Lynn, comment on @TheBlackP_MCR Channel Twitter, "Honey, This Mirror Isn't Big Enough for the Two of Us," YouTube, 2015, https://www.youtube.com/watch?v=T5_492D-tLA.

43. Aesthetic? More Like Ass-Pathetic, comment on @TheBlackP_MCR Channel Twitter, "Honey, This Mirror Isn't Big Enough for the Two of Us," YouTube, 2016, https://www.youtube.com/watch?v=T5_492D-tLA.

44. princess nicole, comment on Fall Out Boy, "Just One Yesterday," YouTube, 2016, https://www.youtube.com/watch?v=dSfKSUd31MM.

45. J Cubed, comment on Fall Out Boy, "Just One Yesterday," YouTube, 2018, https://www.youtube.com/watch?v=dSfKSUd31MM.

46. John Brady, comment on Fall Out Boy, "Just One Yesterday," YouTube, 2017, https://www.youtube.com/watch?v=dSfKSUd31MM.

47. Eric's Comic's, comment on Fall Out Boy, "Just One Yesterday,"

YouTube, 2018, https://www.youtube.com/watch?v=dSfKSUd31MM.

48. SHARLA PINK, comment on My Chemical Romance, "Teenagers," YouTube, 2018, https://www.youtube.com/watch?v=k6EQAOmJrbw.

49. 409 in your coffee maker, comment on My Chemical Romance, "Teenagers," YouTube, 2018, https://www.youtube.com /watch?v=k6EQAOmJrbw; Ophelia Ivy, comment on My Chemical Romance, "Teenagers," YouTube, 2018, https://www.youtube.com /watch?v=k6EQAOmJrbw.

50. Gloupyli, comment on Fueled by Ramen, "Panic! At The Disco: Girls/Girls/Boys [OFFICIAL VIDEO]," YouTube, 2018, https://www .youtube.com/watch?v=Yk8jV7r6VMk.

51. OneLoneVoice, comment on Fueled by Ramen, "Panic! At The Disco: Girls/Girls/Boys [OFFICIAL VIDEO]," YouTube, 2017, https://www .youtube.com/watch?v=Yk8jV7r6VMk.

52. ZanktheGreat, comment on Fueled by Ramen, "Panic! At The Disco: Girls/Girls/Boys [OFFICIAL VIDEO]," YouTube, 2017, https://www .youtube.com/watch?v=Yk8jV7r6VMk.

53. Sandy Jones, comment on Fueled by Ramen, "Panic! At The Disco: Girls/Girls/Boys [OFFICIAL VIDEO]," YouTube, 2017, https://www .youtube.com/watch?v=Yk8jV7r6VMk.

54. Fall Out Josie, comment on Sail Set, "Fall Out Boy 'The Story' 2004 FULL," YouTube, 2016, https://www.youtube.com/watch?v=z8Z4qbj5B48.

55. DJ Spooky Maddi, comment on Sail Set, "Fall Out Boy 'The Story' 2004 FULL," YouTube, 2016, https://www.youtube.com /watch?v=z8Z4qbj5B48.

56. Amira L. Berdouk, comment on Sail Set, "Fall Out Boy 'The Story' 2004 FULL," YouTube, 2018, https://www.youtube.com /watch?v=z8Z4qbj5B48.

57. Gabriel Player, comment on Fall Out Boy, "Dance, Dance," YouTube, 2018, https://www.youtube.com/watch?v=C6MOKXm8x5o.

58. Justin Dowdy, comment on Fall Out Boy, "Dance, Dance," YouTube, 2018, https://www.youtube.com/watch?v=C6MOKXm8x5o.

59. Ranjit Singh, comment on Fall Out Boy, "Dance, Dance," YouTube, 2018, https://www.youtube.com/watch?v=C6MOKXm8x5o.

60. Chantal Robert, comment on My Chemical Romance, "Welcome to the Black Parade," YouTube, 2018, https://www.youtube.com /watch?v=RRKJiM9Njr8.

61. Isabella Adelmann, comment on My Chemical Romance, "Welcome to the Black Parade," YouTube, 2018, https://www.youtube.com/watch?v=RRKJiM9Njr8.

62. Evellyn Winters, comment on My Chemical Romance, "Welcome to the Black Parade," YouTube, 2018, https://www.youtube.com/watch?v=RRKJiM9Njr8.

63. Johnx, comment on Hail Pala, "My Chemical Romance- Vampires Will Never Hurt You-Video (HQ)," YouTube, 2017, https://www.youtube.com/watch?v=Z1FHpCs8tD4.

64. T J Williams, comment on Fall Out Boy, "I Don't Care," YouTube, 2018, https://www.youtube.com/watch?v=Alh6iIvVN9o.

65. Charlotte Boyd, comment on Fueled by Ramen, "Fall Out Boy: Dead On Arrival [OFFICIAL VIDEO]," YouTube, 2017, https://www.youtube.com/watch?v=qLo2p9KhABo.

66. Roanisawstr, comment on Fueled by Ramen, "Fall Out Boy: Dead On Arrival [OFFICIAL VIDEO]," YouTube, 2016, https://www.youtube.com/watch?v=qLo2p9KhABo.

67. sophia craig, comment on Fueled by Ramen, "Fall Out Boy: Dead On Arrival [OFFICIAL VIDEO]," YouTube, 2016, https://www.youtube.com/watch?v=qLo2p9KhABo.

68. Roanisawstr, comment on Fueled by Ramen, "Fall Out Boy: Dead On Arrival [OFFICIAL VIDEO]," YouTube, 2016, https://www.youtube.com/watch?v=qLo2p9KhABo.

69. Justin Yee, comment on My Chemical Romance, "My Chemical Romance - Welcome to the Black Parade [Official Music Video]," YouTube, 2018, https://www.youtube.com/watch?v=RRKJiM9Njr8.

70. Trinity Urie, comment on Fueled by Ramen, "Panic! at the Disco: Lying Is the Most Fun . . . [OFFICIAL VIDEO]," YouTube, 2018, https://www.youtube.com/watch?v=8AZxUtZ2ZgI.

71. Better stay on that side of the street, comment on Fueled by Ramen, "Panic! at the Disco: Lying is the Most Fun . . . [OFFICIAL VIDEO]," YouTube, 2018, https://www.youtube.com/watch?v=8AZxUtZ2ZgI.

72. Trinity Urie, comment on Fueled by Ramen, "Panic! at the Disco: Lying Is the Most Fun . . . [OFFICIAL VIDEO]," YouTube, 2018, https://www.youtube.com/watch?v=8AZxUtZ2ZgI.

73. Better stay on that side of the street, comment on Fueled by

Ramen, "Panic! at the Disco: Lying Is the Most Fun . . . [OFFICIAL VIDEO]," YouTube, 2018, https://www.youtube.com/watch?v=8AZxUtZ2ZgI.

74. antonio.gor, "MCR Life on the Murder Scene," YouTube, September 29, 2011, https://www.youtube.com/watch?v=-JmsTIJhMOA.

75. Gerard Way, "This is well written," Twitter, April 26, 2016, https://twitter.com/gerardway/status/725093778638274560; Gerard Way, "This fanfic gets right to the point. Absolutely no fucking around here. Milk enema like I guessed. No big," Twitter, April 26, 2016, https://twitter.com/gerardway/status/725092965467586560.

76. Night Senpai, comment on CrankThatFrank, "REACTING TO EMO BANDS ON CRACK 61!," YouTube, 2018, https://www.youtube.com/watch?v=DzJBgT6bOwo.

77. CrankThatFrank, comment on Fall Out Boy, "Wilson (Expensive Mistakes)," YouTube, 2018, https://www.youtube.com/watch?v=wH-by1ydBTM.

78. brooke, comment on Panic! at the Disco, "Emperor's New Clothes," YouTube, 2018, https://www.youtube.com/watch?v=7qFF2v8VsaA.

79. The first published real person fiction fan fic can be reliably dated to 1968. See https://fanlore.org/wiki/Visit_to_a_Weird_Planet.

80. Jo Zhang, video description on Jo Zhang, "[Fall Out Boy] Novocaine (fan-made music video)," YouTube, 2015, https://www.youtube.com/watch?v=6RRXtpz4C3.

81. Joe Trohman, "THIS IS MEANT OUT OF RESPECT AND LOVE, NOT ANGER OR DISREGARD," This Is a Blog, Tumblr, June 22, 2013, https://mrtrohman.tumblr.com/post/53642674543/this-is-meant-out-of-respect-and-love-not-anger.

82. Baym, *Playing to the Crowd*, 130.

CHAPTER 4

1. Kelly Bergstrom, "'Don't Feed the Troll': Shutting Down Debate about Community Expectations on Reddit.com," *First Monday* 16, no. 8 (2011), https://firstmonday.org/article/view/3498/3029.

2. Ibid.

3. Reddit, "Moderator Guidelines for Healthy Communities," Reddit Wiki, 2017, https://www.reddit.com/wiki/healthycommunities.

4. Gabriella Coleman, "Our Weirdness Is Free," *Triple Canopy* 15 (2012), https://www.canopycanopycanopy.com/contents/our_weirdness_is_free.

5. Lee Knuttila, "User Unknown: 4chan, Anonymity and Contingency," *First Monday* 16, no. 10 (2011), https://firstmonday.org/ojs/index.php/fm/article/view/3665/3055.

6. Ibid.

7. Whitney Phillips, "The House That Fox Built: Anonymous, Spectacle, and Cycles of Amplification," *Television & New Media* 14, no. 6 (2013): 494–509; Coleman, "Our Weirdness Is Free"; Knuttila, "User Unknown."

8. Knuttila, "User Unknown."

9. Matthew Trammell, "User Investment and Behavior Policing on 4chan," *First Monday* 19, nos. 2–3 (2014), https://firstmonday.org/ojs/index.php/fm/article/view/4819/3839.

10. gottam, comment on "My Chemical Romance," Reddit, r/emo, 2018, https://www.reddit.com/R/Emo/comments/9b0i97/my_chemical_romance/.

11. ouralarmclock, comment on "Fall Out Boy—The Patron Saint Of Liars And Fakes (2003, Fueled By Ramen)," Reddit, r/emo, 2019, https://www.reddit.com/R/Emo/comments/adrg09/fall_out_boy_the_patron_saint_of_liars_and_fakes/.

12. 4chan, discussion in Video Games (/v/), 2018, https://boards.fireden.net/v/thread/424803240/#424806514. Because users are anonymous, 4chan discussions are referenced by date and links.

13. Hills, *Fan Cultures*; Julie Levin Russo, "Textual Orientation: Queer Female Fandom Online," in *The Routledge Companion to Media and Gender*, ed. Cindy Carter, Linda Steiner, and Lisa McLaughlin (Oxon: Routledge, 2013), 450–60; Kristina Busse, "Geek Hierarchies, Boundary Policing, and the Gendering of the Good Fan," *Participations: A Journal of Audience and Reception Studies* 10, no. 1 (2013): 73–91; Zubernis and Larson, *Fandom at the Crossroads*; Fathallah, *Fanfiction and the Author*.

14. No doubt a play on "circlejerk," a disparaging term for a community in which everyone simply compliments and flatters themselves and everyone else, thus the image of mutual masturbation.

15. r/emo Wiki, Reddit, 2019, https://www.reddit.com/R/Emo/wiki/index.

16. Ibid.

17. Sarcastasaurus, "Emo History Lesson Part 5- Emo Pop," Reddit, r/emo, 2016, https://www.reddit.com/r/Emo/comments/4913pt/emo

_history_lesson_part_5_emo_pop/.

18. Ibid.

19. kilar277, "My Chemical Romance," Reddit, r/emo, 2016, https://www.reddit.com/R/Emo/comments/3q5x9t/my_chemical_romance/.

20. toke81, comment on "My Chemical Romance," Reddit, r/emo, 2016, https://www.reddit.com/R/Emo/comments/3q5x9t/my_chemical__romance/.

21. 2relad, comment on "Emo 1984-2014, a Playlist Including the Map of Emo Voting Thread (166 bands)," Reddit, r/emo, 2005, https://www.reddit.com/R/Emo/comments/2z2izb/emo_19842014_a_playlist_including_the_map_of_emo/.

22. Rentington, comment on "Emo is the preferred genre of 91,000 of Spotify's 83 million users, around 0.1%," Reddit, r/emo, 2019, https://www.reddit.com/R/Emo/comments/a3qtzt/emo_is_the_preferred_genre_of_91000_of_spotifys/.

23. 4chan, discussion in Music (/mu/), April 12, 2015, https://4archive.org/board/mu/thread/60800476/anybody-here-like-blood-on-the-dance-floor.

24. 4chan, discussion in Television & Film (/tv/), 2016, http://archive.4plebs.org/tv/thread/71142492/.

25. twavisdegwet, comment on "What do you guys think of the newer and mainstream bands that people consider 'emo'?," Reddit, r/emo, 2018, https://www.reddit.com/r/Emo/comments/6ur7pa/what_do_you_guys_think_of_the_newer_and/.

26. 4chan, discussion in Television & Film (/tv/), March 14, 2019, https://archive.4plebs.org/tv/thread/111380343/.

27. kage6613, comment on "AMA Request: u/kage6613, the legend behind the REAL REAL EMO copypasta," Reddit, r/emo, 2018, https://www.reddit.com/R/Emojerk/comments/9i3at8/ama_request_ukage6613_the_legend_behind_the_real/.

28. TheLampSalesman, "AMA Request: u/kage6613, the legend behind the REAL REAL EMO copypasta," Reddit, r/emo, 2018, https://www.reddit.com/R/Emojerk/comments/9i3at8/ama_request_ukage6613_the_legend_behind_the_real/.

29. Anonymous, comment on "This is a real struggle," Reddit, r/emo, 2018, https://www.reddit.com/R/Emo/comments/8hl5j3/this_is_a_real_struggle/dymkflq/?context=8&depth=9.

30. kage6613, comment on "AMA Request."

31. Giga_Alex, comment on "Need I say anything?," Reddit, r/emojerk, 2019, https://www.reddit.com/R/Emojerk/comments/b34d7d/need_i _say_anything/.

32. Wulcan_WTF, comment on "Need I say anything?," Reddit, r/ emojerk, 2019, https://www.reddit.com/R/Emojerk/comments/b34d7d /need_i_say_anything/.

33. EET FUK, comment on "Fall Out Boy—The Patron Saint Of Liars And Fakes (2003, Fueled By Ramen)," Reddit, r/emo, 2019, https://www .reddit.com/R/Emo/comments/adrg09/fall_out_boy_the_patron_saint _of_liars_and_fakes/.

34. in_san1ty, "Are we an elists?," Reddit, r/emo, 2018, https://www .reddit.com/r/Emo/comments/7h8vdo/are_we_an_elists/.

35. hotdogtacos187, comment on "Are we an elists?," Reddit, r/emo, 2018, https://www.reddit.com/r/Emo/comments/7h8vdo/are_we_an_elists/.

36. 4chan, discussion in Music (/mu/), June 23, 2016, https://4archive .org/board/mu/thread/65887411/itt-guilty-pleasures#p65887800.

37. Duodecim, "BEST eMO ALBUMS OF ALL TIME," Reddit, r/emo, 2016, https://www.reddit.com/r/Emo/comments/4cukoe/best_emo _albums_of_all_time/.

38. GroundbreakingWest7, "This new fanbase . . . ," Reddit, r/ mychemicalromance, 2019, https://www.reddit.com/r /MyChemicalRomance/comments/b36jzn/this_new_fanbase/. *I Brought You My Bullets, You Brought Me Your Love* (2002) is MCR's first album, and the least well known, being released on the independent label Eyeball.

39. Comment on "My Chemical Romance," Reddit, r/emo, 2016, https://www.reddit.com/r/Emo/comments/3q5x9t/my_chemical _romance/.

40. 4chan, discussion in Fashion (/fa/), August 8, 2018, https://warosu .org/fa/thread/S8616765#p8616765.

41. 4chan, discussion in Fashion (/fa/), September 27, 2018. https:// warosu.org/fa/thread/13716195.

42. 4chan, discussion in Video Games (/v/), 2018, https://boards .fireden.net/v/thread/428381342/#428385703.

43. Ibid.

44. Ibid.

45. 4chan, discussion in Fashion (/fa/), September 27, 2018, https://

warosu.org/fa/thread/13716195.

46. 4chan, discussion in Fashion (/fa/), November 21, 2015, https://warosu.org/fa/thread/10630275.

47. See de Boise, "Cheer Up Emo Kid."

48. 4chan, discussion in Music (/mu/), June 23, 2016, https://4archive.org/board/mu/thread/65887411/itt-guilty-pleasures#p65887800.

49. *Death of a Bachelor*, an album by Panic! at the Disco (Fueled by Ramen, 2015).

50. Norabedamned, "Rediscovering Panic," Reddit, r/panicatthedisco, 2019, https://www.reddit.com/r/panicatthedisco/comments/alklto/rediscovering_panic/.

51. 4chan, discussion in Fashion (/fa/), November 21, 2015, https://warosu.org/fa/thread/10630275#p10631047.

52. 4chan, discussion in Fashion (/fa/), August 14, 2013, https://warosu.org/fa/thread/6692677.

53. A_Good_Kitty, "For a concert, how far is too far?," Reddit, r/panicatthedisco, 2018, https://www.reddit.com/r/panicatthedisco/comments/8yqoxa/for_a_concert_how_far_is_too_far/.

54. WaitQuietly, comment on "For a concert, how far is too far?," Reddit, r/panicatthedisco, 2018, https://www.reddit.com/r/panicatthedisco/comments/8yqoxa/for_a_concert_how_far_is_too_far/.

55. willworkforkitties, comment on "For a concert, how far is too far?," Reddit, r/panicatthedisco, 2018, https://www.reddit.com/r/panicatthedisco/comments/8yqoxa/for_a_concert_how_far_is_too_far/.

56. A_Good_Kitty, comment on "For a concert, how far is too far?," Reddit, r/panicatthedisco, 2018, https://www.reddit.com/r/panicatthedisco/comments/8yqoxa/for_a_concert_how_far_is_too_far/.

57. damnitschecky, comment on "For a concert, how far is too far?," Reddit, r/panicatthedisco, 2018, https://www.reddit.com/r/panicatthedisco/comments/8yqoxa/for_a_concert_how_far_is_too_far/.

58. Joshua Brown, "No Homo," *Journal of Homosexuality* 58, no. 3 (2011): 299–314.

59. 4chan, discussion in Fashion (/fa/), October 13, 2014, https://warosu.org/fa/thread/8944085.

60. 4chan, discussion in Random (/b/), "God Tier Emo Albums," March 23, 2016, https://randomarchive.com/board/b/thread/675422735.

61. Ibid.

62. 4chan, discussion in Fashion (/fa/), October 21, 2014, https://warosu.org/fa/thread/8978085.

63. 4chan, discussion in Fashion (/fa/), November 21, 2015, https://warosu.org/fa/thread/10630275.

64. Ibid.

65. 4chan, discussion in Fashion (/fa/), September 27, 2018, https://warosu.org/fa/thread/13716195.

66. bastardjames, "We randomly got each other the same album . . . and of course, it was Best Buds," Reddit, r/emo, 2019, https://www.reddit.com/r/Emo/comments/a9gl6f/we_randomly_got_each_other_the_same_album_and_of. *Best Buds* is an album by the band Mom Jeans.

67. Static1185, comment on "We randomly got each other the same album . . . and of course, it was Best Buds," Reddit, r/emo, 2019, https://www.reddit.com/r/Emo/comments/a9gl6f/we_randomly_got_each_other_the_same_album_and_of.

68. Mlb3621, comment on "We randomly got each other the same album . . . and of course, it was Best Buds," Reddit, r/emo, 2019, https://www.reddit.com/r/Emo/comments/a9gl6f/we_randomly_got_each_other_the_same_album_and_of.

69. Afieldoftulips, comment on "Emo band admits to never playing sport they're named after," Reddit, r/emo, 2019, https://www.reddit.com/r/Emo/comments/acmv1g/emo_band_admits_to_never_playing_sport_theyre/.

70. Theselfescaping, comment on "Emo 1984-2014, a playlist including the Map of Emo Voting Thread (166 bands)," Reddit, r/emo, 2015, https://www.reddit.com/r/Emo/comments/2z2izb/emo_19842014_a_playlist_including_the_map_of_emo/.

71. garethom, comment on "Emo 1984-2014, a playlist including the Map of Emo Voting Thread (166 bands)," Reddit, r/emo, 2015, https://www.reddit.com/r/Emo/comments/2z2izb/emo_19842014_a_playlist_including_the_map_of_emo/.

72. Ibid.

73. 2relad, comment on "Emo 1984-2014, a playlist including the Map of Emo Voting Thread (166 bands)," Reddit, r/emo, 2015, https://www.reddit.com/r/Emo/comments/2z2izb/emo_19842014_a_playlist_including_the_map_of_emo/.

74. GoodMoleManToYou, comment on "Emo 1984-2014, a playlist

including the Map of Emo Voting Thread (166 bands)," Reddit, r/emo, 2015, https://www.reddit.com/r/Emo/comments/2z2izb /emo_19842014_a_playlist_including_the_map_of_emo/.

75. Andrew Fleck, "The Father's Living Monument: Textual Progeny and the Birth of the Author in Sidney's 'Arcadias,'" *Studies in Philology* 107, no. 4 (2010): 520–47.

76. Ibid., 529.

77. unicornurine, comment on "Least Favorite Emo/Screamo band? Post Emo bands you don't like or don't think are that good (or any unpopular opinions)," Reddit, r/emo, 2018, https://www.reddit.com/r /Emo/comments/9qq0s4/least_favorite_emoscreamo_band_post_emo _bands_you/.

78. 4chan, discussion in Fashion (/fa/), November 21, 2015, https:// warosu.org/fa/thread/10630275#p10632906.

79. What_is_life, "Am I emo?," Reddit, r/emo, 2019, https://www .reddit.com/r/Emo/comments/ash1ja/am_i_emo/.

80. BreakingBondage, comment on "Am I emo?," Reddit, r/emo, 2019, https://www.reddit.com/r/Emo/comments/ash1ja/am_i_emo/.

81. fronkelele, comment on "Am I emo?," Reddit, r/emo, 2019, https:// www.reddit.com/r/Emo/comments/ash1ja/am_i_emo/.

82. 4chan, discussion in Fashion, (/fa/), June 26, 2014, https://warosu .org/fa/last50/8410859.

83. 4chan, discussion in Fashion (/fa/), November 21, 2015, https:// warosu.org/fa/thread/10630275#p10632906.

84. Cyborg 2d, comment on "What bands do you listen to these days," Reddit, r/mychemicalromance, 2018, https://www.reddit.com/r /MyChemicalRomance/comments/8y4r47/what_bands_do_you_listen _to_these_days/.

85. Rzorbloods, comment on "Are there any fans of MCR that aren't emo on here? I'm just saying I just really like their music and I'm not emo," Reddit, r/mychemicalromance, 2018, https://www.reddit.com/r /MyChemicalRomance/comments/axg86w/are_there_any_fans_of_mcr _that_arent_emo_on_here/.

86. Zooropa_Station, comment on "Is panic at the disco emo?," Reddit, r/panicatthedisco, 2018, https://www.reddit.com/r/panicatthedisco /comments/a44k1i/is_panic_at_the_disco_emo/.

87. saintollie, comment on "What bands do you listen to these days,"

Reddit, r/mychemicalromance, 2018, https://www.reddit.com/r
/MyChemicalRomance/comments/8y4r47/what_bands_do_you_listen
_to_these_days/.

88. BlueElectivire, comment on "What bands do you listen to these
days," Reddit, r/mychemicalromance, 2018, https://www.reddit.com/r
/MyChemicalRomance/comments/8y4r47/what_bands_do_you_listen
_to_these_days/.

89. -y-y-y, comment on "Is panic at the disco emo?," Reddit, r/
panicatthedisco, 2018, https://www.reddit.com/r/panicatthedisco
/comments/a44k1i/is_panic_at_the_disco_emo/.

90. Cleave Warsaw, comment on "Still not sure why people associate
FOB, MCR, and Panic! together," Reddit, r/falloutboy, 2018, https://www
.reddit.com/r/FallOutBoy/comments/7ujx9g/still_not_sure_why
_people_associate_fob_mcr_and/.

91. puckle-knuck, comment on "Modern Bands like my chem," Reddit,
R/mychemicalromance, 2019, https://www.reddit.com/r
/MyChemicalRomance/comments/ax566w/modern_bands_like_my
_chem/.

92. Andrxw_A, comment on "Opinion: MCR isn't 'emo' music, but is
has obvious emo influences and it's timing, demographic, and impact
should be taken into account before dismissing it as simply 'fake emo,'"
Reddit, r/mychemicalromance, 2019, https://www.reddit.com/r
/MyChemicalRomance/comments/a7q5fa/opinion_mcr_isnt_emo
_music_but_is_has_obvious_emo/.

93. Sarcastasaurus, "Emo History Lesson Sidebar: Scenecore," Reddit,
r/emo, 2017, https://www.reddit.com/r/Emo/comments/52znsf/emo
_history_lesson_sidebar_scenecore/.

94. Amyftw, comment on "Emo History Lesson Sidebar: Scenecore,"
Reddit, r/emo, 2017, https://www.reddit.com/r/Emo/comments/52znsf
/emo_history_lesson_sidebar_scenecore/.

95. Alineinasong, comment on "Still not sure why people associate
FOB, MCR, and Panic! Together," Reddit, r/falloutboy, 2018, https://www
.reddit.com/r/FallOutBoy/comments/7ujx9g/still_not_sure_why
_people_associate_fob_mcr_and/.

## CHAPTER 5

1. *Alternative Press*, "Product Description," issue 352, 2017, https://shop
.altpress.com/products/the_ultimate_guide_to_emo_magazine_352.

2. *Kerrang!*, issue 1409, April 7, 2012.

3. Jesse Richman, "What Is Emo, Anyway? We Look at History to
Define a Genre," *Alternative Press*, January 24, 2018, https://www.altpress
.com/features/what_is_emo_history_definition/; emphasis in original.

4. Ibid.

5. *Alternative Press*, "Chiodos' Craig Owens and the Emo Nite Founders
Explain What Makes the Emo Scene so Special," *Alternative Press*, May 20,
2017, https://www.altpress.com/features/chiodos_craig_owens_emo
_nite_founders_interview/.

6. Ibid.

7. Ibid.

8. Urban Outfitters, "UO Interviews: Barbara Szabo of Emo Nite," UO
Blog, 2019, https://blog.urbanoutfitters.com/blog/uo_interviews
_barbara_szabo_of_emo_nite.

9. *Alternative Press*, "Chiodos' Craig Owens."

10. *Alternative Press*, "AP Staff Share Their Spotify Time Capsule
Playlists, and There's a Lot of Emo," September 29, 2017, https://www
.altpress.com/features/spotify_time_capsule_playlist_staff_list/.

11. Devon Hannan, "If You Remember These 10 Emo Memes, You
Deserve a Senior Discount," *Alternative Press*, July 16, 2018, https://www
.altpress.com/features/list/emo-memes-senior-discount/.

12. *Kerrang!*, "How 10 of Rock's Most Beloved Subgenres Have Evolved,"
*Kerrang!*, 2017, https://www.kerrang.com/features/how-10-of-rocks-
most-beloved-subgenres-have-evolved/.

13. Amy Ebeling, "Four Things to Expect at the Anniversary of Emo
Night LA/Taking Back Tuesday," *Alternative Press*, December 1, 2015,
https://www.altpress.com/features/four_things_to_expect_at_the
_anniversary_of_emo_night_la/.

14. My Chemical Romance, "It's Not a Fashion Statement It's a Fucking
Death Wish," track 11 on *Three Cheers for Sweet Revenge*, Reprise, 2004,
CD.

15. Taylor Markarian, "13 Throwback Emo Lyrics That Broke Your
Heart," *Alternative Press*, February 11, 2019, https://www.altpress.com

/features/list/sad-emo-lyrics-throwback-2000s/.

16. Lycia Shrum, "Low Profile: My Chemical Romance," *Alternative Press*, April 2003, archived at fan site.

17. Jenny Eliscu, "My Chemical Romance: The Most Miserable, Catchiest New Band of the Year," *Rolling Stone*, October 14, 2004, archived at fan site.

18. *Kerrang!*, issue 1045, February 26, 2005.

19. *Alternative Press*, issue 193, August 2004.

20. *NME*, "Hot New Band: Live Special," January 2004, archived at fan site.

21. Eliscu, "My Chemical Romance."

22. Eliscu, "High School Musical," *Rolling Stone*, February 8, 2007, 46–50, 48.

23. Ibid.

24. *SPIN*, March 2007.

25. Brian Hiatt, "Fall Out Boy: The Fabulous Life and Secret Torment of America's Hottest Band," *Rolling Stone*, March 8, 2007, https://www .rollingstone.com/music/music-news/fall-out-boy-the-fabulous-life-and -secret-torment-of-americas-hottest-band-182660/.

26. Brian Rafferty, "It's Swing Time: The Brand Extensions. The Celebrity Hookups. And What's with the R&B? Fall Out Boy Grow Up in Public," *SPIN*, March 2007, 53–57, 54.

27. Hiatt, "Fall Out Boy."

28. Rafferty, "It's Swing Time," 56.

29. Hiatt, "Fall Out Boy."

30. Rafferty, "It's Swing Time," 57.

31. Ibid.

32. Quoted in Hiatt, "Fall Out Boy."

33. Rafferty, "It's Swing Time," 54.

34. Ibid., 56.

35. Sarah Sands, "EMO Cult Warning for Parents," *Daily Mail* Online, August 16, 2006, https://www.dailymail.co.uk/news/article-400953 /EMO-cult-warning-parents.html.

36. Andrew Levy, "Girl, 13, Hangs Herself after Becoming Obsessed with 'Emo Suicide Cult' Rock Band," *Daily Mail*, May 7, 2008, https:// www.dailymail.co.uk/news/article-1018516/Girl-13-hangs-obsessed-Emo -suicide-cult-rock-band.html.

37. Phillipov, "'Generic Misery Music.'"

38. *NME*, November 1, 2006; *Kerrang!*, April 7, 2012.

39. Thornton, *Club Cultures*, 129–36.

40. *Kerrang!*, "Emo Fights Back," *Kerrang!*, issue 1127, September 30, 2006, 34–35, 35.

41. Sarah Boden, "Nobody Likes Us, We Care," *Observer Music Monthly* (December 2006): 51–53, 51.

42. Ibid., 53.

43. Hill, "Is Emo Metal?," 310.

44. Ibid.

45. Luke Lewis, "Kings of the Wild Frontier," *NME*, November 13, 2010, 18–22, 22.

46. Dan Martin, "My Chemical Romance: The Black Parade," *NME*, October 13, 2006, https://www.nme.com/reviews/album/reviews-my -chemical-romance-8050.

47. Luke Dean, "My Chemical Romance Saved My Life," *Alternative Press*, June 6, 2017, https://www.altpress.com/features/my_chemical _romance_saved_my_life/.

48. Ibid.

49. Marianne Eloise, "From Lil Peep to Paramore, Emo and Rap Have Been Related for Years," *Kerrang!*, September 5, 2017, https://www .kerrang.com/features/from-lil-peep-to-paramore-emo-and-rap-have -been-related-for-years/.

50. Ibid.

51. Joe Price, "The Artists Redefining Emo," *Complex*, June 5, 2018, https://www.complex.com/music/2018/06/artists-redefining-emo-2018/.

52. Elias Leight, "How ILoveMakonnen, Lil Peep and Fall Out Boy Made 'I've Been Waiting,'" *Rolling Stone*, January 31, 2019, https://www .rollingstone.com/music/music-features/lil-peep-ilovemakonnen-fall -out-boy-ive-been-waiting-786808/.

53. *Kerrang!*, "Watch Rapper Post Malone Playing Welcome to the Black Parade at Emo Night," *Kerrang!*, October 4, 2017, https://www.kerrang .com/video/watch-rapper-post-malone-playing-welcome-to-black-parade -at-emo-night/.

54. Good S U C C, comment on "Post Malone Plays My Chemical Romance at Emo Nite," YouTube, 2018, https://www.youtube.com /watch?v=VzJa8Eql6A8.

55. Destiny Lawson, comment on "Post Malone Plays My Chemical Romance at Emo Nite," YouTube, 2018, https://www.youtube.com/watch?v=VzJa8Eql6A8.

56. Hill, *Gender, Metal and the Media*, location 2335.

57. Devin Hannan, "Emos vs. Rap Gods—Is It an Emo Lyric or a Hip-Hop Lyric?," *Alternative Press*, July 27, 2018, https://www.altpress.com/quizzes/emo-hip-hop-lyric-quiz/.

58. Whitney Shoemaker, "Study Ranks Songs by How Emo the Lyrics Are," *Alternative Press*, September 2, 2017, https://www.altpress.com/news/study-ranks-songs-emo-lyrics/.

59. Matt Daniels, "Quantifying Emotional Lyrics in Emo Rap vs Dashboard Confessional," *Pudding*, April 30, 2018, https://pudding.cool/2018/08/emo-rap/.

60. Lindsay Zoladz, "All the Young Sadboys: XXXTentacion, Lil Peep, and the Future of Emo," *The Ringer*, August 30, 2017, https://www.theringer.com/music/2017/8/30/16225968/emo-xxxtentacion-lil-peep-brand-new.

61. Ibid.

62. Tom Breihan, "Juice WRLD Turns SoundCloud Rap into Toxic Emo-Pop," *Stereogum*, June 13, 2018, https://www.stereogum.com/2001216/juice-wrld-toxic-masculinity/franchises/status-aint-hood/.

63. Fall Out Boy, "Nobody Puts Baby in the Corner," track 5 on *From Under the Cork Tree*, Island, 2005, CD.

64. Spencer Kornhaber, "The Classic Queer Paradox of Tyler, the Creator," *The Atlantic*, July 21, 2017, https://www.theatlantic.com/entertainment/archive/2017/07/tyler-the-creator-flower-boy-coming-out-queerness/534486/.

65. Booth, *Playing Fans*.

# BIBLIOGRAPHY

_tune_you_out. Untitled post. LiveJournal, December 22, 2004. https://
    chemicalromance.LiveJournal.com/329646.html.

A_Good_Kitty. "For a concert, how far is too far?" Reddit, r/
    panicatthedisco, 2018. https://www.reddit.com/r/panicatthedisco
    /comments/8yqoxa/for_a_concert_how_far_is_too_far/.

Alsaksen, Matthew J. "Middle Class Music in Suburban Nowhere Land:
    Emo and the Performance of Masculinity." MA thesis, Bowling Green
    State University, 2006.

*Alternative Press*. "AP Staff Share Their Spotify Time Capsule Playlists, and
    There's a Lot of Emo." *Alternative Press*, September 29, 2017. https://
    www.altpress.com/features/spotify_time_capsule_playlist_staff_list/.

———. "Chiodos' Craig Owens and the Emo Nite Founders Explain
    What Makes the Emo Scene so Special." *Alternative Press*, May 20, 2017.
    https://www.altpress.com/features/chiodos_craig_owens_emo_nite
    _founders_interview/.

———. "Product Description." Issue 352, 2017. https://shop
    .altpress.com/products/the_ultimate_guide_to_emo_magazine_352.

Attu, Rose, and Melissa Terras. "What People Study When They Study
    Tumblr: Classifying Tumblr Related Academic Research." *Journal of
    Documentation* 73, no. 3 (2017): 528–54.

Austin, John Langsaw. *How to Do Things with Words*. Oxford: Clarendon
    Press, 1962.

Azzopardi, Chris. "Panic! Frontman on Being a Little Gay, Bisexual

Anthem & Getting Naked." PrideSource, November 6, 2013. https://
pridesource.com/article/63018-2/.

Bacon-Smith, Camille. *Enterprising Women: Television Fandom and the
Creation of Popular Myth*. Philadelphia: University of Pennsylvania
Press, 1992.

Baldry, Arthur P. "Phase and Transition, Type and Instance: Patterns
in Media Texts as Seen Through a Multimodal Concordancer." In
*Multimodal Discourse Analysis: Systemic Functional Perspectives*, ed. Kay
L. O'Halloran, 83–108. London: Continuum, 2006.

Barthes, Roland, "Rhetoric of the Image." In Roland Barthes, *Image, Music,
Text*, 32–51. London: Fontana Press, 1977.

Barton, David. "Tagging on Flickr as a Social Practice." In *Discourse and
Digital Practices: Doing Discourse Analysis in the Digital Age*, ed. Rodney
H. Jones, Alice Chik, and Christopher A. Hafner, 47–65. New York:
Routledge, 2015.

Bastardjames. "We randomly got each other the same album . . . and of
course, it was Best Buds." Reddit, r/emo, 2019. https://www.reddit
.com/r/Emo/comments/a9gl6f/we_randomly_got_each_other_the
_same_album_and_of.

Baym, Nancy. *Playing to the Crowd: Musicians, Audiences, and the Intimate
Work of Connection*. New York: New York University Press, 2018.

Bayton, Mavis. "How Women Become Musicians." In *On Record: Rock, Pop
and the Written Word*, ed. Simon Frith and Andrew Goodwin, 201–19.
London: Routledge, 2006.

Bennett, Andy. "Subcultures or Neo-Tribes? Rethinking the Relationship
between Youth, Style and Musical Taste." *Sociology* 33, no. 3 (1999):
599–617.

Benson, Phil. "YouTube as Text: Spoken Interaction and Digital
Discourse." In *Discourse and Digital Practices: Doing Discourse Analysis
in the Digital Age*, ed. Rodney H. Jones, Alice Chik, and Christopher A.
Hafner, 80–96. New York: Routledge.

Bergstrom, Kelly. "'Don't Feed the Troll': Shutting Down Debate about
Community Expectations on Reddit.com." *First Monday* 16, no. 8
(2011). https://firstmonday.org/article/view/3498/3029.

Biddle, Ian, and Gibson Kirsten, eds. *Masculinity and Western Musical
Practice*. Farnham, Surrey: Ashgate, 2009.

Bietermen, Sallie. "'I'm Not Like Other Girls': The Motivations and

Consequences of Saying It." The Odyssey, May 31, 2016. https://www
.theodysseyonline.com/not-like-other-girls.

Bloor, Meriel, and Thomas Bloor. *The Practice of Critical Discourse Analysis:
An Introduction.* London: Hodder and Arnold, 2007.

Boden, Sarah. "Nobody Likes Us, We Care." *Observer Music Monthly*
(December 2006): 51–53.

Booth, Paul. *Crossing Fandoms: SuperWhoLock and the Contemporary Fan
Audience.* London: Palgrave Macmillan, 2016.

———. *Digital Fandom 2.0.* New York: Peter Lang, 2017.

———. "Narractivity and the Narrative Database." *Narrative Inquiry* 19,
no. 2 (2009): 372–92.

———. *Playing Fans: Negotiating Fandom and Media in the Digital Age.*
Iowa: University of Iowa Press, 2015. Kindle edition.

Bourdieu, Pierre. *Distinction: A Social Critique of the Judgement of Taste.*
London: Routledge and Kegan Paul, 1984.

Breihan, Tom. "Juice WRLD Turns SoundCloud Rap into Toxic Emo-Pop."
*Stereogum*, June 13, 2018. https://www.stereogum.com/2001216/juice
-wrld-toxic-masculinity/franchises/status-aint-hood/.

Brickell, Chris. "Masculinities, Performativity, and Subversion: A
Sociological Reappraisal." *Men and Masculinities* 8, no. 24 (2005): 24–43.

Brockmeier, Siri C. "'Not Just Boys' Fun?': The Gendered Experience of
American Hardcore." MA thesis, Universitet I Oslo, 2009.

Brown, Joshua. "No Homo." *Journal of Homosexuality* 58, no. 3 (2011): 299–314.

Bryant, Tom. *The True Lives of My Chemical Romance: The Definitive
Biography.* Basingstoke: Sidgwick and Jackson, 2014.

Burgess, Jean, and Jonathan Green. *Youtube: Online Video and
Participatory Culture.* Cambridge: Polity, 2009.

Bury, Rhiannon. *Cyberspaces of Their Own: Female Fandoms Online.* New
York: Peter Lang, 2005.

———. "The X-Files, Online Fan Culture, and the David Duchovny
Estrogen Brigades." In *The Post-Subcultures Reader*, ed. David
Muggleton and Rupert Weinzierl, 285–96. Oxford: Berg, 2004.

Busse, Kristina. "Geek Hierarchies, Boundary Policing, and the Gendering
of the Good Fan." *Participations: A Journal of Audience and Reception
Studies* 10, no. 1 (2013): 73–91.

Butler, Judith. *Bodies That Matter: On the Discursive Limits of "Sex."*
London: Routledge, 2014.

Cann, Victoria. *Girls Like This, Boys Like That: The Reproduction of Gender in Contemporary Youth Cultures*. London: Tauris, 2018.

Carabine, Jean. "Unmarried Motherhood 1830–1990: A Genealogical Analysis." In *Discourse as Data: A Guide for Analysis*, ed. Margaret Wetherell, Stephanie Taylor, and Simeon J. Yates, 267–307. London: Sage, 2001.

Carrillo-Vincent, Matthew. "Wallflower Masculinities and the Peripheral Politics of Emo." *Social Text* 31, no. 3 (2013): 35–55.

Chiew, Arthur Kok Kum. "Multisemiotic Mediation in Hypertext." In *Multimodal Discourse Analysis: Systemic Functional Perspectives*, ed. Kay O'Halloran, 131–59. London: Continuum, 2006.

Coates, Norma. "(R)Evolution Now? Rock and the Political Potential of Gender." In *Sexing the Groove*, ed. Sheila Whitely, 50–64. New York: Routledge, 1997.

Coleman, Gabriella. "Our Weirdness Is Free." *Triple Canopy* 15 (2012). https://www.canopycanopycanopy.com/contents/our_weirdness_is_free.

Daniels, Matt. "Quantifying Emotional Lyrics in Emo Rap vs Dashboard Confessional." *Pudding*, April 30 2018. https://pudding.cool/2018/08/emo-rap/.

Davisson, Amber. "Mashing Up, Remixing, and Contesting the Popular Memory of Hillary Clinton." *Transformative Works and Cultures* 22 (2016). https://journal.transformativeworks.org/index.php/twc/article/view/965.

Dean, Luke. "My Chemical Romance Saved My Life." *Alternative Press*, June 6, 2017. https://www.altpress.com/features/my_chemical_romance_saved_my_life/.

De Boise, Sam. "Cheer Up Emo Kid: Rethinking the 'Crisis of Masculinity' in Emo." *Popular Music* 33, no. 2 (2014): 225–42.

———. *Men, Masculinity, Music and Emotions*. London: Palgrave Macmillan, 2015.

De Kosnik, Abigail. *Rogue Archives: Digital Cultural Memory and Media Fandom*. Cambridge, MA: MIT Press, 2016.

Doty, Alexander. *Making Things Perfectly Queer: Interpreting Mass Culture*. Minneapolis: University of Minnesota Press, 1993.

Douglas, Nick. "It's Supposed to Look Like Shit: The Internet Ugly Aesthetic." *Journal of Visual Culture* 13, no. 3 (2014): 314–39.

Duodecim. "BEST eMO ALBUMS OF ALL TIME." Reddit, r/emo, 2016.
https://www.reddit.com/r/Emo/comments/4cuk0e/best_emo
_albums_of_all_time/.

Ebeling, Amy. "Four Things to Expect at the Anniversary of Emo Night
LA/Taking Back Tuesday." *Alternative Press*, December 1, 2015. https://
www.altpress.com/features/four_things_to_expect_at_the
_anniversary_of_emo_night_la/.

Ehrenreich, Barbara, Elizabeth Hess, and Gloria Jacobs. "Beatlemania:
Girls Just Want to Have Fun." In *The Adoring Audience: Fan Culture and
Popular Media*, ed. Lisa A. Lewis, 84–105. London: Routledge, 1992.

electroclash. "An Open Letter to the Warped Tour." LiveJournal, July 11,
2005. https://chemicalromance.LiveJournal.com/1046898
.html?page=3.

Eliscu, Jenny. "High School Musical." *Rolling Stone*, February 8, 2007, 46–50.

———. "My Chemical Romance: The Most Miserable, Catchiest New
Band of the Year." *Rolling Stone*, October 14, 2004.

Eloise, Marianne. "From Lil Peep to Paramore, Emo and Rap Have Been
Related for Years." *Kerrang!*, September 5, 2017. https://www.kerrang
.com/features/from-lil-peep-to-paramore-emo-and-rap-have-been
-related-for-years/.

ex_i_amcland189. Untitled post. LiveJournal, 2004. Accessed via the
Internet Archive Wayback Machine.

———. Untitled post. LiveJournal, June 21, 2004. https://
chemicalromance.LiveJournal.com/96360.html.

Fairclough, Norman. *Analysing Discourse: Textual Analysis for Social
Research*. London: Routledge, 2003.

———. *Discourse and Social Change*. London: Polity, 1993.

Fall Out Boy. 2004. Untitled post at falloutboyrock.com. Available via the
Internet Archive Wayback Machine.

———. 2005. Untitled post at falloutboyrock.com. Available via the
Internet Archive Wayback Machine.

Fathallah, Judith. *Fanfiction and the Author: How Fanfic Changes Popular
Cultural Texts*. Amsterdam: Amsterdam University Press, 2017.

Fiske, John. *Understanding Popular Culture*. London: Routledge, 1989.

Fleck, Andrew. "The Father's Living Monument: Textual Progeny and the
Birth of the Author in Sidney's 'Arcadias.'" *Studies in Philology* 107, no. 4
(2010): 520–47.

Foucault, Michel. *The Archaeology of Knowledge*.Trans. A. M. Sheridan Smith. London: Routledge, [1969] 1989.

———. "The Discourse on Language." *Social Science Information* 10, no. 2 (1971): 7–30.

———. *The Order of Things*. London: Routledge, [1966] 2002.

———. *The Will to Knowledge*. Trans. Robert Hurley. In *The History of Sexuality*, vol. 1. London: Penguin, [1976] 1998.

Frith, Simon, and Angela McRobbie. "Rock and Sexuality." In *On Record: Rock, Pop and the Written Word*, ed. Simon Frith and Andrew Goodwin, 317–32. London: Routledge, 2006.

Fueled by Ramen. "Cobra Starship: Send My Love To The Dancefloor . . . [OFFICIAL VIDEO]." YouTube, 2008. https://www.youtube.com /watch?v=84saYemcJQY.

Furguson, Aaron Robert. "Surfing for Punks: The Internet and the Punk Subculture in New Jersey." PhD diss., Rutgers State University of New Jersey, 2008.

Greenwald, Andy. *Nothing Feels Good: Punk Rock, Teenagers, and Emo*. New York: St. Martin's Press, 2012. Kindle edition.

Grossberg, Lawrence. "Is There Rock after Punk?" *Critical Studies in Mass Communication* 3 (1986): 50–74.

GroundbreakingWest7. "This new fanbase . . . " Reddit, r/ mychemicalromance, 2019. https://www.reddit.com/r /MyChemicalRomance/comments/b36jzn/this_new_fanbase/.

Hannan, Devon. "Emos vs. Rap Gods—Is It an Emo Lyric or a Hip-Hop Lyric?" *Alternative Press*, July 27, 2018. https://www.altpress.com /quizzes/emo-hip-hop-lyric-quiz/.

———. "If You Remember These 10 Emo Memes, You Deserve a Senior Discount." *Alternative Press*, July 16, 2018. https://www .altpress.com/features/list/emo-memes-senior-discount/.

Haydn, Reindhart. *My Chemical Romance: This Band Will Save Your Life*. London: Plexus, 2013.

Hebdidge, Dick. *Subculture: The Meaning of Style*. London: Routledge, 1979.

Herring, Susan C., Inna Kouper, John C. Paolillo, Lois Ann Scheidt, Michael Tyworth, Peter Welsch, Elijah Wright, and Ning Yu. "Conversations in the Blogosphere: An Analysis 'From the Bottom Up.'" In *Proceedings of the Thirty-Eighth Hawai'i International Conference on System Sciences* (HICSS-38), 1–11. Los Alamitos: IEEE Press, 2005.

Hiatt, Brian. "Fall Out Boy: The Fabulous Life and Secret Torment of America's Hottest Band." *Rolling Stone*, March 8, 2007. https://www.rollingstone.com/music/music-news/fall-out-boy-the-fabulous-life-and-secret-torment-of-americas-hottest-band-182660/.

Hill, Rosemary. "Emo Saved My Life: Challenging the Mainstream Discourse of Mental Illness around My Chemical Romance." In *Can I Play with Madness? Metal, Dissonance, Madness and Alienation*, ed. Colin McKinnon, Niall Scot, and Kirsten Sollee, 143–54. Oxford: Interdisciplinary Press, 2011.

———. *Gender, Metal and the Media: Women Fans and the Gendered Experience of Music*. London: Palgrave Macmillan, 2016. Kindle edition.

———. "Is Emo Metal? Gendered Boundaries and New Horizons in the Metal Community." *Journal for Cultural Research* 15, no. 3 (2011): 297–313.

Hills, Matt. *Fan Cultures*. London: Routledge, 2002.

———. Foreword. In Paul Booth, *Digital Fandom 2.0*, i–xxiii. New York: Peter Lang, 2017.

———. "Review of *Fans: The Mirror of Consumption*, by Cornel Sandvoss, and *Media Audiences and Identity: Self-Construction and the Fan Experience*, by Steve Bailey." *Popular Communication* 5, no. 2 (2007): 149–54.

Hodkinson, Paul. "'Net.Goth': Internet Communication and (Sub)Cultural Boundaries." In *The Post-Subcultures Reader*, ed. David Muggleton and Rupert Weinzierl, 285–98. Oxford: Berg, 2004.

Holt, Fabian. 2007. *Genre in Popular Music*. Chicago: University of Chicago Press.

How_u_disappear. "I wonder what's the surprise." LiveJournal, August 21, 2005. https://chemicalromance.LiveJournal.com/1218335.html.

Hutcheon, Linda. *A Theory of Parody*. Urbana: University of Illinois Press, 2000.

In_san1ty. "Are we an elists?" Reddit, r/emo, 2018. https://www.reddit.com/r/Emo/comments/7h8vdo/are_we_an_elists/.

Jenkins, Henry. *Textual Poachers: Television Fans and Participatory Culture*. London: Routledge, 1992.

Jenkins, Henry, et al. "When Fan Boys and Fan Girls Meet . . ." Confessions of an Aca-Fan (blog), 2007. http://henryjenkins.org/2007/05/when_fan_boys_and_fan_girls_me.html.

Jones, Rodney H., Alice Chik, and Christopher A. Hafner. Introduction.

In *Discourse and Digital Practices: Doing Discourse Analysis in the Digital Age*, ed. Rodney H. Jones, Alice Chik, and Christopher A. Hafner, 1–16. New York: Routledge, 2015.

*Kerrang!* "Emo Fights Back." *Kerrang!*, issue 1127, September 30, 2006, 34–35.

———. "How 10 of Rock's Most Beloved Subgenres Have Evolved." *Kerrang!*, 2017. https://www.kerrang.com/features/how-10-of-rocks -most-beloved-subgenres-have-evolved/.

———. "Watch Rapper Post Malone Playing Welcome to the Black Parade at Emo Night." *Kerrang!*, October 4, 2017. https://www.kerrang.com /video/watch-rapper-post-malone-playing-welcome-to-black-parade -at-emo-night/.

kilar277. "My Chemical Romance." Reddit, r/emo, 2016. https://www .reddit.com/R/Emo/comments/3q5x9t/my_chemical_romance/.

Knuttila, Lee. "User Unknown: 4chan, Anonymity and Contingency." *First Monday* 16, no. 10 (2011). https://firstmonday.org/ojs/index.php/fm /article/view/3665/3055.

Kornhaber, Spencer. "The Classic Queer Paradox of Tyler, the Creator." *The Atlantic*, July 21, 2017. https://www.theatlantic.com/entertainment /archive/2017/07/tyler-the-creator-flower-boy-coming-out -queerness/534486/.

Laclau, Ernesto, and Chantal Mouffe. *Hegemony and Socialist Strategy: Towards a Radical Democratic Politics*. London: Verso, 1985.

leadtheflock. Untitled post. LiveJournal, June 13, 2005. https:// chemicalromance.LiveJournal.com/982420.html.

Leight, Elias. "How ILoveMakonnen, Lil Peep and Fall Out Boy Made 'I've Been Waiting.'" *Rolling Stone*, January 31, 2019. https://www .rollingstone.com/music/music-features/lil-peep-ilovemakonnen-fall -out-boy-ive-been-waiting-786808/.

Levin Russo, Julie. "Textual Orientation: Queer Female Fandom Online." In *The Routledge Companion to Media and Gender*, edited by Cindy Carter, Linda Steiner, and Lisa McLaughlin, 450–60. Oxon: Routledge, 2013.

Levy, Andrew. "Girl, 13, Hangs Herself after Becoming Obsessed with 'Emo Suicide Cult' Rock Band." *Daily Mail*, May 7, 2008. https://www .dailymail.co.uk/news/article-1018516/Girl-13-hangs-obsessed-Emo -suicide-cult-rock-band.html.

Lewis, Luke. "Kings of the Wild Frontier." *NME*, November 13, 2010, 18–22.

Mack, Ryan. "Fluid Bodies: Masculinity in Emo Music." MA thesis, Carleton University, 2014.

Marchart, Oliver. "Bridging the Micro-Macro Gap: Is There Such a Thing as a Post-Subcultural Politics?" In *The Post-Subcultures Reader*, ed. David Muggleton and Rupert Weinzierl, 83–97. Oxford: Berg, 2004.

marionnettes. "Pop Stars, eh?" LiveJournal, October 17, 2005. https://chemicalromance.LiveJournal.com/1427456.html.

Markarian, Taylor. "13 Throwback Emo Lyrics That Broke Your Heart." *Alternative Press*, February 11, 2019. https://www.altpress.com/features/list/sad-emo-lyrics-throwback-2000s/.

Marsh, Jackie. "The Discourses of Celebrity in the Fanvid Economy of Club Penguin Machinima." In *Discourse and Digital Practices: Doing Discourse Analysis in the Digital Age*, ed. Rodney H. Jones, Alice Chik, and Christopher A. Hafner, 192–208. New York: Routledge, 2015.

Martin, Dan. "My Chemical Romance: The Black Parade." *NME*, October 13, 2006. https://www.nme.com/reviews/album/reviews-my-chemical-romance-8050.

McClary, Susan. *Feminine Endings: Music, Gender, & Sexuality*. Minneapolis: University of Minnesota Press, 1991.

McRobbie, Angela. "Settling Accounts with Subculture. A Feminist Critique." *Screen Education*, 34 (1980): 37–49.

McRobbie, Angela, and Jenny Garber. "Girls and Subcultures." In *Feminism and Youth Culture*, 2nd ed., ed. Angela McRobbie, 12–25. Basingstoke: Macmillan, 2000.

Moisala, Pirkko, and Beverely Diamond, eds. *Music and Gender*. Champaign: University of Illinois Press, 2000.

Mortara, Ariela, and Simona Ironico. "Deconstructing Emo Lifestyle and Aesthetics: A Netnographic Research." *Young Consumers* 14, no. 4 (2013): 351–59.

myxinfinitexromance. "Gerard and Frank POP Interview." YouTube, 2011. https://www.youtube.com/watch?v=hNUs43YxmeY.

Newman, Michael Z. "'Say *Pulp Fiction* One More Goddamn Time': Quotation Culture and an Internet-Age Classic." *New Review of Film and Television Studies* 12, no. 2 (2013): 125–42.

Nicholas, Lucy, and Christine Agius. *The Persistence of Global Masculinism:*

*Discourse, Gender and Neo-Colonial Re-Articulations of Violence*. Cham, Switzerland: Palgrave Macmillan, 2018.

Norabedamned. "Rediscovering Panic." Reddit, r/panicatthedisco, 2019. https://www.reddit.com/r/panicatthedisco/comments/alklto /rediscovering_panic/.

O'Connell, Emily. "I'm Not Like Other Girls, Because 'Other Girls' Don't Exist." *Thought Catalog*, July 27, 2016. https://thoughtcatalog.com /emily-oconnell/2015/07/im-not-like-other-girls-because-other-girls -dont-exist/.

O'Halloran, Kay L. "Introduction." In *Multimodal Discourse Analysis: Systemic Functional Perspectives*, ed. Kay L. O'Halloran, 1–10. London: Continuum, 2006.

Overell, Rosemary. "Emo Online: Networks of Sociality/Networks of Exclusion." *Perfect Beat* 11, no. 2 (2010). https://journals.equinoxpub .com/index.php/PB/article/view/7483.

Panic! at the Disco. Post to panicatthedisco.com. 2006a. Accessed via the Internet Archive Wayback Machine.

———. 2006b. Post to panicatthedisco.com. Accessed via the Internet Archive Wayback Machine.

Papparchissi, Zizi. *Affective Publics: Sentiment, Technology and Politics*. Oxford: Oxford University Press, 2015.

Peters, Brian M. "Emo Gay Boys and Subculture: Postpunk Queer Youth and (Re)thinking Images of Masculinity." *Journal of LGBT Youth* 7, no. 2 (2010): 129–46.

Phillipov, Michelle. "'Generic Misery Music': Emo and the Problem of Contemporary Youth Culture." *Media International Australia Incorporating Culture & Policy* 136 (2010): 60–70.

———. "'Just Emotional People'? Emo Culture and the Anxieties of Disclosure." *M/C Journal* 12, no. 5 (2009). http://journal .media-culture.org.au/index.php/mcjournal/article/view/181.

Phillips, Whitney. "The House That Fox Built: Anonymous, Spectacle, and Cycles of Amplification." *Television & New Media* 14, no. 6 (2013): 494–509.

———. *This Is Why We Can't Have Nice Things: Mapping the Relationship between Online Trolling and Mainstream Culture*. Cambridge, MA: MIT Press, 2015.

Phillips, Whitney, and Ryan M. Milner. *The Ambivalent Internet: Mischief,*

*Oddity and Antagonism Online*. Cambridge: Polity, 2017.

Price, Joe. "The Artists Redefining Emo." *Complex*, June 5, 2018. https://www.complex.com/music/2018/06/artists-redefining-emo-2018/.

R/Emo Wiki. Reddit, 2019. https://www.reddit.com/R/Emo/wiki/index.

Rafferty, Brian. "It's Swing Time: The Brand Extensions. The Celebrity Hookups. And What's With the R&B? Fall Out Boy Grow Up in Public." *SPIN*, March 2007, 53–57.

Raha, Maria. *Cinderella's Big Score: Women of the Punk and Indie Underground*. Emeryville, CA: Seal Press, 2005.

Red, Magdalena. "Who Are the 'Emos' Anyway? Youth Violence in Mexico City and the Myth of the Revolution." *Journal of Popular Music Studies* 26, no. 1 (2014): 101–20.

Reddington, Helen. 2003. "Lady Punks in Bands: A Subculturette?" In *The Cultural Study of Music: A Critical Introduction*, ed. Martin Clayton, Trevor Herbert, and Richard Middleton, 239–51. New York: Routledge, 2013.

Reddit. Moderator Guidelines for Healthy Communities. Reddit wiki, 2017. https://www.reddit.com/wiki/healthycommunities.

Richman, Jesse. "What Is Emo, Anyway? We Look at History to Define a Genre." *Alternative Press*, 2018. https://www.altpress.com/features/what_is_emo_history_definition/.

Rohde, Achim. "Gays, Cross-Dressers and Emos: Non-Normative Masculinity in Militarized Iraq." *Journal of Middle Eastern Women's Studies* 12, no. 3 (2016): 433–49.

*Rolling Stone*. "My Chemical Romance's Gerard Way Taps Another Nail into 'Emo' Coffin." *Rolling Stone*, September 20, 2007. http://www.rollingstone.com/music/news/my-chemical-romances-gerard-way-taps-another-nail-into-emo-coffin-20070920.

Ryalls, Emily. "Emo Angst, Masochism, and Masculinity in Crisis." *Text and Performance Quarterly* 33, no. 2 (2013): 83–97.

Sands, Sarah. "EMO Cult Warning for Parents." *Daily Mail* Online, August 16, 2006. https://www.dailymail.co.uk/news/article-400953/EMO-cult-warning-parents.html.

Sarcastasaurus. "Emo History Lesson Part 5- Emo Pop." Reddit, r/emo, 2016. https://www.reddit.com/R/Emo/comments/4913pt/emo_history_lesson_part_5_emo_pop/.

———. "Emo History Lesson Sidebar: Scenecore." Reddit, r/emo, 2017.

https://www.reddit.com/r/Emo/comments/52znsf/emo_history
_lesson_sidebar_scenecore.

Scuzz TV. "Scuzz Meets Fall Out Boy." YouTube, 2013. https://www
.youtube.com/watch?v=L85yQhIOkB8&t=484s7.

Selwyn, Neil. "The Discursive Construction of Education in the Digital
Age." In *Discourse and Digital Practices: Doing Discourse Analysis in
the Digital Age*, ed. Rodney H. Jones, Alice Chik, and Christopher A.
Hafner, 225–40. New York: Routledge, 2015.

Separateskies. "My Chemical Romance Slam Fame-Hungry Musicians on
New Album (Source: Spinner.com)." LiveJournal, November 30, 2009.
https://chemicalromance.LiveJournal.com/3273187.html.

Shiffman, Limor. *Memes in Digital Culture*. Cambridge, MA: MIT Press,
2014.

Shoemaker, Whitney. "Study Ranks Songs by How Emo the Lyrics Are."
*Alternative Press*, September 2, 2017. https://www.altpress.com/news
/study-ranks-songs-emo-lyrics/.

Shrum, Lycia. "Low Profile: My Chemical Romance." *Alternative Press*,
April 2003.

*South Park*. "Member Berries." Season 20, episode 1. Directed by Trey
Parker. Written by Trey Parker. Comedy Central, September 14, 2016.

Spanos, Brittany. "Mark Hoppus, Chris Carrabba on How Emo Night
Vindicated the Scene." *Rolling Stone*, November 23, 2015. http://www
.rollingstone.com/music/features/mark-hoppus-chris-carrabba-on
-how-emo-night-vindicated-the-scene-20151123.

Stanfill, Mel. "'They're Losers, But I Know Better': Intra-Fandom
Stereotyping and the Normalization of the Fan Subject." *Critical
Studies in Media Communication* 30, no. 2 (2013): 117–34.

Stein, Louisa E. *Millennial Fandom: Television Audiences in the Transmedia
Age*. Iowa City: University of Iowa Press, 2015.

taijutsu_queen. "Mikey is such a blog whore." LiveJournal, March 8, 2006.
https://chemicalromance.LiveJournal.com/1609243.html.

TheLampSalesman. "AMA Request: u/kage6613, the legend behind the
REAL REAL EMO copypasta." Reddit, r/emojerk, 2018. https://www
.reddit.com/R/Emojerk/comments/9i3at8/ama_request_ukage6613
_the_legend_behind_the_real/.

Thomas-Jones, Angela. "Emo Is Not the New Black: Current Affairs
Journalism and the Marking of Popular Culture." *Metro Magazine:*

*Media & Education Magazine* 156 (2008): 72–77.

Thornton, Sarah. *Club Cultures: Music, Media and Subcultural Capital.* Cambridge: Polity, 1995.

Trammell, Matthew. "User Investment and Behavior Policing on 4chan." *First Monday* 19, nos. 2–3 (2014). https://firstmonday.org/ojs/index .php/fm/article/view/4819/3839.

TV Tropes. "Not Like Other Girls." n.d. Accessed December 10, 2018. https://tvtropes.org/pmwiki/pmwiki.php/Main/NotLikeOtherGirls.

Vasquez, Camilla. "Intertextuality and Interdiscursivity in Online Consumer Reviews." In *Discourse and Digital Practices: Doing Discourse Analysis in the Digital Age,* ed. Rodney H. Jones, Alice Chik, and Christopher A. Hafner, 65–80. New York: Routledge, 2015.

Way, Gerard. Homepage update to mychemicalromance.com, 2002. Accessed via the Internet Archive Wayback Machine.

———. "I actually knocked and Pete's door and said 'Do you wanna take a legends of emo selfie.'" Twitter, April 14, 2015. https://twitter.com /gerardway/status/588026811000426497.

———. "This fanfic gets right to the point. Absolutely no fucking around here. Milk enema like I guessed. No big." Twitter, April 26, 2016. https://twitter.com/gerardway/status/725092965467586560.

———. "This is well written." Twitter, April 26, 2016. https://twitter.com /gerardway/status/725093778638274560.

———. "A Vigil, On Birds and Glass." Twitter, March 25, 2013. http:// www.twitlonger.com/show/n_1rjdh4f.

Welch, Ben. *Fall Out Boy: Our Lawyer Made Us Change the Name of This Book so We Wouldn't Get Sued. The Biography.* London: Music Print Press, 2016.

Wentz, Pete. Update to the falloutboyrock.com homepage. 2005. Accessed via the Internet Archive Wayback Machine.

What_is_life. "Am I emo?" Reddit, r/emo, 2019. https://www.reddit .com/r/Emo/comments/ash1ja/am_i_emo/.

Williams, Rebecca. *Post-Object Fandom: Television, Identity and Self-Narrative.* New York: Bloomsbury, 2015.

Williams, Sarah F. "'A Walking Open Wound': Emo Rock and the 'Crisis' of Masculinity in America." In *Oh Boy!: Masculinities and Popular Music,* ed. Freya Jarmen-Ivens, 145–60. London: Routledge, 2007.

xpistolax. "I WANNA TAKE YOU TO A GAY BAR." LiveJournal, December

23, 2004. https://patd.LiveJournal.com/8182.html.

Young, Robert J. C. *Postcolonialism: An Historical Introduction*. Oxford: Blackwell, 2001.

Zoladz, Lindsay. "All the Young Sadboys: XXXTentacion, Lil Peep, and the Future of Emo." *The Ringer*, August 30, 2017. https://www.theringer .com/music/2017/8/30/16225968/emo-xxxtentacion-lil-peep-brand -new.

Zubernis, Lynn, and Kathy Larsen. *Fandom at the Crossroads: Celebration, Shame and Fan/Producer Relationships*. Newcastle Upon Tyne: Cambridge Scholars, 2012.

# INDEX

# FANDOM & CULTURE